EXPLORATIONS
IN
FEMINIST ETHICS

EXPLORATIONS

IN

FEMINIST ETHICS

THEORY AND PRACTICE

EDITED BY

EVE BROWNING COLE

AND

SUSAN COULTRAP-MCQUIN

INDIANA UNIVERSITY PRESS
BLOOMINGTON AND INDIANAPOLIS

The paper used in this publication meets the minimum requirements of American
National Standard for Information Sciences—Permanence of Paper for Printed
Library Materials, ANSI Z39.48-1984.

∞ ™

Manufactured in the United States of America

Library of Congress Cataloging-in-Publication Data

Explorations in feminist ethics : theory and practice / edited by Eve
  Browning Cole and Susan Coultrap-McQuin.
      p.   cm.
  Includes bibliographical references and index.
  ISBN 0-253-31384-8. — ISBN 0-253-20697-9 (pbk.)
    1. Feminism—Moral and ethical aspects.   2. Social ethics.
I. Cole, Eve Browning, date.   II. Coultrap-McQuin, Susan
Margaret.
HQ1221.E96   1992
305.42—dc20   91-21235

1 2 3 4 5 96 95 94 93 92

CONTENTS

III. Constructing an Ethical Life

IV. Working within a Feminist Ethic

V. New Directions in Theory

PREFACE

Feminist ethics is a flourishing interest across many disciplines in women's studies. It challenges traditional moral theories, particularly those that focus on justice and rights, and calls into question many ethical assumptions about how we live and work. Our own excitement and that of many others about the revolutionary implications of the theorizing in this field inspired us to put together this anthology.

Our introduction to the book, "Toward a Feminist Conception of Moral Life," provides an overview of terms, traces historical antecedents, explains various debates and new developments, and speculates about the future of the field. The essays in the anthology provide excellent examples of the developments we discuss in feminist ethics today. They are grouped in sections according to their theoretical or practical aims.

We begin with essays contributing to "The Care Debate." These are concerned with defining and defending an ethic of care, comparing it with an ethic of justice and rights, and criticizing the concept of care. The next group of essays examines some past and present ethical theories providing theoretical insights that may be helpful as feminists move forward in creating feminist ethics. "Comparisons across Theories" suggests that feminist ethics may have many and diverse roots.

The third group of essays, "Constructing an Ethical Life," focuses on particularities of an ethical self including self-knowing, moral vision, and emotional work. Attention to such details gives a rich and complex understanding of moral life. Essays in the fourth section, "Working within a Feminist Ethic," illustrate the ways in which people use a feminist ethic in work situations. These essays link the theoretical and the practical in instructive ways.

The essays in the final section, "New Directions in Theory," represent major developments in feminist ethical thinking. They examine the application of maternal thinking to peace politics, female agency in lesbian ethics, an alternative moral epistemology, and the need to recognize global diversity in articulating feminist ethics. We conclude the anthology with a bibliography of suggestions for further reading in the field.

Much more can be said about the essays in this anthology than we have offered in our introduction. Individually and in comparison with each other they provide the basis for much fruitful discussion. We believe they will inspire good work in the future as well.

Acknowledgments

The essays in this anthology originated in presentations at the conference "Explorations in Feminist Ethics: Theory and Practice" held in Duluth, Minnesota, in October 1988. Almost 350 people from the United States, Canada, the Netherlands, and Great Britain attended; more than 50 papers were presented by people in both academic and nonacademic fields.

For help in planning and organizing this conference we are indebted to Maureen Riley and Teri Williams of the Office of Continuing Education and Extension, University of Minnesota, Duluth. We are grateful for the financial support provided by a grant from the Minnesota Humanities Commission. Many friends and colleagues helped with program selection and contributed their time to various conference-related activities; we especially thank Elizabeth Bartlett, Robert Evans, Helen Hanten, Georgia Keeney, Loren Lomasky, Jane Maddy, Jane Ollenburger, Tineke Ritmeester, Cindy Spillers, and Karla Ward.

A grant from the University of Minnesota Graduate School supported the preparation of the bibliography for this anthology, and Elizabeth Blakesley's research assistance is much appreciated. The Interlibrary Loan Office at our university was an invaluable help for this part of the project, and we are grateful to Susan Kesti, Mary Palzer, and all of its staff. Substantial clerical support came from Karla Ward and Janet Stanaway. Editorial suggestions from Elizabeth Bartlett, Tineke Ritmeester, and Loren Lomasky were extremely helpful. We also appreciate our families' encouragement and support. Our sincerest thanks to these and to all others who work and live in feminist ethics.

EXPLORATIONS
IN
FEMINIST ETHICS

Toward a Feminist Conception of Moral Life

EVE BROWNING COLE AND
SUSAN COULTRAP-McQUIN █████████████

Twenty years ago there was no field called feminist ethics; today discussions about this subject cross continents and academic disciplines. Although much of the work originates in philosophy, other fields including sociology, psychology, education, medicine, theology, and business have recently entered the debate about the meaning and application of feminist ethics. Developing against a background of diverse feminist theories and criticism, feminist ethics deal specifically with moral questions such as: How can we resolve moral conflicts, both personal and social, in feminist ways? What is the place in ethics of the moral traits traditionally associated with women such as sympathy, nurturance, care, and compassion? What are the ethical ramifications of human relationships? And how can feminist principles be lived in the workplace, the classroom, and the world at large? Discussions of these and many other questions are part of the inquiry called feminist ethics. The essays in this anthology represent both present concerns and new directions.

What characterizes feminist ethics as presently conceived? A simple description is impossible to provide because theories and approaches are diverse and rapidly evolving; however, we can identify several key features as basic characteristics of current thinking. First, and perhaps most obvious, the discussion of feminist ethics grows out of a commitment to feminism, particularly to two basic assumptions relevant to moral life: (1) women and their values are of profound moral significance in and of themselves; (2) social institutions and practices have encouraged discrimination against women and the suppression of their moral views.[1] Those two assumptions have led to demands for a new ethical outlook as well as for social change. There are, however, significant disagreements over exactly what kind of moral outlook most naturally emerges from feminist thinking and practice. As the essays reveal, lively controversies arise over such issues as: whether an ethic that emphasizes the centrality of *care* can be developed into a coherent and satisfying feminist ethic; whether *justice* as defined within classical liberal political theory can have its usual hegemonic role when one is working within a feminist ethical context; whether the concepts of the *moral agent* and of *moral action* need radical redefinition; and whether a relational ethic that emphasizes personal bonds between people can be adapted to larger-scale, necessarily impersonal situations. Feminists have a wide range of opinions on these particular issues, but they are united in their endorsement of the basic assumptions mentioned above.

A second characteristic of feminist ethics is that those working in the field call into question many traditional moral perspectives and seek to construct moral views more congenial to women. They argue that traditional moral philosophy has been a largely male-directed enterprise and has reflected interests derived predominantly from men's experience. In other words, because men's experience has often involved market transactions, their moral theories concentrate on promise-keeping, property rights, contracts, and fairness.[2] As Patricia Ward Scaltsas explains in her essay "Do Feminist Ethics Counter Feminist Aims?": "The project of criticizing, analyzing and when necessary replacing the traditional categories of moral philosophy in order to eradicate the misrepresentation, distortion, and oppression resulting from the historically male perspective is, broadly speaking, the project of feminist ethics." She maintains, as do many others, that most traditional moral theories have implicitly excluded and silenced women and their moral perspectives and, thus, must be replaced with an ethic that reinterprets and validates both.

Many have turned to women's experiences with care-giving—whether in child-care, friendships, or work—for concrete demonstrations of feminist ethics. They view the willingness to nurture and a ready capacity for emotional involvement as essential to a humane moral stance in a world of injustice and alienation. They also argue that those values can be expressed in ways that are liberating to women. Thus, Sara Ruddick, whose work on maternal thinking has contributed greatly to the development of feminist ethics, argues in "From Maternal Thinking to Peace Politics" that the thinking that arises from women's traditional experience with childcare can be transformed into a liberating political and ethical stance of global significance.

In addition to honoring care as potentially liberating, many thinkers in feminist ethics argue that moral decision-making should not focus narrowly on the mechanical application of abstract principles but must be sensitive to the ways in which various specific human relationships generate different varieties of responsibility. Finding the desirable moral response requires an assessment of role responsibilities in light of an enriched account of human needs. For instance, in "Just Caring" Rita Manning points out that "[a] pressing need calls up an immediate obligation to care for; roles and responsibilities call up an obligation to respond in a caring manner. . . . Sometimes [as in the case of homelessness] it is better to organize a political response." In feminist ethics, thinkers emphasize that the particular context, not abstract principles of right and wrong, must shape and inform morally appropriate choices.[3]

Finally, many working in feminist ethics have begun the process of reassessing the meaning of important moral concepts. For example, Sarah Lucia Hoagland ("Lesbian Ethics and Moral Agency") stresses the constructive nature of altruism. According to her, moral action, even when prompted by a desire to benefit another, can be the creation of, rather than the relinquishing of, a good for the moral agent. This conception contrasts with the traditional view of altruism as the sacrifice of a benefit to another in a finite system of goods. Her argument leads to a reassessment of the notion of altruism itself, and the accompanying action of self-sacrifice as it is traditionally associated with the female role.[4]

In sum, feminist ethics as currently discussed display the following basic characteristics: they are grounded in a feminist perspective; they seek to challenge traditional, some would say "masculinist," moral assumptions; they frequently seek to reinterpret the moral significance of women's cultural experiences as care-givers; they emphasize the importance of particularity, connection, and context; and they strive to reinterpret moral agency, altruism, and other relevant concepts from a feminist perspective.[5] The development of feminist ethics along these lines received a special impetus from research that began appearing in the United States, Canada, and elsewhere in the early 1980s.

Although many works might be cited as setting the initial agenda in feminist ethics, the contributions of two women—Carol Gilligan and Nel Noddings—were especially important, both for providing powerful feminist critiques of traditional ethical theories of rights and justice and for articulating the earliest descriptions of an ethic of care. Although the works of both women have been subject to criticism, revision, and sometimes outright rejection by others working in the area, their theories, nevertheless, remain central to understanding the origins of, and many directions within, feminist ethics today.[6]

Carol Gilligan, a Harvard psychologist who began her career working with Lawrence Kohlberg on his studies of moral development, became concerned in the 1970s that women appeared not to score as well as men on Kohlberg's moral development scale. After conducting some of her own studies on college students and on women considering abortions, she concluded that women actually mature through different stages than men do because the moral priorities of each gender differ. In her book *In a Different Voice* (1982), Gilligan writes, "The moral imperative that emerges repeatedly in interviews with women is an injunction to care, a responsibility to discern and alleviate the 'real and recognizable trouble' of this world. For men the moral imperative appears rather as an injunction to respect the rights of others and thus to protect from interference the rights to life and self-fulfillment." Therefore, she argues, women's moral judgments are "contextual and narrative rather than formal and abstract"; they are concerned with "responsibility and relationships" not with "rights and rules" (*Different Voice*, 19).[7]

Similarly, Nel Noddings, a Stanford philosopher of education, puts caring, responsibility, and relationship at the center of her descriptions of an ethic of care. In *Caring: A Feminine Approach to Ethics and Moral Education* (1984), she claims caring "is feminine in the deep classical sense—rooted in receptivity, relatedness, and responsiveness" (*Caring*, 2). She argues that ethical caring arises out of the memory of "natural" caring—the "relation in which we respond as one-caring out of love or natural inclination" (*Caring*, 5). In an ideal caring relationship the one-caring is receptive to and engages with the cared-for by trying to understand the latter's point of view, needs and expectations; empathy is of crucial importance. In response, the one cared for recognizes the concern and feels encouraged to develop him/herself. The ethic describes a process, not a fixed state, in which feeling, not rationality, is central to the relationship. In the process of caring for others, the one-caring learns to care for her/himself. Like Gilligan's theory, Noddings's ethics of care is not a system of principles, rules or universalizable maxims; instead, it is a mode of human responsiveness that is manifest in particular concrete situations and types of relationships.

Both women contrast their views of morality with those of theorists like Immanuel Kant, John Rawls, and Lawrence Kohlberg, who are working in the tradition of an ethic of rights and justice. For instance, Gilligan explains the difference between her theory and that of Kohlberg as follows: "The conception of morality as concerned with the activity of care centers moral development around the understanding of responsibility and relationships, just as the conception of morality as fairness ties moral development to the understanding of rights and rules" (*Different Voice*, 19). Noddings affirms that distinction and also points out a related contrast that results from the two different methods of moral reasoning. According to Noddings, when operating within an ethic of rights and justice, a person's consideration of a moral situation "moves immediately to abstraction where its thinking can take place clearly and logically in isolation from the complicating factors of particular persons, places, and circumstances"; by contrast, when using an ethic of care, a person's consideration of a moral situation "moves to concretization where its feelings can be modified by the introduction of facts, the feeling of others, and personal histories" (*Caring*, 36–37). Gilligan claims the ethic of care is different from, but not necessarily superior to, an ethic of justice and rights; Noddings argues that the ethic of care is much preferable to an ethic of rights.

Many theorists have built on the work of Gilligan and Noddings to explore more extensively the differences between an ethic of care and an ethic of justice and rights.[8] In this collection Roger Rigterink uses a specific historical example in "Warning: The Surgeon Moralist . . . " to argue that the concept of rights is incapable of accommodating itself to the particularities of real-life moral situations, in which what is "within one's rights" may still be profoundly wrong. Margaret Walker in "Moral Understandings: Alternative 'Epistemology' for a Feminist Ethics," argues that there are important differences, originating in their epistemologies, between feminist ethics (which she does not limit to an ethic of care) and traditional ethics. She argues that the alternative (feminist) moral epistemology "does not imagine our moral understandings congealed into a compact theoretical instrument of impersonal decision for each person, but as deployed in shared processes of discovery, expression, interpretation, and adjustment between persons."[9]

Similarly, we believe that an important difference exists between the ethics in their respective assumptions about the process of moral decision-making. In an ethic of care a guiding assumption is that the moral agent never loses sight of the personal elements in the situation at hand; the feelings and opinions of the relevant others, their relationships, their histories, their individuality and their connectedness are all taken into account. In an ethic of justice it is assumed that the moral agent adjudicates between conflicting demands of "persons *qua* persons," devoid of morally relevant individualities, present in a kind of ethical silhouette. In other words, the justice-centered ethic emphasizes detachment, impersonality, objectivity, and individual autonomy at the expense of attachment, particularity, emotion, and intersubjectivity.[10]

Theoretical presentations of the process of moral decision-making itself make the contrast clear. Much of modern moral philosophy takes as its focal point a hypothetical moral quandary in which someone is enmired. Several possible courses of action are presented, after which the moral agent deliberates, weighing possible costs in suffering (her or his own and that of others), evaluating the comparative goods to be gained, and ultimately *choosing*. Throughout the process, the moral agent is pictured as operating in relative isolation to make her/his decision; the agent must, above all, preserve her/his autonomy in the decision-making process. Because reaching a moral decision results from a process of delicate intellectual calculation of the benefits to be derived from one's choices, emotions are sources of potential disturbance, and other particularities of the situation, like relationships and individual histories, are distracting marginalia to be ignored insofar as possible.

This model of moral decision-making does not seem to fit the phenomena of moral life, as we view them, nor convincingly portray a moral ideal toward which we think most feminists wish to strive. Human beings are constantly affecting and being affected by particular other human beings whose lives run alongside or converge with their own. As a result, the moral quality of their lives is in some deep sense a shared project, in which others play constructive roles. Such particular bonds to others constitute contexts of commitment, of reciprocal understandings and expectations, which are not readily accommodated within the model of justice-centered ethics. Furthermore, women's traditional commitments to nurturing and care-giving in various cultural contexts are seen by most feminists as valuable attributes of a moral life. Thus, to devalue particular attachments to others, and the emotions that shape them, in the process of moral decision-making is at odds with a feminist vision of ethical life.

Although there is much to be said from a feminist perspective in favor of adopting an ethic of care, there are also substantial grounds for caution.[11] We will mention just three significant, but we think not defeating, objections that have been raised. First, women's traditional activities of care-giving have been historically defined not in accordance with women's freely chosen moral commitments, but in response to the needs of patriarchal institutions. These demand that the sensitive and caring woman support, nurture, and reproduce the bruised male warrior and his scions. Given this origin, it may be perilous to valorize the very traits and behaviors that have propped up vast inequities in past society. On the other hand, to reject caring for that reason may be only reactive, not liberating. Caution, but not outright rejection, would appear to be in order.

Second, an ethic of care might seem to enshrine the very image of what the patriarchal male desires to see in women's moral commitments: an Angel in the

House. As such, the ethic would present only a mirror of a male moral fantasy. This problem, however, may be mitigated by a more detailed and theoretically rich expression of the ethic than stereotypical representations allow. This is what Dianne Romain calls for in her essay "Care and Confusion." Finally, though it might work well in the context of private relationships, the ethic of care may not be easily applicable to a public arena of decision-making. In legislation and social policy, both the size of the population involved and the necessity for maintaining equity make it difficult to envision how an ethic of care might be fairly applied.[12] Sara Ruddick responds to this criticism by advocating alterations in social institutions to make them more accommodating to caring human values.[13] Nevertheless, these two cautions also must be acknowledged.

And while there are reasons for being cautious about an ethic of care, there are also reasons not to reject an ethic of rights completely—a tendency some thinkers have when characterizing them as opposites. An ethic of rights provides, as Rita Manning suggests, a moral minimum for interpersonal behavior. In addition, with its emphasis on justice, fairness, and respect, an ethic of rights has in many cases provided a workable, if not always perfect, foundation for social and political institutions that must balance the competing claims of persons unknown to each other. Finally, the concept of "human rights" has had an important influence globally as a rallying cry for those working toward the elimination of grossly inequitable practices like apartheid and the torture of political prisoners. As such it has had enormous value.[14]

In fact, current thinkers in feminist ethics, including those whose work is represented in this anthology, show a variety of attitudes toward an ethic of care and an ethic of rights and justice. Some, like Roger Rigterink, have rejected rights as an adequate perspective for a moral life. Others, like Charlotte Bunch, want us to recognize the equal worth of both ethics. Still others, like Robin S. Dillon and Elizabeth Ann Bartlett, argue the importance of integrating the two perspectives for a fuller moral outlook.[15]

As many of these essays suggest, feminist ethical theories are moving beyond their early, singular focus on the care/justice controversy in at least three ways: (1) Some thinkers are exploring ways in which other ethical traditions may provide at least partial models for a feminist ethic; (2) others are analyzing specific attributes of a moral life; and (3) some even are reconceptualizing the moral situation itself. We view many of these developments as promising and will discuss each briefly.

First of all, many have begun to ask: Can traditional moral philosophy, present or past, be of help in the effort to construct a feminist ethical vision? Several authors here represented answer in the affirmative. Marilyn Friedman in "Feminism and Modern Friendship: Dislocating the Community," for example, focuses attention on the communitarian tradition, recently revived in the well-known work of Alasdair MacIntyre.[16] Communitarian theories criticize liberal political philosophies for their excessive emphasis on abstract individualism; communitarians argue that the genuine human self is constituted by real relationships, and by membership and participation in communities. Yet, Friedman argues, this valuable starting point is rendered troublesome to feminists by the communitarians' uncritical acceptance of the idea of given, rather than chosen, communities, because many given communities (national, religious, familial, and so on) are oppressive. Friedman suggests that communitarians' theoretical stance can be rendered useful to feminists if it attends to *communities of choice*, and to the ways in which we constantly reform and reconstitute ourselves *via* voluntary community memberships.

Another modern philosophical outlook being examined for potential contributions to feminist ethics is existentialism. Elizabeth Ann Bartlett in "Albert Camus and a Theory of Feminist Ethics" argues that Camus's concept of rebellion—"an action which simultaneously rejects injustice and oppression, and affirms human dignity"—is useful to consider because it affirms both justice and care, saving each ethic from its own excesses. The ethic of rebellion also gives one a standpoint that reconciles conflicts between public, political commitments and individual, personal ones.

Ancient philosophy has also yielded some suggestive material. Julie K. Ward's "*Harmonia* and *Koinonia*: Moral Values of Pythagorean Women," describes a community of choice among the women members of the ancient Pythagorean schools similar to that which Friedman advocates. Ward locates a type of care ethic among the women that enabled them to apply the tenets of their mystico-mathematical philosophy to their lives as women and to support one another in times of philosophical and personal tribulation. In her paper, Scaltsas includes Aristotle among those philosophers who have something to offer feminist ethics, because he also stressed sensitivity to context, the deep significance of friendship, and the centrality of emotion in the moral life.

Another development in feminist ethics is occurring at a more specific level: some thinkers are offering reconceptions of key components in a moral life. These discussions may provide a basis for a more satisfactory moral theory than we have yet seen. In "Emotional Work," Cheshire Calhoun draws attention to and analyzes the process of helping others to sort out their own emotional responses and to direct those responses in salutary ways. Emotional work, as she describes it, includes "soothing tempers, boosting confidence, fueling pride, preventing friction, and mending ego wounds"—aspects of moral experience that have been largely neglected by moral theorists but which she thinks ought to be recognized in a feminist ethic. Ellen Fox in her essay, "Seeing through Women's Eyes," calls our attention to those dimensions of moral life that are represented in the metaphor of vision: empathy and moral imagination. She asks feminists to more fully consider "[w]hich particular contents of the soul, which elements of the fat, relentless ego, must be dispensed with for the sake of loving vision and which must be retained in order for there to be a self which views."[17]

While Calhoun and Fox focus on particular aspects of moral behavior, Winnie Tomm focuses on the meaning of the moral person. "Ethics and Self-knowing" maintains that the crucial characteristic of the moral person is self-knowing, the process by which one becomes aware of and expresses both subjective and reflective aspects of the self. Self-knowing arises in interaction with others and involves respecting both individual autonomy and social interdependence.

A third promising development in feminist ethics is the reconceptualization of the moral situation itself. Rather than thinking of moral situations as primarily dilemmas or crises during which one must deliberate and choose, many feminists emphasize morality as a way of being in relationship with others. Thus, what is admirable is not a particular choice but the larger field of interaction that constitutes shared life. This reconceptualization is illustrated in the essays by Margaret Urban Walker and Robin S. Dillon as well as others.

The concept of moral community itself has undergone a variety of reappraisals that emphasize the recognition of diversity within community.[18] Thus, in "A Global Perspective on Feminist Ethics and Diversity" Charlotte Bunch calls for the development of a feminist ethic that acknowledges the interconnectedness of the global community yet recognizes and embraces cultural diversity. In a different direction, Sarah Lucia Hoagland insists on articulating an ethics for lesbians, rather than purporting to develop an ethics for all women. In "Some Issues in the Ethics of Collaborative Work," the members of the feminist ethics project in CRIAW (Canadian Research Institute for the Advancement of Women) affirm the importance of their struggle to express their individualities in genuinely collective work. All three approaches affirm diversity.

Perhaps most important, the feminist reconceptualization of ethics includes some attempts to collapse the long-accepted distinctions between public and private morality. Writers like Sara Ruddick believe women can bring what has been a private way of relating to people into public discussions of peace. Practitioners consciously applying feminist ethics in work situations also are blurring the borders between public and private. Both those collaborating in the CRIAW project and those who worked with Mary Raugust on the Kennedy Aging Project, discussed in "Womanist Ethics and Workplace Values," seek to construct working lives that embody feminist ethics.

As we look to the future in feminist ethics we anticipate several further developments. First, we expect continued dialogue about an ethic of care and an ethic of justice. Whereas earlier comparisons between the ethics characterized them as in opposition, future comparisons will probably find them theoretically more compatible. As feminists continue to search for an ethic that promotes women's welfare, ends oppression against women, and humanizes all social institutions, we predict the emergence of an ethic of something like "care respect," as Robin Dillon calls it. We envision an ethic based on a conception of the person that embraces emotion alongside rationality, intersubjectivity as well as autonomy, and particularity in addition to abstract human value.

Second, we anticipate that many more people will seek ways to apply feminist ethical thinking to work-related situations, as Mary Raugust and the CRIAW group have done. In the bibliography at the end of this book, articles on the applications of feminist ethics in work situations are cited in such areas as medical ethics, academic research, and moral education. Other important theorizing cited in our bibliography that also has potential for work-related applications is being done in environmental ethics, religious ethics, and women's spirituality. As examples of applications like Mary Raugust's become more well known, we anticipate that more people will be thinking about integrating ethical theory and practice from a feminist perspective.

In addition we hope to see greater attention paid to the possibilities of interdisciplinary inquiry. In spite of the fact that interest in feminist ethics is found in many and diverse disciplines, and although Gilligan's work demonstrated the usefulness of seeing connections between psychology, literature, and myth, much other work in feminist ethics remains discipline-based. Just as other areas of feminist thinking have been enriched when they have integrated the materials and insights of more than one field, feminist ethics will benefit from a more extensive sharing of insights from various intellectual orientations. For instance, a fruitful area for interdisciplinary exploration is the domain of art and literature, in which representations of the particularity of moral life so valued by feminist ethics can be examined, often with more specificity than we would have about any actual human experience.

Finally, we hope to see greater attention paid to the issue of human diversity in relation to ethical thinking. Many questions in this regard remain unanswered: Can there be or should there be an ethical theory shared by all? What difference does cultural background, sexual orientation, or economic class, for example, make in the conception or application of ethical theories? How do we construct a moral outlook that affirms human diversity as a good, without fragmenting the larger communities we also value? The search for answers to such questions will certainly deepen our understanding of feminist moral life.

NOTES

1. There are of course many branches of feminism—liberal, socialist, lesbian, postmodernist, and so forth—but we would expect widespread agreement around the two basic assumptions we have just stated.

2. This marketplace orientation of moral philosophy and its exclusion of women and other oppressed groups from ethical discourse are discussed by Annette Baier in "Trust and Antitrust," *Ethics* 96 (1986), 231–260. See also Cheshire Calhoun, "Justice, Care, and Gender Bias," *Journal of Philosophy* 85 (1988), 451–463.

3. Seyla Benhabib, for example, argues for a moral theory that will recognize human worth and dignity by acknowledging individual particularity. See "The Generalized and the Concrete Other: The Kohlberg-Gilligan Controversy and Feminist Theory," *Praxis International* 5 (1986), 402–424.

4. For another feminist view of self-sacrifice, see Joan Straumanis, "Duties to Oneself: An Ethical Basis for Self-Liberation?" *Journal of Social Philosophy* 15 (1984), 1–13.

5. Many examples illustrating these characteristics can be found in the bibliography at the end of this book.

6. All the papers in the anthology *Women and Moral Philosophy*, edited by Eva Feder Kittay and Diana T. Meyers (Totowa, N.J.: Rowman and Littlefield, 1987), deal directly or indirectly with debates inspired by Gilligan and Noddings. Volume 50.3 (1983) of *Social Research* was devoted entirely to responses to Gilligan's work. Critical responses to Gilligan can be found in, for example, Linda K. Kerber et al. "On *In a Different Voice*: An Interdisciplinary Forum," *Signs* 11.2 (1986), 304–333; Betty A. Sichel, "Women's Moral Development in Search of Philosophical Assumptions," *Journal of Moral Education* 14.3 (1985), 149–161; Susan F. Parsons, "Feminism and the Logic of Morality: A Consideration of Alternatives," *Radical Philosophy* 47 (1987), 2–12. Critical responses to Noddings can be found in, for example, Winnifred A. Tomm, "Gender Factor or Metaphysics in a Discussion of Ethics," *Explorations: A Journal for Adventurous Thought* 6.1 (1987); Leslie Wilson, "Is a 'Feminine' Ethic Enough?" *Atlantis* 13.2 (1988), 15–23.

7. An excellent comparison of Gilligan and Kohlberg can be found in Lawrence A. Blum, "Gilligan and Kohlberg: Implications for Moral Theory," *Ethics* 98 (1988), 472–491. See also Owen Flanagan and Kathryn Jackson, "Justice, Care, and Gender: The Kohlberg-Gilligan Debate Revisited," *Ethics* 97 (1987), 622–637.

8. For example, see Seyla Benhabib, "The Generalized and the Concrete Other . . . " (cited in note 3 above).

9. See also Lorraine Code, "Responsibility and the Epistemic Community: Woman's Place," *Social Research* 50 (1983), 537–555, and her *Epistemic Responsibility* (Hanover: Press of New England for Brown University, 1987) for an examination of the feminist ethical implications of epistemologies.

10. For an excellent critique of the liberal foundations of traditional moral thinking, see Seyla Benhabib, "Methodological Illusions of Modern Political Theory: The Case of Rawls and Habermas," *Neue Hefte für Philosophie* 21 (1982), 47–74.

11. A compelling critique of the ethic of care, particularly for its inability to account for the possibility of violence within caring relationships, is offered by Claudia Card, "Women's Voices and Ethical Ideals: Must We Mean What We Say?" *Ethics* 99 (1988), 125–135. A different critique and suggestions for a defense of an ethic of care are offered by Joan C. Tronto, "Beyond Gender Difference to a Theory of Care," *Signs* 12.4 (1987), 644–663.

12. Discussion of this problem is found in Mary G. Dietz, "Citizenship with a Feminist Face: The Problem with Maternal Thinking," *Political Theory* 13.1 (1985), 19–37. Nancy Fraser argues that an ethic of solidarity is superior to an ethic of care for larger political contexts; see her article "Toward a Discourse Ethic of Solidarity," *Praxis International* 5.4 (1986), 425–429.

13. Sara Ruddick, "Maternal Thinking," reprinted in Joyce Trebilcot, *Mothering: Essays in Feminist Theory* (Totowa, N.J.: Rowman & Allanheld, 1983), esp. 224–227.

14. A general rights-justice framework has also facilitated many political reforms of undeniable importance to women, such as suffrage and abortion rights. See Zillah Eisenstein, *The Radical Future of Liberal Feminism* (New York: Longman, 1981).

15. Another integrationist approach can be found in Meredith W. Michaels, "Morality Without Distinction," *Philosophical Forum* 17.3 (1986), 175–187. She argues that the assumed dichotomy between reason and emotion can be reconciled in a concept of vision. Annette Baier argues that the concept of trust may serve as a theoretical basis for integrating love (care) and obligation (rights/duties), in "What Do Women Want in a Moral Theory?" *Nous* 19 (1985), 53–63. Susan Parsons argues for a reinterpretation of the relation between fact and value in "Feminism and Moral Reasoning," *Australasian Journal of Philosophy* 64 Suppl. (1986), 75–90.

16. Alasdair MacIntyre, *After Virtue: A Study in Moral Theory* (Notre Dame, Ind.: University of Notre Dame Press, 1981).

17. On the concept of vision, particularly as it relates to cultural diversity, see Maria Lugones, "Playfulness, 'World-Travelling,' and Loving Perception," *Hypatia* 2 (1987), 3–19.

18. Cheshire Calhoun has written, "Unless moral theory shifts its priority to knowledgeable discussions of human differences—particularly differences tied to gender, race, class, and power—lists and rank orderings of basic human interests and rights as well as the political deployment of these lists are likely to be sexist, racist, and classist." "Justice, Care, and Gender Bias," *Journal of Philosophy* 85.9 (1988), 456.

I. The Care Debate

Do Feminist Ethics Counter Feminist Aims?

PATRICIA WARD SCALTSAS ▬▬▬▬▬▬▬

In a preliminary phase of deconstruction, feminist theorists focused on and developed the distinction between *sex* (the biological determination of female and male) and *gender* (the socially constructed characteristics and roles of women and men). They then exposed the gender blindness and gender biases of the Western intellectual heritage by showing the confusion of sex with gender in the writings of philosophers like Aristotle, Aquinas, Rousseau, and Schopenhauer (to name a few of the worst offenders).[1] This confusion of sex with gender still appears in contemporary philosophical writings. In his 1973 article "Because You Are a Woman," John Lucas says, "However much I, a male, want to be a mother, a wife or a girlfriend, I am disqualified from those roles on account of my sex, and I cannot reasonably complain. Not only can I not complain if individuals refuse to regard me as suitable in those roles, but I have to acknowledge that it is reasonable for society generally to do so, and for the state to legislate accordingly. . . . For exactly the same reasons, women are debarred from being regarded in a fatherly or husbandly light."[2] In addition to the continuing deconstruction of men's thought, there is the need to build better theories. This task of feminist theoretical reconstruction has now begun.[3]

A major part of this task is the development of feminist ethics. Carol Gilligan's book *In a Different Voice* documents the disparity between women's experience and the representation of human moral development throughout the psychological literature. The theoretical and observational bias of psychologists in general, and moral developmental psychologists in particular, leads to the pervasive, though often only implicit, adoption of the male life as the norm.[4] Subsequently women's lives, development and values, insofar as they are different from men's, are judged deviant and are devalued. Hence the need for a reexamination of the moral concepts and presuppositions of current standard ethical theory and the construction of ethical theory more in tune with women's actual experience of morality and their moral concerns.

Gilligan argues that there is a misrepresented voice that expresses a valid, mature mode of ethical thought different from that currently recognized as valid and mature. She further argues that it is "characterized not by gender but by theme"; its association with women is just an "empirical observation."[5] Annette Baier points

out in "What Do Women Want in a Moral Theory?" that a few men who are
moral philosophers have also recently been proclaiming discontent with the standard approach in moral philosophy, but that by and large it is women moral
philosophers who are articulating this different voice uncovered by Gilligan in her
studies of moral development.[6] In Gilligan's analysis, this different voice expresses
an ethic of care and responsibility which focuses on maintaining interconnections
between particular personalities and on their particular welfare. Because this is
often seen (especially by moral psychologists such as Lawrence Kohlberg)[7] as in
direct opposition to the standard, traditional (empirically male) voice that expresses
an ethic of justice and rights focusing on universal principles and independent
individuals, the different, contextual approach is either dismissed as not valid as
ethics or relegated to an immature stage of moral development. Gilligan argues
that the ethic of care and responsibility is at least as valid and mature as the ethic
of justice and rights.[8] The project of criticizing, analyzing, and when necessary
replacing the traditional categories of moral philosophy in order to eradicate the
misrepresentation, distortion, and oppression resulting from the historically male
perspective is, broadly speaking, the project of feminist ethics. Jean Grimshaw
identifies three main themes that have been developed in feminist ethics.[9]

(1) A critique of "abstraction," and the belief that women's thinking *is* (and moral
    thinking in general *should be*) more contextualized, less bound to abstract rules,
    more "concrete."[10]

(2) A stress on the values of empathy, nurturance or caring, which are seen as
    qualities that women both value more and tend more commonly to display.[11]

(3) A critique of the idea that the notions of *choice* and *will* are central to morality,
    and of a sharp distinction between fact and value; a stress, instead, on the
    idea of the *demands* of a situation, which are discovered through a process of
    attention to it and require an appropriate response.[12]

Given the laudable aims of feminist ethics, do feminist ethics in fact endorse a
restrictive rather than an emancipatory view of women's place? Let us examine to
what extent the development of these three main themes in feminist ethics does
or does not endorse a restrictive view.

I

    Theme (1) is a critique of *abstraction* and the promotion of more contextual,
more "concrete" moral thinking, believed to be more pervasive among women
than men. Feminists must develop this theme very carefully because maintaining
a sharp distinction between "abstract" and "concrete" thinking has a tendency to
replicate sexist dichotomies. If women's moral thinking, insofar as it is seen to
differ from men's, is seen as context-bound or situational in the sense of being

directly opposed to abstract thinking, there is a real danger that the representation of women's moral reasoning may degenerate into the belief that women perceive and act intuitively, pragmatically, emotionally, and that women's processes of reasoning, if they exist at all, are "nebulous" or "unfathomable" because unprincipled.[13] Being more concrete in one's thinking may indicate greater concern for the particular persons and circumstances but may also be seen to indicate *inability* to conduct abstract thinking. Such characterizations have been used to try to justify women's exclusion from participation in public and professional life, to say nothing of education. Hence, feminists should be ever so vigilant to challenge rather than assume those characterizations. Grimshaw argues, for the reasons just mentioned, that it is much better to see these gender differences as differences in ethical concerns and priorities than as differences in mode or style of reasoning. She suggests that sometimes it is "not [that] women do not act on principles, but that the principles on which they act are not recognized (especially by men) as valid or important ones."[14] Sometimes there is not even recognition of any *implicit* principle, valid or invalid. However, two principles are commonly given priority in women's moral thinking: (i) it is wrong to hurt anyone and (ii) it is right to sustain human relationships.[15] The concrete, contextual aspect of women's moral thinking can be seen to result from this perceived responsibility to appropriately respond to actual people in actual situations, to ensure that this particular person is not hurt and that this particular relationship is sustained. The moral dilemmas faced by women in Gilligan's studies reveal just how difficult it is, given the complexities of real life, to determine precisely what action will satisfy those two principles in any actual situation (especially situations in which someone will inevitably be hurt or a relationship inevitably be broken). Women's moral thinking, then, differs from men's mainly in the different priority of principles acted on. The concrete, contextual aspect of moral thinking is a *necessary* stage in applying any principle, whether by women or men. Feminist ethics can redirect attention to the importance and difficulty of this aspect of moral thinking without presenting women as unprincipled.

In his paper "Gilligan and Kohlberg: Implications for Moral Theory," Lawrence Blum points out that, in an important sense, a morality of care *is* based on universal principles (that *everyone* should be kind and caring, responsible to those to whom they are connected), but the notion of moral action is *enlarged*. This enlarged notion, he argues,

> encompasses emotional response [and] acknowledges that moral action—acting to that principle—requires a care for particular persons which can **not** be exhaustively codified into universal principles. . . . It acknowledges that other moral capacities, involving perception and sensitivity to particulars, care and concern for individual persons, which cannot be accounted for by that in the moral agents which generates principles, are equally central to moral agency. . . . [But, of course,] if "moral" is **defined** in terms of impartiality, then anything outside impartiality—even what is a necessary condition of it—is excluded.[16]

It is this *narrow* definition of "moral" that effectively excludes what the different voice identified by Gilligan expresses.

The restrictiveness of the argument from impartiality can be seen from its effects in the deontological moral tradition.[17] Iris Young argues that the deontological tradition assumes that normative reason is impartial and universal (abstract). She shows that this generates artificial polarities by expelling desire and feeling from moral reason. As a result, *all* feelings, inclinations, needs, and desires are deemed equally irrational, hence equally inferior.[18] In his book *Friendship, Altruism and Morality*, Blum argues that because deontological reason opposes duty to feeling, it fails to recognize that altruistic emotions (sympathy, compassion, and concern) can and *do* provide reasons for, and motivate, moral action.[19] Consequently, a whole sector of reasons and motives for moral action are defined out of court. Hence, moral decisions grounded in considerations of compassion, caring, and a recognition of differences in need (as those documented by Gilligan) are *defined* as not rational and are dismissed as merely sentimental.[20] But premodern philosophy, in particular virtue-based moral theories, did recognize these factors as legitimate in moral thinking and tried to develop standards for distinguishing good from bad interests and noble from base sentiments.[21] For example, consider Aristotle's discussion of the virtue of friendship. As Terence Irwin points out, Aristotle argues that friendship "includes the *favourable attitudes* of business partners and associates and of fellow-citizens for each other," (my italics) and "it also requires some FEELING, actual FONDNESS for the other, not mere goodwill and benevolence."[22] In an Aristotelian conception of ethics, the situations that call for concern and caring, as well as many moral situations, defy universalizing. The stress in such a system is not for the exercise of codified courses of action that are dictated by the identification of the equally codifiable moral predicaments of the agent; rather, what is required is the development of moral sensitivity and dispositions that will enable the individual to respond to each situation according to the demand it makes. Aristotle argues, "All law is universal, but in some areas no universal rule can be correct. . . . And this is the nature of what is decent—rectification of law in so far as the universality of law makes it deficient. . . . For the standard applied to what is indefinite is itself indefinite, as the lead standard is in Lesbian building, where it is not fixed, but adapts itself to the shape of the stone."[23]

Iris Young further argues that the dichotomy between deontological reason and feeling is expressed in the distinction between the public realm of the state and the private realm of the family that dominates modern political theory. The consequence of this division is that women have been so effectively confined to the private.[24] Hence, feminist ethics, which retain a sharp opposition between moral reason and feeling, and universal and particular, also retain the basis for generating gendered dichotomies that have been used to try to justify a restrictive view of women's place. But feminist ethics like Iris Young's, which aim to develop a conception of normative reason that does not oppose moral reason to feeling, challenge rather than endorse this restrictive view.[25]

Annette Baier is pursuing an alternative strategy in developing a more adequate moral theory that will bring together men's theories of obligation and justice and women's theories of love and care. She advances the concept of appropriate trust as the implicit theoretical foundation of both moralities. Her concept of trust mediates well between reason and feeling by being both "belief-informed and action-influencing."[26] Her strategy also avoids endorsing a restrictive view of women's place. Baier observes that women's responsibility for the care of others is imposed on them by asymmetrical power relations in society; however, although the received contractarian[27]–Kantian moral theory implicitly presupposes this imposition, it does not acknowledge or attempt to justify it.[28] If voluntary agreement is the paradigm source of moral obligation in liberal morality, Baier argues, women are either excluded from the class of moral subjects or the theory must admit internal contradiction.[29]

I I

Theme (2) emphasizes the values of empathy, nurturance, or caring as particularly female virtues. These virtues are seen to develop from women's experience and activities as the carers for others' welfare. It is argued by some feminists that these virtues enable women to perceive, more easily than men perceive, the dangerous and inhuman nature of ideologies and actions that have led to so much corruption and destruction.[30] The recognition and application of these values are deemed vital for the improvement of social and political life.[31] In praising the value of care, feminists must be extremely cautious to avoid endorsing notions of care that can be used oppressively. Gilligan documents cases where women submerge their own identities, interests, and needs as they struggle to fulfill their prescribed roles as nurturers of others and to avoid accusations of selfishness. So, although the traditional role of women in society might have led to the development of certain virtues, the *confinement* of women to that role has had destructive results in their development as individuals in society. Indeed, the view of women solely as the nurturers of other people at the expense of what was seen as their own personal development and self-realization was the focus of feminist criticism in the 1960s and early 1970s.[32] This could be a serious problem for feminist ethics, especially when women's ethical values are seen as arising principally out of the practice and traditions of mothering, as Sara Ruddick argues.[33] To isolate mothering from fathering or, in general, parenting, is to isolate women as a sex as *the* sex best suited to the role of nurturer. From here it is but a short step to asserting that mothering is the *only* role for which women are suitable.[34]

Although Ruddick wants to remain neutral on the question of a biological basis of maternal thinking, she does believe that "the 'biological body' (in part a cultural artifact) *may* foster certain features of maternal practice, sensibility, and thought."[35] She argues that although "some men express maternal thinking in various kinds of working and caring with others," *all* women's maternal thought "exists in a radically different way" from men's because the mother-daughter relationship is

radically different from the mother-son relationship. (She bases this claim mainly
on Nancy Chodorow's (1978) *The Reproduction of Mothering*.)[36] But what does
Ruddick mean? If some men manage to escape patriarchal genderization and acquire
maternal thinking, why does it differ from women's maternal thinking? If those
men are still to some degree genderized males, then perhaps they do not really
acquire maternal thinking. But if Ruddick means that some men really do acquire
maternal thinking, the only difference between women's maternal thinking and
men's maternal thinking must be biological. Despite her declaration of neutrality
on the issue of biological determinism, her argument seems to imply it.[37] If the
virtues of empathy and care are considered to be, or are in any way implied to be,
sex-determined, then women are trapped biologically in a restrictive, feminine
stereotype and men are biologically excluded. If these virtues are considered to be
linked to gender, then men as well as women could develop these virtues with the
right social conditioning. Given the phenomenon of postnatal depression, the
virtues of mothering seem to be learned rather than innate. Some might want to
argue that postnatal depression is a phenomenon of oppressive patriarchal societies
that suppress a woman's natural virtues of empathy and care. One could likewise
argue that patriarchal societies also suppress a *man's* natural virtues of empathy
and care. In both cases, encouragement, support, and training could lead to the
cultivation of these natural capacities. Apparently chimpanzees also must *learn* to
care appropriately for their young. A special place in Texas is set up for chimps
to be in their typical social organization so the females can learn "mothering" and
then be used as breeders in captivity. Females taken from their mothers early on
do not know how to care for their own newborns.[38] The biological fact that women
are the ones who give birth to babies does not guarantee that mothers develop
naturally the virtues of empathy and care expected of them. If parental care is
recognized as a social rather than a natural virtue, it becomes very important, as
Grimshaw points out, "that men should participate more fully in, and take more
responsibility for, the tasks of physical and emotional maintenance."[39]

Ruddick also wants to remain neutral on the question of "essential and inerad-
icable difference between female and male parents," but does believe "there are
features of mothering experience which are invariant and nearly unchangeable."[40]
Ruddick sympathizes "with the anger that insists upon and emphasizes the oppressive
nature of maternal practices," but wants to articulate and celebrate "those conditions of mothering that allow for happiness and efficacy."[41] However, in her en-
thusiasm to show that mothers are *not* "principally victims of a kind of crippling
work,"[42] she argues that the traditional dichotomy between mothering and fathering
and between female virtues and male virtues in patriarchal society seems to persist.
She says "a mother typically considers herself and is considered by others to be
responsible for the maintenance of the life of her child," and "although rarely
given primary credit, a mother typically holds herself and is held by others to be
responsible for the *malfunction* of the growth process."[43] Where is the challenge to
this tradition which relegates full responsibility for childcare to the mother? Is it
natural that mothers feel this responsibility and fathers do not, "even if it were

not demanded of [one] by [one's] community?"[44] Ruddick goes on to say that if some mothers do not display "interested participation in the practices of mothering," it is "because of emotional, intellectual, or physical disability," "severe poverty," or disaffection because of "the derogation and confinement of women in maternal practice."[45] Where is the challenge to the tradition that labels women *abnormal* for not displaying "interested participation" in childcare but labels men *normal* for that same lack of "interested participation"? Even Ruddick's discussion of "inauthenticity" in maternal practice, where "it is taken as an achievement to fulfill the ["psychologically and physically damaging"] values of the dominant culture," does not go far enough.[46] To avoid this inauthenticity, Ruddick argues that "maternal thought will have to be transformed by feminist consciousness" and quotes from Sandra Bartky's article that the feminist rejects certain, intolerable features of social reality "in behalf of a transforming project for the future."[47] But Ruddick then warns against letting men participate fully in childcare. She argues that as long as "a mother is not effective publicly and self-respecting privately," "it does a woman no good to have the power of the Symbolic Father brought right into the nursery, often despite the deep, affectionate egalitarianism of an individual man."[48] Even the children are seen to suffer under paternal childcare. Ruddick argues that "so long as a mother—even if she is no more a parent than a father—is derogated and subordinate outside the home, children will feel angry, confused, and 'wildly unmothered'."[49] For someone who accepts that "*all* thought arises out of social practice,"[50] it should seem that the father's full participation in childcare is one of the *essential means to end* the subordination and derogation of women both at home and outside the home. At the very least, there is a dialectic between theory and practice from which social values and beliefs emerge and are transformed. Feminist transformations would seem much more effective and extensive if they were to operate as simultaneously as possible in both public and domestic spheres— the one reinforcing the other. Hence, sharing family care can only help break down sexist stereotypes and contribute toward the emancipation of both women and men: women will be freer to pursue other activities and develop other capacities; men will gain sensitizing experience, which will develop the virtues of empathy and care. As long as "fathering" implies patriarchal values and practices rather than shared values and practices with female parenting, the dichotomy between fathering and mothering will persist, as will the dichotomy between "male" virtues and "female" virtues. Hence the restrictive traditional stereotypes will persist as well.

The stress feminist ethics places on the values of empathy and nurturance or care *does* potentially endorse a restrictive view of women's position when these virtues are taken to be, or are in any way implied to be, sex-determined. However, when these virtues are taken to be linked to gender, it is also imperative to consider them in the broader socioeconomic context that generates gendered dichotomies and to explicitly reject any possible implications of a restrictive view of women's position, as well as the features of the socioeconomic structure which reproduce gendered stereotypes. Neither ethical nor political theory can *settle* the question of the extent to which our propensities to behavior are biologically rooted. However, so far, the weight of the evidence of behavior modification through controlled environments of positive and negative reinforcement gives us *no reason to assume* that any virtues are biologically determined but *does give us reason to challenge that view.* Furthermore, given the oppressive results (the restrictive roles women were delegated) throughout history in societies where virtues were assumed to be biologically determined, we should be very careful, first, to scrutinize any theory that proposes or in any way implies the biological determination of some virtues; if it were to turn out to be true, we should be even more concerned about the *use* to which such a discovery would be put in society. After all, if, for example, potential athletes are in no way segregated to restrictive roles in society, why should potential empathizers?

I I I

The third main theme developed in feminist ethics is a critique of the idea that the notions of "choice" and "will" are central to morality, and of a sharp distinction between fact and value. Sara Ruddick argues that women especially are often in situations which *demand* appropriate kinds of responses. Childrearing is the reality that confronts most women; the demands of childrearing are for the "preservation, growth, and acceptability" of children.[51] The physical, emotional, intellectual, and social needs of children *require* attention and response. They are not a matter of choice or will. Ruddick goes on to argue that the task of mothering develops the skills and capacities required in the dailiness of care and concern for others. Hence, the "maternal" priorities, attitudes, and virtues are not a matter of choice or will.[52] Although it is a very important recognition that much of behavior is the response to demands of reality, it is equally important to recognize ways that "demands of reality are not just given but are related to ways reality is socially constructed."[53] As Grimshaw points out, "Ruddick's account tends to isolate mother and child as a self-contained unit of demand and response," as if interpretations of the child's needs were not informed by particular conceptions of the maternal role which in turn are related to particular conceptions of the sort of society to be realized or maintained.[54] The very fact that it is *women* who are faced with the *reality* of childrearing is a social fact, not an eternal natural law. As Annette Baier sharply observes, "the liberal system would receive a nasty spanner in its works should women . . . choose not to abort, and then leave their newborn children on their fathers' doorsteps."[55] Let the demands of childrearing fall on the men. Unless the socioeconomic context is also considered in the feminist advancement of the idea of the demands of the situation, the demands of childrearing can be seen as an inescapably female "reality," which can then be used to try to justify excluding women from educational, professional, and political opportunities.

Ruddick argues that the moral domain should not be confined only to situations that call for the exercise of choice and will, but we should recognize that it extends to include situations in which the agent recognizes the moral demands that are made on her. Recognizing moral demands and acting on them *is*, on this conception, *being* a moral agent. However, Ruddick does not make the further, but essential, following distinction. The difference between *recognizing* not only moral choices but also *moral demands*, on the one hand, and having *a responsibility imposed* on one, on the other, is a fine but crucial distinction for the autonomy of women as moral agents. *Being allocated a responsibility* is the exercise of someone else's choice being imposed on oneself. It is not the recognition by the agent herself of a moral demand made by the situation she is in, but the arbitrary assignment of the responsibility of caring for others by another agent on her. In an *ethical system which does not assume or in any way imply a restrictive view of women's place*, new and future members of the community would be trained to register the moral demands made on them by the situations they find themselves in and to respond to them. But this would be sharply distinguished from the imposition of responsibilities on them by other members of the community.

I V

The project of feminist ethics is to construct a more adequate moral theory: one that informs women's actual experience of morality and their moral concerns; one that does not devalue and dismiss the role of emotions, demands, and contextual thinking in morality; one that does not lead to a distorted assessment of women as morally immature. Some feminists argue that current moral theory is too narrowly focused and needs to be broadened to encompass the full scope of morality; others argue that the very foundations of current (contractarian-Kantian) moral theory are wrongheaded to begin with and must be totally reconstructed in order to accommodate previously excluded, but morally central values and considerations. Whichever approach is taken, feminists should be constantly vigilant to reject explicitly any possible implications of a restrictive view of women's position. Stressing the values of empathy and nurturance or care and contextual thinking as distinctly female and arising out of a distinctly female reality is potentially dangerous to the feminist cause if these can be seen in any way to imply that they are sex-linked or biologically rooted. The danger is that these female values, ways of thinking, and experiences will degenerate into the traditional dichotomies between male and female capacities and characteristics which have been used to try to justify excluding women from educational, professional, and political opportunities and locking them into roles of irrational love-givers or love-giving simpletons. There is *no necessary* connection between the belief that women are biologically disposed to be more empathetic and caring than men and the belief that the traditional division of labor between men and women should be maintained. But historically, the former belief has always been used to try to justify, albeit mistakenly, the latter belief. Why should we assume or imply the biological determination of these virtues when in fact the issue has *not been settled* by psychology and physiology or social anthropology *and* when male chauvinists have so effectively *misused* the belief in biological determination to oppress women? On the other hand, when these values, ways of thinking, and experiences are seen as gender-linked, to a large extent as results of social conditioning and socially constructed "reality," these values, ways of thinking, and experiences are seen as more or less available to men, too, depending on the extent of changes in social conditioning and social "reality." In addition, they are more resistant to degeneration into damaging stereotypes. On these terms, the recognition and vastly overdue appreciation of the values of empathy and nurturance and contextual thinking as valid and central components of morality advocated by feminist ethics contribute toward freeing moral theory from the distortion of a historically male perspective and promote feminist aims of emancipation.

NOTES

I would like to thank the following people for their useful comments and criticisms of earlier drafts of this essay: Antony Duff, Ellen Fox, Ronald Hepburn, Tamara Horowitz, Peter Jones, Sandra Marshall, Carol McAllister, Frances Olsen, and Timothy Sprigge. I am also grateful for the opportunity to have presented and discussed earlier versions of this essay at the Conference on *Explorations in Feminist Ethics: Theory and Practice* (University of Minnesota, Duluth); the University of Pittsburgh; University of Stirling; University of Edinburgh; and UCLA.

1. See especially S. M. Okin, *Women in Western Political Thought* (Princeton, N.J.: Princeton University Press, 1979); L. M. G. Clark and L. Lange, eds., *The Sexism of Social and Political Theory* (Toronto: University of Toronto Press, 1979); M. L. Osborne, ed., *Woman in Western Thought* (New York: Random House, 1979); M. Mahowald, ed., *Philosophy of Woman* (Indianapolis: Hackett, 1978, 1983).

2. John R. Lucas in J. Rachels, ed., *Moral Problems* (New York and London: Harper & Row, 1975), 140; also in *Philosophy* 48 (April 1973), 161–171.

3. S. Harding and M. B. Hintikka, eds., *Discovering Reality: Feminist Perspectives on Epistemology, Metaphysics, Methodology and Philosophy of Science* (Boston: D. Reidel, 1983): x.

4. See also Jean Baker Miller, *Toward a New Psychology of Women* (Boston: Beacon Press, 1976); Juliet Mitchell, *Psychoanalysis and Feminism* (New York: Pantheon Books, 1974); Naomi Scheman, "Individualism and the Objects of Psychology" in Harding and Hintikka, 225–244.

5. Carol Gilligan, *In a Different Voice* (Cambridge, Mass.: Harvard University Press, 1982), 2.

6. Annette Baier, "What Do Women Want in a Moral Theory?," *Nous* (March 1985), 53–63, plus unpublished section, 53–54; Lawrence Blum is notably one of these few men moral philosophers.

7. Lawrence Kohlberg, *Essays on Moral Development*, Vol. 1, *The Philosophy of Moral Development* (New York: Harper & Row, 1981), xiii, 22, 30–31, and *Essays on Moral Development*, Vol. 2, *The Psychology of Moral Development* (New York: Harper & Row, 1984), 216, 293–296, 305, 360.

8. Gilligan, 19, 21–22, 37, 62, 132.

9. Jean Grimshaw, *Feminist Philosophers* (Brighton: Wheatsheaf Books, 1986), 203.

10. See especially Seyla Benhabib, "The Generalized and the Concrete Other: The Kohlberg-Gilligan Controversy and Feminist Theory," and Iris M. Young, "Impartiality and the Civic Public: Some Implications of Feminist Critiques of Moral and Political Theory," both in S. Benhabib and D. Cornell, eds., *Feminism as Critique* (Minneapolis: University of Minnesota Press, 1987).

11. See especially Sara Ruddick, "Maternal Thinking," *Feminist Studies*, no. 2 (Summer 1980): 342–367, and "Preservative Love and Military Destruction: Some Reflections on Mothering and Peace," in J. Trebilcot, ed., *Mothering: Essays in Feminist Theory* (Totowa, N.J.: Rowman & Allanheld, 1983), and Jean Elshtain, *Public Man, Private Woman* (Oxford: Martin Robertson, 1981).

12. See especially Ruddick, "Maternal Thinking."

13. Grimshaw, 211.

14. Ibid., 210.

15. Gilligan, 100, 149.

16. Lawrence Blum, "Gilligan and Kohlberg: Implications for Moral Theory," *Ethics* 98, no. 3 (April 1988), 488–489.

17. Deontological moral theories take duty as the basis of morality. Kant's moral theory is one of the most influential of this type.

18. Iris M. Young, "Impartiality and the Civic Public: Some Implications of Feminist Critiques of Moral and Political Theory," in S. Benhabib and D. Cornell, 63.

19. Lawrence Blum, *Friendship, Altruism and Morality* (London: Routledge & Kegan Paul, 1980), 15, 117–121.

20. Gilligan, 165; see M. W. Jackson, "Oscar Schindler and Moral Theory" in *Journal for Applied Philosophy* 5, no. 2 (1988): 175–182, for further discussion of the inadequacy of deontological and utilitarian moral theories.

21. Young, 63.

22. Aristotle, *Nicomachean Ethics*, translated by T. Irwin (Indianapolis: Hackett, 1985), 403.

23. Ibid., 1137b12–32.

24. Young, 63–66.

25. For further discussion of the merits of abstraction as theorizing in general, as not intrinsically masculine, see Frances Olsen, "Feminist Theory in Grand Style," *Columbia Law Review* 89, no. 5 (1989), 1166–1177.

26. Baier, 57.

27. Contract theory focuses on the obligation to fulfill an agreement, when made freely by autonomous persons.

28. Annette Baier, "Trust and Antitrust," *Ethics* 96, no. 2 (January 1986), 247, 252.

29. Ibid., 247.

30. Grimshaw, 194.

31. Ruddick, "Maternal Thinking," 353, 359.

32. This damagingly restrictive view of women's position was most famously criticized by Betty Friedan in *The Feminine Mystique* (New York: W. W. Norton, 1963).

33. Ruddick, "Maternal Thinking," and "Preservative Love and Military Destruction."

34. For legal implications, see Frances Olsen, "The Politics of Family Law," *Law and Equality: A Journal of Theory and Practice* 2, no. 1 (1984).

35. Ruddick, "Maternal Thinking," 346.

36. Ibid., 346, 347, 359, footnote 12.

37. Ruddick also argues in "Preservative Love and Military Destruction" that "we cannot preclude the possibility that some aspects of maternal thinking derive from the infant's, and perhaps from the mother's, *biological* constitution and experience" (235, my emphasis).

38. American TV program about the feared extinction of the chimpanzee, "20/20" Friday, 27 May 1988.

39. Grimshaw, 225.

40. Ruddick, "Maternal Thinking," 346.

41. Ibid., 344.

42. Ibid., 344.

43. Ibid., 348–349.

44. Ibid., 357.

45. Ibid., 349.

46. Ibid., 354, 355.

47. Ibid., 356; Bartky's quote is from her article "Toward a Phenomenology of Feminist Consciousness," in M. Vetterling-Braggin, F. A. Elliston, and J. English, eds., *Feminism and Philosophy* (Totowa, N.J.: Littlefield Adams, 1977).

48. Ruddick, 361.

49. Ibid., using the expression of Adrienne Rich, *Of Woman Born* (New York: Norton, 1976).

50. Ruddick, 347.

51. Ibid., 348.

52. Ibid., 347–348, 351.

53. Grimshaw, 247.

54. Ibid., 246, 247.

55. Baier, 56d, unpublished section.

Care and Confusion

DIANNE ROMAIN ███████████████████

I planned to write this essay about feminist ethics in Carol Gilligan's book *In a Different Voice*.[1] However, the more I think about Gilligan's book the more confused I become about its relation to feminist ethics. Instead of presenting a view of feminist ethics, I am going to articulate my confusion.

I wonder about the extent to which Gilligan's work is feminist. More fundamentally, I am unclear about the relation between her work and ethics. What, I wonder, is the relationship between moral philosophical questions like "What ought I value?" "What is morality?" "How ought I think about moral questions?" and empirical questions like "What do women say they value?" "How do women describe morality?" "How do women think about moral questions?" Gilligan puzzles me, for she proceeds as if there is no need to clarify the relation between social science and moral philosophy.

In what follows I raise some difficulties with Gilligan's methodology. First, I question whether one can produce a feminist ethic, a theory of women's *moral* development, or a list of women's values by asking the above empirical questions. Second, I question whether Gilligan has produced a *clear (meaningful)* theory by asking these empirical questions.[2] I conclude with some reflections on the value of Gilligan's work.

VOICING FEMINIST VALUES?

If one were trying to describe a feminist ethic, one might begin by asking questions of paradigmatic feminists. These feminists could include male feminists like John Stuart Mill, as well as contemporary female feminist activists like Alice Walker, or female feminist theorists like Alison Jaggar. One would not, I assume, seek a feminist ethic by questioning women in general raised in a sexist society, for one could not assume women in general would express feminist values.

Yet this is the very approach Gilligan takes. She interviews twenty-nine women considering abortion and twenty-five college students and asks them questions to elicit their reasoning about moral dilemmas.[3] Gilligan then organizes their responses into three perspectives, with transitions between them. She summarizes the three perspectives as follows: "The sequence of women's moral judgment proceeds from an initial concern with survival to a focus on goodness and finally to a reflective understanding of care as the most adequate guide to the resolution of conflicts in human relationships."[4] The "goodness" of the second perspective is the conventional feminine ideal of goodness, caring for others at the expense of self.[5] The "reflective understanding of care" in the third perspective recognizes the worth of the caregiver and allows for care for self as well as other.[6] In each of these perspectives, preventing and responding to harm and suffering is valued.[7] Although Gilligan calls these three points of view "perspectives," they represent for her different degrees (or stages) of moral development.

DEVELOPMENT WITHOUT VALUE?

I have questioned whether one can produce a feminist ethic by studying what women say. But Gilligan doesn't say she's trying to describe a feminist ethic. She's studying the moral development of women. My question then is "How do we find *moral* order among these perspectives?" Gilligan appears to do so by observation. But suppose we observe that women respond from the first perspective, then a few years later respond from the second perspective, then a few years later respond from the third perspective? Can we conclude that the third perspective is the most *morally* developed perspective? We cannot unless we equate moral and temporal progression. To order the perspectives morally, we need to make some assumptions about the value of goodness. For example, a recent study shows that Nazi women assume that female goodness is self-sacrifice to family and community.[8] With this assumption, the second of Gilligan's perspectives is the most morally developed, not the third. One who moved to the third perspective would be judged to have regressed morally.

I would be less confused by Gilligan's approach had she related her stages of development to a philosophical ethical theory. The one that seems the most appropriate, given her subjects' concern with harm, is utilitarianism. Utilitarianism tells us to do those acts that increase happiness and decrease misery for all concerned. Persons would become more morally developed (better utilitarians) the more they are able to recognize the existence of pain (in others as well as in themselves) and the more they recognize that all pains (whether their own pain or someone else's) should be treated equally.

Why doesn't Gilligan relate her perspectives to any philosophical theory of morality or value? Gilligan rejects Lawrence Kohlberg's approach because she believes his framework distorts our perception of women's thinking. Gilligan notes that within Kohlberg's framework, the girl child Amy's response to Heinz's dilemma seems "evasive and unsure."[9] To Gilligan the problem is not with the child's thinking, it stems from the interviewer's "failure to imagine a response not dreamt of in Kohlberg's moral philosophy."[10] Gilligan wants to find a way of understanding Amy's answer that finds value in her response. I believe utilitarian ethical theory would do so, but I don't think this would satisfy Gilligan. Why? Here's my conjecture. Gilligan is not merely looking for how to find value in Amy's response, she's listening for *voice*. She wants to know how women give voice to value. She wants to be ready to hear values and ways of thinking and talking that academic philosophies have not called attention to. She assumes that by listening to women talk about their choices, their values will emerge.

Suppose, for the sake of argument, that one could discover women's values by listening to them talk. Can one discover the values required to judge moral development by listening to women make decisions? I think not. If one hears different values, then how are we to select (from women's point of view) the most morally developed? On the other hand, if women have the same values, there would be no separate stages of moral development. Thus I do not see how one can produce a theory of moral development merely by listening to women's voices (without making additional independent value assumptions).[11]

MORALITY, VOICE, AND BEHAVIOR

In the preface of *Mothers in the Fatherland*, Claudia Koonz describes her interview with Gertrud Scholtz-Klink, the chief of the Women's Bureau under Hitler. Koonz writes:

> I sat face-to-face, over tea and cakes, with the everyday banality of evil, gazing at a woman who had embraced an ideology and surrendered responsibility to a closed system that left no doubts—or at least none that she would admit to. Never had she overstepped her bounds. Always she had followed the law. Never did she admit to pondering the ramifications of anything. She translated orders from above into obedience from below. And she had not broken the criminal code or the Geneva Convention. Thinking back on the archives I had visited, a new picture of the Third Reich began to take shape. Next to the dominant motif of male brutality, Gertrud Scholtz-Klink and millions of followers created the social side of tyranny. Busily administering welfare services, educational programs, leisure activities, ideological indoctrination, and consumer organizations, Nazi women mended while Nazi men marched.[12]

In *Obedience to Authority*, Stanley Milgram writes:

> Forty women were also studied. . . . The level of obedience was virtually identical to the performance of men; however, the level of conflict experienced by the women was on the whole higher than that felt by our male subjects.[13]

In a footnote Milgram adds:

> Recently, I have learned that other experimenters (Sheridan and King, 1972) have replicated the obedience experiments but with this difference: in place of a human victim, they used a genuine victim, a puppy, who actually received the

electric shock and who yelped, howled, and ran when he was shocked. Men and women were used as subjects, and the authors found that the women were more compliant than the men. Indeed, they write, "Without exception, female S's (subjects) complied with instructions to shock the puppy all the way to the end of the scale."[14]

Milgram and Koonz prevent me from concluding that women, as such, have answers to the questions "What moral values or ways of thinking ought I adopt?" and "What can I do to act on my commitments in the face of authority or other challenges?" Their work reminds me that though women may voice caring values, we do not necessarily live up to them. It doesn't follow that women don't value caring, but these reminders of how women behave prevent us from concluding too hastily from women's voices that care is our ultimate value.[15]

VALUE FROM VOICE?

I want to say more about using what women say when making decisions to derive what women value.[16] Let's put Milgram and Koonz aside for the moment and assume that women voice caring values and engage in caring activities. Can we conclude that women value maintaining relationships and caring? Can we infer that caring and maintaining relationships are women's primary values?

If someone looked at what I talk about and how I spend my time, they might well conclude that relationships are important to me. I belong to a women's writing group and a group that plans the campus nuclear-issues class, and I spend time talking with these people outside of the groups, working on maintaining our relationships. I also have a companion whom I set aside special time for to engage in activities that reinforce our relationship. When teaching, I have my students work in groups to build constructive connections with each other, while I go from group to group to give more individual attention to them. I also engage in more solitary activities of playing the piano and writing. Often when I describe my life I find I emphasize building and maintaining relationships. But I wonder, "Would I focus so much on relationship, if I had the opportunity to become a writer or an adventurer, climbing volcanos around the world?"

Intellectual and creative work give me the most pleasure and satisfaction. How do I know this? Because the only time I think "Don't let me die now" (other than when I'm facing immediate danger, like climbing an active volcano) is when I'm engaged in some creative project. I feel this way regardless of whether the project I'm working on has any obvious value to others. I love to be alone in my study all day with only the hum of my Mac to keep me company. I love to read my writing again and again, to find thoughts to elaborate, structure to develop. I love to sound my words and sentences, to listen to the pattern of phrases. I could spend hours on a single paragraph. But I rarely do. I rarely spend hours on a single essay or story. And why?

When am I to find the time to breathe, to think, to create, when I teach in an institution where full-time work is teaching four courses (most of them service courses) and when in that institution I am a lecturer, hired (if I am lucky) year after year, with no opportunities for sabbaticals or release time for research? I can take time off, without pay, but if I do, I take the chance of losing my toe-in-the-door status that gives me the negligible right to be rehired. Is it any wonder that in this precarious professional and economic context, I focus more on relationships than on writing? In the last few years I've chosen to teach part-time to give myself the chance to begin to write again. But I can do this (and live in comfort) only because of my companion. I have a Ph.D., I am a respected teacher and colleague, and yet I remain one man away from poverty. And I sometimes wonder if I value my relationship with him for its own sake or because my relationship with him allows me to spend an occasional entire day in my study alone with the hum of my Mac (not to mention an occasional hike up a volcano).

Should I apply for a job at a research institution to allow me more time to write, even if this means long separations from my companion or asking him to give up his tenured position and follow me? How many women (or men) receive tenure in such places? Can I jeopardize both our chances for financial security because of my love of writing? If I do not, does my decision show that I care more about maintaining relationships than about writing?

"Ah," you say, "but if women really valued solitude and creative projects, we would hear them say so." I didn't used to say so, either, in quite this way, and I'm not sure how different my values were then. I began to question the meaning of my own talk about caring a number of years ago while reading Margaret Adams's "The Compassion Trap."[17]

In her article Adams raises questions about whether women should focus on caring for the near and dear in a society headed for destruction. She also raises questions about whether our choices show that we do prefer caring or whether we are making the best of limited opportunities. She notes that the "helping professions" of teaching, social work, and nursing welcome women. She explains our willingness to enter these professions as follows: "This overriding need to feel useful in a social system that in other respects accords little opportunity for significant participation makes most women leap at an offer of involvement, even when it means stifling their underlying frustration and disappointment at the soothing rationalization that personal ambition and success are corrupting."[18] I began to question whether I believed (what I said) that teaching was intellectually satisfying when Adams questions whether women receive sufficient intellectual satisfaction from teaching (as many say they do). We teach instead of create, she suggests, because our perception of ourselves as care givers prevents us from finding the time for "the single-minded concentration that writing and other creative ventures require."[19]

The Adams article raises the questions: Do we talk about valuing relationships and caring because we place the highest priority on them or because these are qualities we use in the societal roles open to us? Do we not talk about other creative work because we don't want to feel frustration? Do we hope to find satisfaction by ignoring the wish for a room of our own? Are we embarrassed to admit economic security dictates our choices between creativity and care?

How can we answer these questions?[20] Ideally we would look at what women say and choose when they have the opportunity to play noncaring roles. Short of that we might take an imaginative look at those who came before us.

REVISIONED VOICE

I have in mind here the type of revisioning that Alice Walker does in "In Search of Our Mothers' Gardens." Walker describes her mother's work:

> She made all the clothes we wore, even my brother's overalls. She made all the towels and sheets we used. She spent the summers canning vegetables and fruits. She spent the winter evenings making quilts enough to cover all our beds.
> During the "working" day, she labored beside—not behind—my father in the fields. Her day began before sunup, and did not end until late at night. There was never a moment for her to sit down, undisturbed, to unravel her own private thoughts; never a time free from interruption—by work or the noisy inquiries of her many children.[21]

How, one might wonder, could one find art in this woman's life? Through traditional lenses Walker's mother was no artist. Her works could not be preserved in museums for generations to see. Walker herself did not recognize the artist in her mother for many years, though throughout her childhood Walker had seen her mother's art. By revisioning, Alice Walker came to see her mother's art in her mother's garden:

> Whatever she planted grew as if by magic, and her fame as a grower of flowers spread over three counties. Because of her creativity with her flowers, even my memories of poverty are seen through a screen of blooms—sunflowers, petunias, roses, dahlias, forsythia, spirea, delphiniums, verbena . . . and on and on. . . .
> I notice that it is only when my mother is working in her flowers that she is radiant, almost to the point of being invisible—except as Creator: hand and eye. She is involved in work her soul must have. Ordering the universe in the image of her personal conception of Beauty.
> Her face, as she prepares the Art that is her gift, is a legacy of respect she leaves to me, for all that illuminates and cherishes life. She has handed down respect for the possibilities—and the will to grasp them.[22]

I think of my own mother raising seven children in a small Missouri town where motherhood was the one challenging occupation for a woman. The closest my mother came to a room of her own was a sewing area off the kitchen, where she sat alone late at night making dresses for her five daughters. Was her sewing a way to show her care for us? Or was it a way to express her creativity within the limits of her society? I have no doubt of her love, but neither do I doubt her driving desire for other modes of expression.

When on a beautiful day I sit on my deck and dream and know I will not be interrupted by the sweet face of a child, I smile and think, "How lucky I am that I have no children!" And I wonder now as I write, "Is this my mother's voice within me?"[23] Is the voice that gives me permission to glory in my freedom from motherhood the familiar voice of my own mother? Yet how can this be, given her life and what she would say about it, that she has no regrets over the twenty years she spent caring for her family before she went to college? Like Alice Walker I know from my mother's look, by her joyful concentration when searching for the latest delicate bloom in her wildflower garden, by the pleasure it gives her to paint, by the light in her eyes when her oldest and only childless daughter kisses her good-bye, and she tells me, "I am so proud of you."

CLARITY WITHOUT QUESTION?

I want now to turn to my second methodological question: Can one produce a *clear* (*meaningful*) theory by listening to women talk about moral questions? In the following quotation Gilligan is describing and quoting Claire, a participant in the college-student study. Listen to how Claire talks:

> (S)he (Claire) believes that Heinz should steal the drug, whether or not he loves his wife, "by virtue of the fact that they are both there." Although a person may not like someone else, "you have to love someone else, because you are inseparable from them. In a way it's like loving your right hand; it is part of you. That other person is part of that giant collection of everybody." Thus she articulates an ethic of responsibility that stems from an awareness of interconnection: "The stranger is still another person belonging to that group, people you are connected to by virtue of being another person."[24]

Here's my puzzlement. I can't imagine reading a student paper or listening to a student say, "You have to love someone else, because you are inseparable from them," or "That other person is a part of that giant collection of everybody," without wondering what they mean. In what sense I wonder are persons inseparable from one another? Unless they are Siamese twins or fetus and mother, they are not physically connected the way one's hand is connected to the rest of one's body. And how, I might add, is loving a person (whom you don't like) like loving your hand? I'm not sure I know what it means to love my hand, but I suspect it's a different type of thing from loving a person.

If Claire were my student, I might not ask her these questions. I may want to adopt a less intrusive way of moving her to clarify her meaning. But if she did not clarify her meaning, I would have to conclude I did not know what she meant. Gilligan doesn't seem to recognize a lack of clarity in Claire's language. In the passage above she summarizes Claire's view, as if she understands what Claire is saying.

Here are two other student quotations that are difficult for me to understand:

> I never feel that I can condemn anyone else. I have a very relativistic position. The basic idea that I cling to is the sanctity of human life. I am inhibited about impressing my beliefs on others.

> I could never argue that my belief on a moral question is anything that another person should accept. I don't believe in absolutes. If there is an absolute for moral decisions, it is human life.[25]

How, I wonder, can one be a relativist and cling to the sanctity of human life? Again, how can one not believe in absolutes, yet imply that human life may be an absolute? If someone said these things to me, I would want clarification. Yet Gilligan uses these quotes to describe: "The reticence about taking stands on 'controversial issues,' a willingness to 'make exceptions all the time.' "[26] She adds, "What emerges in these voices is a sense of vulnerability that impedes these women from taking a stand."[27] I don't doubt that these women are vulnerable. But I don't see how one can understand what they think from these quotes.

I have difficulty throughout In A Different Voice understanding the meaning of key terms Gilligan uses. I puzzle over "relationship," "connection," "responsibility," "caring,"[28] "self," "contextual judgment." All are abstract terms that have a variety of meanings. Yet Gilligan does not specify which meaning or meanings she intends.

Perhaps Gilligan's failure to clarify meaning results from her methodology. If she is listening to women speak in order to record their voice, she might use their language for accuracy of description, and it would be inappropriate to critique or clarify the language. Gilligan would then be speaking in her voice, not the voice of the women she interviewed.[29] Unfortunately, Gilligan's careful process results in a deeply muddled voice.

CARING IS FEMINIST?

It is largely because I could not understand what Gilligan was saying that I gave up my efforts to figure out whether the highest, the third moral perspective was feminist.[30] But in spite of my confusion I'd like to present an example for your consideration. Suppose I have a baby who needs her diapers changed. I respond to her cry, not by moving from my study, but by sending my husband while I continue writing a lecture. Am I not caring for self and other as the third perspective requires? Am I a feminist? What if the lecture I am writing is against the ERA?

I am also concerned about Gilligan's description of persons. Again I am not clear about her view, but she seems to hold that persons (in the third perspective) define themselves in relationships. I have two recommendations. First, I would like to see an interpretation of this view of persons in which "sacrificing oneself" does not become meaningless. I believe there are times when fully morally developed women (and men) genuinely and freely sacrifice their interests for another, and I would like to see them get credit for doing so. Second, Gilligan's notion of responsibility, as far as I understand it, appears to describe an individual's responsibility.[31] She talks about relationship as it further defines individual responsibility. My responsibility is to my relationship to my child, its father, and so on. I find it particularly strange that Gilligan does not discuss shared responsibility, given her description of how third-perspective persons define themselves. I want to know how Gilligan's description affects responsibility. Among other things, Gilligan might discuss shared responsibility for pregnancy and birth control.[32]

Finally I want to voice a feminist concern about stereotyping women. An anthropologist colleague of mine, Mildred Dickemann, read Gilligan and pronounced her view "the same old tune, sung upside down."[33] I, too, worry about stereotyping women, even when the stereotyped characteristics are laudable. And though Gilligan says in her introduction, "The different voice I describe is characterized not by gender but theme," she talks all the way through her book about women's voice. My concern is not merely with women once again being separated from men, but with myself once again being separated from women. Although I hear a familiar tone in the voice Gilligan describes,[34] her women's voice fails to express my longing for a room of my own and my love of theoretical questioning. Do I not, in Gilligan's view, "think (at least in part) like a man"? Isn't it time we stopped classifying characteristics as feminine or masculine when we have no evidence that all and only females or males have such characteristics?

THE VALUE OF VOICES

I work under the assumption that insight and creativity follow from confusion. Thus I value Gilligan's work. The very ambiguity Gilligan records invites interpretation and exploration. Her work has motivated other voices to speak up, to clarify, and to develop moral philosophy. I hope that Gilligan and other social scientists will continue to work on moral questions. They can provide philosophers information to help us create views that make sense to the ear, heart, and mind. A continuing dialogue must be our goal, if we want moral philosophy to have any useful effect on the morality of our day.[35]

NOTES

I am indebted to members of the Society of Women in Philosophy for their comments when I read this essay at their April 1988 meeting in Los Angeles. I also benefited from the comments of Mildred Dickemann and Ellen Kay Trimberger. I am grateful to Mary Ann

Warren for her constructive response to an early draft and to Edward F. Mooney and P. S. Page Bennett for helping me with finishing touches.

1. Carol Gilligan, *In a Different Voice: Psychological Theory and Women's Development* (Cambridge: Harvard University Press, 1982).

2. Ironically, while describing women's alleged discomfort with abstract principles, Gilligan produces a theory of moral development that itself (of necessity) abstracts from the stories she hears.

3. Gilligan, 3. (Gilligan also notes here that she further refined her conclusions in a rights and responsibilities study of 144 males and females.)

4. Ibid., 105.

5. Ibid., 74.

6. Ibid.

7. Ibid., 95.

8. Claudia Koonz describes Nazi women's values in her book *Mothers in the Fatherland: Women, the Family, and Nazi Politics* (New York: St. Martin's Press, 1987).

9. Gilligan, 28.

10. Ibid., 29.

11. The value assumption Gilligan makes may well be feminist. The assumption that women are equal in worth to those they care for would explain why the third perspective is more morally developed than the second.

12. Koonz, xxxiii.

13. Stanley Milgram, *Obedience to Authority: An Experimental View* (New York: Harper & Row, 1974), 62–63.

14. Milgram, 206.

15. See also Claudia Card, "Women's Voices and Ethical Ideals: Must We Mean What We Say?" *Ethics* 99 (October 1988): 125–135. She notes studies of women's violence against other lesbian women and against children and white women's violence against black people during American slavery, and writes, "The point is neither that we act against our values nor that women's voices should not be taken seriously. It is that taking seriously what we *say* when we are disadvantaged requires of us special critical scrutiny. Widespread resort to violence after a history of subordination indicates that women, like men, value power and resent impotence, rhetoric to the contrary notwithstanding."

16. Here I'm using "voice" to mean "talk" or "conversation." Writing teachers sometimes use the expressions "writing with voice" or "writing in one's own voice" to refer to writing that in some way reflects the character of the author. One *speaks* in one's voice when one speaks in a tone or manner that reflects one's character or values. See, for example, "Writing and Voice" in Peter Elbow, *Writing with Power: Techniques for Mastering the Writing Process* (Oxford: Oxford University Press, 1981), 281–303. With these two senses of "voice" in mind, my question becomes "Can one discover voice (in the sense of character) by listening to voices (in the sense of conversation)?"

17. Margaret Adams, "The Compassion Trap," in Martha Lee Osborne, ed., *Woman in Western Thought* (New York: Random House, 1979), 257–263.

18. Ibid., 260.

19. Ibid., 263.

20. For a discussion of how our understanding of what's possible in our society affects our emotions (and how we would describe what matters to us), see chapter 9, "A Rage for Justice," in Carol Tavris, *Anger: The Misunderstood Emotion* (New York: Simon & Schuster, 1982). For a discussion of how we talk ourselves out of or into emotions (and how we would describe what matters to us), see Arlie Hochschild, *The Managed Heart: Commercialization of Human Feeling* (Berkeley: University of California Press, 1983). These books raise questions that must be addressed when trying to figure out how what we say indicates what we want or value.

21. Alice Walker, "In Search of Our Mothers' Gardens," in Alice Walker, *In Search of Our Mothers' Gardens* (San Diego: Harcourt Brace Jovanovich, 1983), 238.

22. Walker, 241–242.

23. In this section I'm using "voice" to represent character.

24. Gilligan, 57.

25. Ibid., 66.

26. Ibid.

27. Ibid.

28. For a clearer discussion of "caring," see Nel Noddings, *Caring: A Feminine Approach to Ethics & Moral Education* (Berkeley: University of California Press, 1984).

29. Gilligan mentions a number of psychologists, including Nancy Chodorow and Jean Baker Miller, who use the language of connection and relationship. I wonder about the extent to which Gilligan listens to her subjects through the language of these theorists and whether she can clearly hear her subjects' own voices. Virginia Warren asked me to consider whether a teacher might not help a student discover her own voice by questioning her and offering her other language. Yes, I do this. But I also believe the questions I raised above, if asked in a certain tone, would have silenced Claire. I am also puzzled over the difference between "discovering one's own voice," and "developing a new voice."

30. I realize that Gilligan regards the care approach as incomplete. She discusses the relation between care and justice approaches in "Moral Orientation and Moral Development," in Eva Feder Kittay and Diana T. Meyers, eds., *Women and Moral Theory* (Totowa, N.J.: Rowman & Littlefield, 1987), 19–33.

31. For a wonderful discussion of the meaning of "responsibility" in *In a Different Voice*, see Mary Ann O'Loughlin, "Responsibility and Moral Maturity in the Control of Fertility— or, A Woman's Place is in the Wrong," *Social Research* 50 (Autumn 1983), 556–576.

32. Ibid.

33. Mildred Dickemann, "Mythical Women: The Political Economy of the New Women's Ideologies," a talk given at Sonoma State University, March 1988, during Women's History Week.

34. I wonder whether the familiarity of Gilligan's different voice follows from its vagueness. Perhaps it fits me only like my morning horoscope.

35. Kathryn Pyne Addelson gave a paper "Why Can't a Woman Be Like Us?" at the Pacific Division APA in 1975. In this paper, Addelson makes productive use of the work of interactionist sociologists. For insight into the confusion of developing a new moral approach, see Addelson's (Kathryn Pyne Parson's) article "Nietzsche and Moral Change" in Martha Lee Osborne, ed., *Woman in Western Thought* (New York: Random House, 1979), 235–248.

Warning: The Surgeon Moralist Has Determined That Claims of Rights Can Be Detrimental to Everyone's Interests

ROGER J. RIGTERINK ███████████████

The Fond du Lac Commonwealth Reporter, January 3, 1988: The white crow that attracted the attention of bird watchers in a broad area of Fond du Lac's east side and the outlying countryside is dead. The crow was killed at long range with a shot from a .22 caliber rifle by a local hunter during the early part of the small-game hunting season. At the request of the hunter who shot the crow, his name is not used here. He said his decision to shoot the bird is a "touchy thing." "I realize that people who are interested in ornithology are going to be very upset about it. . . . "

One person who is upset about the shooting is Jo Ann Munson. . . . "I was angry about it when I first heard about it, and I still am," she said. "I don't understand why someone feels the need to shoot a bird like that. It should have been left in the wild for all of us to enjoy." She says the bird was a frequent visitor at feeders in her neighborhood. She noted that children on their way to school often saw the white crow flying with the flock. . . .

Asked why he shot the crow, the hunter responded, "I'm a hunter. It's fair game. The opportunity presented itself. People blow these things out of context . . . I had been seeing it for a long time," he said. "I wanted it for a trophy. . . . "[1] The shooting of crows—black or white—is legal. . . . It is illegal to shoot an albino deer. All other albino species may be hunted.

When I presented this news report to a class, I received two sorts of responses. On the one hand, I had students describe the hunter as thoughtless, insensitive, a jerk. In contrast, I also had students claim that the hunter had not done anything wrong. One might think that I had the beginnings of a spirited debate. The fact of the matter is that the class was pretty much of a single piece. Admittedly, there were purists who adhered to only one of the above-mentioned perspectives. But the vast majority of the class thought that both sets of claims were correct. They felt that even though what the hunter had done was morally repugnant, he had not done anything wrong. This seeming contradiction caused discomfort, but the students saw no escape. It is surprising that in order to explain whence their dilemma came, we need to begin with Carol Gilligan.

Gilligan obviously hit a responsive chord when she identified two modes of moral thought: the ethics of justice versus the ethics of care.[2] The distinction raised questions. Can these modes of thought be described with more sharpness? Is the gender differentiation real or do all people appeal to both modes situationally? Where do minorities and members of foreign cultures fit in? Are these the only modes of ethical thought or is a finer-grained analysis needed? All these questions need to be addressed, but my concern is different. How are the two modes of thought related to each other?

The most common view seems to be that the two perspectives are additive. By this I mean that both perspectives are legitimate, but they need to be added together in order to obtain a truly adequate account of morality. The very title of a recent article by Annette Baier, "The Need for More Than Justice," seems to reflect this view. Baier makes both an individualistic and a social claim in favor of the need for combining. On the one hand, she notes that if individuals have nothing more than the conception of justice holding their lives together, their lives may well end up as empty and hollow:

> For the main complaint about the Kantian version of a society with its first virtue justice, construed as respect for equal rights to formal goods . . . is that none of these goods do much to ensure that the people who have and mutually respect such rights will have any other relationships to one another than the minimal relationship needed to keep such a 'civil society' going. They may well be lonely, driven to suicide, apathetic about their work and about participation in political processes, find their lives meaningless and have no wish to leave offspring to face the same meaningless existence.[3]

The harms listed here are real, but the only persons negatively affected are those with the diminished sense of morality. Those who have a sense of caring as well as a sense of justice have nothing to fear. They gain by what Baier is tempted to call "a moral extra."

Things are different, however, with regard to Baier's social complaint. She notes that when a society contains both types of individuals—those with only a sense of justice versus those with a sense of care—it is possible for, in fact it has been the pattern for, the former group to exploit the latter.

> The encouragement of some to cultivate [the ethics of care] while others do not could easily lead to exploitation of those who do. It obviously *has* suited some in most societies well enough that others take on the responsibilities of care (for the sick, the helpless, the young) leaving them free to pursue their own less altruistic goods. . . . As long as women could be got to assume responsibility for the care of home and children, and to train their children to continue the sexist system,

the liberal morality could continue to be the official morality. . . . The long unnoticed moral proletariat were the domestic workers, mostly female.[4]

In this case, the ethics of care cannot be viewed as something that automatically benefits those who possess it, "a moral extra." In fact, the very people who possess a sense of caring are being put at risk. They alone shoulder the burden of meeting the needs of those who are in a state of dependency. They gain this task via the inattentiveness and inaction of those concerned with only their own rights. But even here, Baier sees no need to dispense with an ethics of justice. Rather, if those who only possess such concerns could *augment* them with an ethics of care, they would acquire sympathies that would prod them away from inattentiveness into action. Thus, Baier can still argue that the relationship between the two ethics is additive.

At the close of her article, Baier registers a final complaint about the various theories of justice. She claims that they are based on a "partial myth" that human interactions typically take place between freestanding individuals. In contrast, she claims, "Vulnerable future generations do not choose their dependence on earlier generations. The unequal infant does not choose its place in a family or nation, nor is it treated as free to do as it likes until some association is freely entered into. Nor do its parents always choose their parental role."[5]

Virginia Held makes the same point. She complains that excessive attention has been paid to "rational contractors" or "economic man" as if the primary social relations that we encounter are between fully developed, nondependent equals. Held believes that the more typical human relationship is the one found between mothering person and child: "[Contract] theorists have supposed the context of mothering to be of much less significance for human history and of much less relevance for moral theory than the realms of trade and government, or they have imagined mothers and children as somehow outside human society altogether in a region labelled 'nature,' and engaged wholly in 'reproduction.' But mothering is at the heart of human society."[6] But even in the midst of arguing for a noncontractual society, one modeled on the relationship found between mothering person and child, Held acknowledges that there are some situations, albeit many fewer than normally thought, in which an appeal to the "rational contractor," along with its concomitant concern for rights and justice, is the more appropriate model to adopt. She believes that context will determine when we should appeal to each model. Cancer patients and children are, of necessity, in dependent positions. A business contractor often is not. Since situations dictate to which ethic we should appeal, Held like Baier considers the relationship between the two modes of ethical thought to be additive.

Baier and Held have made a number of significant points. They fall short, however, not because they misrepresent the situations they consider, but because they fail to consider yet another type of situation. This brings us back to the news report presented at the beginning of this essay. The hunter was acting within his rights. He had not harmed anyone, nor done any irreparable damage to the environment, nor brought a reproducible species nearer to extinction. Given what is now viewed as a moral truism—that people acting within their rights are not doing anything wrong—the hunter was able to conclude, with my students concurring, there was no wrongdoing when he shot the crow.

But the hunter was not simply satisfying his own interests. He was causing frustration for everyone but himself. Of course, not everyone really, deeply cared about the white crow. But among those who did not care, most were respectful of those who did. This is why my students considered the hunter's actions morally repugnant. Such feelings stemmed from an ethics of care and concern. But my students, like Baier and Held, presumed the relationship between cares and rights to be additive. No matter how much the students' sympathies extended to those who enjoyed the presence of the white crow, that could not cancel out the fact that the hunter was acting within his rights. As long as the hunter was acting within his rights, that, in and of itself, exonerated him from any wrongdoing.

The death of a single crow, albeit a white one, is not morally earthshaking. Perhaps this whole affair is a mere moral oddity, a unique and isolated occurrence, and a rather trivial one at that. Such notions can be quickly dispelled by listening to who is currently claiming rights. The presumption is that it is people seeking protection from any overzealous interference into their personal affairs. But more likely, it is the cigar smoker who seeks personal pleasure while spoiling the atmosphere of an entire room. Or it is the entrepreneur seeking to put an amusement park in an established neighborhood. It is the chauvinist who wants his *Playboy* in full public display and convenient to buy. It is the camper with a boombox who feels nature ought to be embellished with the heavy rhythms of acid rock. In short, it is boorish people who care nothing about the interests and desires of others. Whenever anyone has the strength to protest, the smoker, the entrepreneur, the chauvinist, the camper all appeal to their rights. Such appeals provide allies—embarrassed but staunch—in proclaiming that a person does indeed have a right to do such things.

The obvious fix to all these difficulties would be to dump the idea that the relationship between rights and cares is additive. Perhaps the two perspectives are competitive in the sense that they present equally legitimate moral claims that have to be adjudicated on a case-by-case basis. This is the position of the moral pluralists.

Thomas Nagel, for example, argued that there were five equally valid moral perspectives: obligations, rights, utility, perfectionist ends, and private commitments. This list is notable because of the absence of any kind of feminist standpoint. It would be hoped that this is only because the list represents Nagel's thinking as of 1979. In any case, Nagel contends that "conflicts can exist within one of these [perspectives], and it may be hard to resolve. But when conflict occurs between them, the problem becomes still more difficult. . . . They cannot be resolved by subsuming [one] of the points of view under [another] or both under a third. Nor can we simply abandon any of them."[7]

The only solution, according to Nagel, is to make an appeal to what he calls *judgment*, "essentially the faculty Aristotle described as practical wisdom, which reveals itself over time in individual decisions rather than in the enunciation of general principles. It will not always yield a solution: there are true practical dilemmas that have no solution. . . . But in many cases it can be relied on to take up the slack that remains beyond the limits of explicit argument."[8]

Owen Flanagan and Kathryn Jackson present a similar position in a recent reappraisal of the Kohlberg-Gilligan debate. They see "moral psychology as variegated, as composed of a wide array of attitudes, dispositions, rules of thumb, and principles that are designed for multifarious sorts of situations."[9] Flanagan and Jackson claim that this collage of attitudes and perspectives not only contains the notions of justice and care described by Gilligan, but a number of other equally valid moral concerns. Like Nagel, Flanagan and Jackson believe that how one adjudicates between the various perspectives is situational. Often the nature of the moral problem can dictate that one perspective is the most appropriate. But in some cases, several perspectives seem equally correct, and this is what creates some of our more intractable moral dilemmas.

The fundamental problem with the competitive view, as outlined above, is that rights, by design, are not meant to be competitive. The whole point of naming things as rights is to remove them from the arena of competition. They are, as Nozick noted, "side constraints"—delimiters that mark off areas in which other moral considerations cannot be used to justify interference.[10] The only thing that can defeat a right is another right.

This notion that rights can be defeated only by rights led to the profusion of alleged rights. Philosophers had recognized long before Gilligan that concerns of care could not be addressed as long as rights were conceived of in the traditional Lockean fashion as freedoms. In order to address matters of care, they invented (and "invented" is the right word) positive rights. They claimed that in addition to the traditional basic freedoms, people also have a right to adequate food, shelter, medical care, and, according to the Universal Declaration of Human Rights of the United Nations, a paid vacation.

But even positive rights proved to be inadequate. Rights must be claimed. But how are infants, the mentally defective and senile, the Karen Ann Quinlans, not to mention the animals and trees within the environment, supposed to speak in behalf of their interests? Philosophers responded by saying that lawyers and other third-party advocates could represent the interests of these parties. But that runs afoul of the fact that the claiming of rights is meant to be optional. Free speech does not obligate people to speak. Likewise, a person might refuse an operation even though she has the right to medical care. But how can an advocate determine what a silent third party would wish with regard to the exercise of a right when the choice of whether to exercise that right is supposed to be the result of a free and independent thought process representing the uniqueness of the individual involved?

I suggest that this and all of the difficulties mentioned in this essay could be solved by presuming that the relationship between rights and cares is neither additive nor competitive, but eliminative. We need to take the hard step of denying that rights exist. This suggestion might strike some not as a solution, but as something on par with "the final solution." Speaking for my opponents, they might concede there are difficulties within the field of rights, but then ask "How can I deny that, amidst all of the turmoil, there are legitimate rights, and that, when humans demanded the enforcement of these rights, it led to some of the greatest achievements in moral progress, while the denial of these very same rights has been responsible for some of history's darkest enterprises?"

But is a theory of rights the only theory capable of asserting that a moral equality exists among individuals? Do we have to have rights in order to claim that a better world results when people are given some free space in order to pursue their own endeavors? Is a theory of rights the only theory that can hold up an autonomous individual as a developmental ideal?

Speaking for one, I believe that such laudable goals can be incorporated into a feminist ethic that emphasizes the reality of concerns and cares, or into what might amount to the same thing, a well-developed moral theory anchored to the concept of virtue. These latter theories have the advantage of being metaphysically less suspicious in that they avoid getting us involved in the ontological commitments that led Jeremy Bentham to label rights as "nonsense on stilts." More important, these theories avoid proclaiming that a certain moral concept is fundamental and inviolable. These properties allowed the hunter, once he had determined that he was acting within his rights, to say that he had done no wrong. Perhaps, if we were to deny that any moral concept can have the status of being absolutely fundamental and, in so doing, deny the existence of rights, we could then say that the hunter had done something wrong after all.

NOTES

1. Michael Mentzer, "Hunter Kills White Crow," *Fond Du Lac Commonwealth Reporter* (January 3, 1988).

2. Carol Gilligan, *In a Different Voice* (Cambridge, Mass.: Harvard University Press, 1982).

3. Annette C. Baier, "The Need for More Than Justice," in Marsha Hanen and Kai Nielsen, eds., *Science, Morality and Feminist Theory* (Calgary, Alberta: University of Calgary Press, 1987), 47.

4. Ibid., 49–50.

5. Ibid., 54.

6. Virginia Held, "Non-Contractual Society," in Marsha Hanen and Kai Nielsen, eds., *Science, Morality and Feminist Theory* (Calgary, Alberta: University of Calgary Press, 1987), 137.

7. Thomas Nagel, *Moral Questions* (Cambridge, England: Cambridge University Press, 1979), 132.

8. Ibid., 132.

9. Owen Flanagan and Kathryn Jackson, "Justice, Care and Gender: The Kohlberg-Gilligan Debate Revisited," *Ethics* 97.3 (April 1987), 627.

10. Robert Nozick, *Anarchy, State and Utopia* (New York: Basic Books, 1974).

Just Caring

RITA MANNING

In this essay, I shall sketch and provide a cursory defense of a model of ethical considerations which I shall call, following Nel Noddings, an ethic of caring.[1]

I shall confess at the outset that this model owes more to my experience as a woman, a teacher, and a mother than to my training and experience in moral philosophy. Over the years, my students have convinced me of the barrenness of standard ethical theories. It has occurred to me only very recently that, in sketching a more adequate model, I might appeal to my own experience as a moral person. I credit Hume,[2] Annette Baier,[3] and Carol Gilligan[4] with waking me from my dogmatic slumber and Nel Noddings with allowing me to take caring, which is central to my moral experience, seriously.

An ethic of caring, as I shall defend it, includes two elements. First is a disposition to care. This is a willingness to receive others, a willingness to give the lucid attention to the needs of others which filling these needs appropriately requires. I see this disposition to care as nourished by a spiritual awareness similar to the awareness argued for by proponents of the women's spirituality movement. As Starhawk describes this awareness: "Immanent justice rests on the first principle of magic: all things are interconnected. All is relationship. Perhaps the ultimate ethic of immanence is to choose to make that relationship one of love . . . love for all the eternally self-creating world, love of the light and the mysterious darkness, and raging love against all that would diminish the unspeakable beauty of the world."[5]

In addition to being sensitive to my place in the world and to my general obligation to be a caring person, I am also obligated to care for. (I am following Noddings in using "care for" to indicate caring as expressed in action.) In the paradigm case, caring for involves acting in some appropriate way to respond to the needs of persons, and animals, but can also be extended to responding to the needs of communities, values, or objects. My obligation to care for is limited by a principle of supererogation, which is necessary to keep an ethic of caring from degenerating into an ethics of total self-sacrifice. I shall argue that we are obligated to adopt this model of caring as far as we can in our moral deliberations. We are morally permitted and sometimes morally obliged to appeal to rules and rights. In Gilligan's idiom, we are required to listen to the voices of both care and justice. In what follows, I shall first fill in some of the details of this model. Specifically, I shall discuss what it is to care for someone or something and when we are obligated to care for. Next, I shall say something about the role of rules and rights in this model.

I. CARING

I have often wondered if taking a class in moral philosophy was the best way for students to become sensitive to moral concerns. It seemed to me that a better way would be to have students work in soup kitchens or shelters for the homeless.[6] I am convinced that taking care of my children has made me more open to moral concerns. In taking care of the hungry, homeless, and helpless, we are engaged in caring for. In the standard case, caring for is immediate; it admits of no surrogates. When I directly care for some creature, I am in physical contact. Our eyes meet, our hands touch. Not every need can be met in this immediate way. In that case, I must accept a surrogate. Not every need can be met by individual action. In those cases, I must seek collective action.[7] But when I can do the caring for myself, I ought to do so, at least some of the time. The need of the other may sometimes require that I do the caring for. If my child needs my attention, I cannot meet this need by sending her to a therapist. Even when the needs of the other do not require my personal attention, I must provide some of the caring for directly in order to develop and sustain my ability to care.

My day-to-day interactions with other persons create a web of reciprocal caring. In these interactions, I am obliged to be a caring person. I am free, to a certain extent, to choose when and how to care for these others. My choice is limited by my relationships with these others and by their needs. A pressing need calls up an immediate obligation to care for; roles and responsibilities call up an obligation to respond in a caring manner. In the first case, I am obligated (though this obligation can be limited by a principle of supererogation) to respond; in the second, I can choose, within limits, when and how to care.

A creature in need who is unable to meet this need without help calls for a caring response on my part. This response needn't always be direct. Sometimes it is better to organize a political response. (Many, for example, who are confronted on the street by homeless people are unsure about how to respond, convinced that their immediate response will not be enough, might even be counterproductive.) Certain relationships obligate me to provide direct caring for. When my daughter falls and asks me to "kiss it and make it better," I can't send her to my neighbor for the kiss.

My roles as mother, as teacher, as volunteer, put me in particular relationships to others.[8] These roles require and sustain caring. My obligation to my infant children and my animals is to meet their basic needs for physical sustenance (food, shelter, clothing, health care) and for companionship and love. My obligation to my students is grounded on my roles as teacher and philosopher and their psycho-logical needs to discover who they are and how they can live with integrity. Here I feel a connection with my students but also with teaching and philosophy. But if one of my students comes to me needing another kind of care, I may be obligated to provide it, though I may not be obligated to do so singlehandedly. My response depends on my ability to care for, my obligation to care for myself, and my sense of the appropriateness of the need and the best way to meet it.

In discharging obligations to care for that are based on role responsibility, I am conscious of my need to fill those roles conscientiously. The role of teacher, for example, requires a certain impartiality; the role of mother requires a fierce devotion to each particular child. But I am free, to a certain extent, to choose my roles. In adopting or reshaping roles, I should be sensitive to my need to be cared for as well as my capacity to care. In critiquing socially designed and assigned roles, we should aim for roles and divisions of roles that make caring more likely to occur.

Caring for can involve a measure of self-sacrifice. The rescuers of Jessica McClure who went without sleep for days, the parents of an infant who go without unin-terrupted sleep for months, are involved in caring for. Caring for involves an openness to the one cared for. Caring for requires that I see the real need and that I satisfy it insofar as I am able. In satisfying it, I am sensitive not just to the need but to the feelings of those in need.

Caring for does not require that I feel any particular emotion toward the one cared for, but that I am open to the possibility that some emotional attachment may form in the caring for. Nor does it require that I have an ongoing relationship with the one cared for.[9] I may meet the one cared for as stranger, though the caring for will change that.

Obviously, a model of caring along the lines I am defending must include an account of needs. I cannot offer a complete account here, but I would draw heavily from biology, psychology, and other relevant social sciences in constructing such an account; there would be an essentially normative component as well. I want to begin by drawing a distinction between what I will call subsistence needs and psychological needs. Subsistence needs will usually be needs that must be filled if physical existence is to continue. Psychological needs are needs that must be filled if human flourishing is to occur. Filling subsistence needs does not automatically benefit both the carer and the cared for. Rather, the carer is likely to feel burdened by filling such needs, though the recognition that one has filled such needs often creates a sense of virtue in the carer. I am reminded here of the ferocious demands for food that infants make on their parents with astonishing regularity. Filling psychological needs can often be more fulfilling. It is more likely to be done in a reciprocal relationship and in such a relationship filling psychological needs requires that both parties share the roles of carer and cared for. I needn't respond to every need. In choosing how and when to respond, I should consider the seriousness of the need, the benefit to the one needing care of filling this particular need, and the competing needs of others, including myself, that will be affected by my filling this particular need.

II. OBJECTS OF CARE

I can care for persons, animals, values, institutions, and objects. My choice of objects of caring about should reflect my own need to be cared for and my capacity to care. But decisions about what to care for should not depend exclusively on my own needs and capacities. I should also be sensitive to the needs that summon the obligation to care for. If I understand my obligation to care for as following from the existence of need and helplessness, I should care for institutions, values, and practices that would diminish such needs. One might argue that we could virtually eliminate the need to care for by creating such institutions, values, and practices and hence undermine our capacity to care. But even in a perfectly just world, children would need care and people and animals would get sick. Furthermore, human needs include more than needs for physical sustenance. Human needs for companionship and intimacy would exist even in a world free from the horrors of war, homelessness, sickness, and disease.

III. DEFENSE OF A GENERAL OBLIGATION TO CARE

The obligation to respond as carer when appropriate can be defended on three grounds. The first is the need. Here I would appeal to Peter Singer's principle, "if it is in our power to prevent something very bad happening without thereby sacrificing anything of comparable moral significance, we ought to do it."[10]

The second is the recognition that human relationships require a continuous kind of caring. This caring involves three components: being receptive to the other, being accepting of the other, and being on-call for the other when s/he is in need.[11] Unless we want to do away with human relationships, we must be open to the demands of caring that such relationships require. But caring in human relationships is, as human relationships are, reciprocal.

The third defense is that I cannot develop and sustain my ability to care unless I do some active caring. This is an empirical claim and we must look both to social science and to our own experience in evaluating it, but there is an obvious way in which caring for enhances our ability to care. When I make the real attempt to care for, I must understand the needs of the one cared for. I must also see how that one wants the needs to be addressed. This ability to notice needs and wants, to empathize as well as sympathize is developed through caring. Of course, one might ask why one should want to develop this capacity to care. It seems to me that the right response is to point out that human lives devoid of caring impulses and responses would be nasty, brutish, short, and lonely.

IV. LIMITATION ON OBLIGATIONS TO CARE

I don't think that we are obligated to be like Mother Teresa. Mother Teresa cares for continuously.[12] We can limit our obligation to care for by focusing on the defenses of this obligation. First, I have a prima facie obligation to care for when I come across a creature in need who is unable to meet that need without help, when my caring is called on as a part of a reciprocal relationship, or when indicated as part of my role responsibility. My actual obligation rests on the seriousness of the need, my assessment of the appropriateness of filling the need, and my ability to do something about filling it. But I must also recognize that I am a person who must be cared for and that I must recognize and respond to my own need to be cared for. The continuous caring for required to respond to needs for physical sustenance is, for most of us, incompatible with caring for ourselves. But not all caring for involves responding to physical needs. The caring for required to sustain relationships, which is usually reciprocal, can be a source of great strength to the person doing the caring for. Finally, allowing myself to suffer caring burnout also diminishes my ability to care for others in the future. I don't mean to argue that caring for requires no sacrifice. Indeed, where the need is great and my ability to meet it sufficient, I am required to sacrifice. But I am not required to adopt this as a form of life.

My obligation to care for is not an all-or-nothing thing. Being unable to care for now does not eliminate the possibility that I may be obligated to meet this need later. This is a general point about obligations. I might owe someone money and be unable to pay it back now, through no fault of my own. If I later come into a windfall, I am obligated to pay the money back then. In addition, there is no one right way to care for. My assessment of the appropriateness of the need, my ability to meet the need, and my sense of the most successful way of doing so provide some guidance here. Perhaps immediate caring for is the best way to meet a need in one case, and cooperative political activity the most successful way of meeting other needs. I would want to leave these kinds of choices up to the agent.

V. RULES AND RIGHTS

In my model, rules and rights serve three purposes. They can be used to persuade, to sketch a moral minimum below which no one should fall and beyond which behavior is condemned, and they can be used to deliberate in some cases.

My attention to rules and rights here does not reflect my unwillingess to make appeals to virtues and practices. I think it is fair to describe caring as a virtue. I do include other virtues and practices as fulfilling each of the three functions that rules and rights play in my model. We certainly can and do persuade by reminding others of virtues: "Would an honest man do that?" We likewise persuade by pointing to practices: "Native Americans don't have that kind of an attitude about the earth." Virtues and practices can serve as minimums: "I can see that you won't be doing me any favors, but at least give me the courtesy of an honest reply."

We don't live in a caring world. By that I mean that not everyone recognizes his or her obligation to care. Our society does not encourage the flourishing of this capacity, but undermines it in various ways. In a world infamous for its lack of caring, we need tools of persuasion to protect the helpless. This is one of the roles that rules and rights fill. We can reason in the language of rules with those who lack a sufficient degree of caring. If their natural sympathies are not engaged by the presence of suffering, we can attempt to appeal to reason: "How would you feel if you were in their place?" "What would be the consequences of such behavior on a large scale?" I am not convinced of the effect of such persuasion, and it is, I think, an empirical question whether such appeals would persuade where caring did not, but I suspect that such socially agreed on minimums could serve as persuasive appeals.

Rules and rights provide a minimum below which no one should fall and beyond which behavior is morally condemned. Rules provide a minimum standard for morality. Rights provide a measure of protection for the helpless. But on this level of moral discourse, morality is, like politics, the art of the possible. In the face of large-scale selfishness and inattention, perhaps the best we can hope for is a minimum below which no one should fall and beyond which behavior is roundly condemned. But we shouldn't fool ourselves into thinking that staying above this minimum is a sufficient condition for being a morally decent person. I don't want to deny the importance of these socially agreed on minimums; in a less than perfect world, they provide some real protection. They are not, in principle, incompatible with caring but can, I think, encourage caring. Much caring requires collective action and without a shared sense of moral minimums it will be difficult to organize such collective action.

Elizabeth Wolgast, in *The Grammar of Justice*, argues against the claim that treating patients in a moral fashion is entirely a matter of respecting their rights.[13] She points out that patients are often sick and in need of caring for. In this situation, she argues, we want doctors and other health-care workers to care for the patient. This involves far more than respecting rights. One could talk, I suppose, about a patient's right to be cared for, but as Wolgast points out, rights talk suggests a minimum below which the doctor should not fall, and in this case, we are less interested in the minimum than in the maximum. We want all our moral citizens to be open to the obligation to care for.

Rules and rights can also be used to deliberate under some conditions. Often we don't need to appeal to rules in deciding whom to care for and how to care for them. A creature's need and our ability to meet it identifies it as a candidate for caring for. We decide how to care for by appeal to the need, the strategies for meeting it, and the desires of the one in need about how best to meet the need. But when I am not in direct contact with the objects of care, my actions cannot be guided by the expressed and observed desires of those cared for, and hence I might want to appeal to rules. In these cases, I must make assumptions about their desires. I shall assume that they do not wish to fall below some minimum. Rules that provide a minimum standard for acceptable behavior ought to be sensitive to the general desires and aims of creatures, so I may take these into account. I am also free to appeal to my needs for care and on that basis decide that I do not wish to violate some socially approved minimum standard of behavior. I can also appeal to rules and rights when care must be allocated. For example, in a hospital emergency room we must make sure that the needs of the first accident victim of the night do not cause us to ignore the later victims. Finally, since rules and rights can express a consensus about morally acceptable behavior, I should be sensitive to the expectations generated in the one cared for by the public recognition of such roles and rights. For example, suppose I want to make sure that my family and friends are happy and involved in the wedding of my son. I might be tempted to ignore the rules of etiquette in making sure that my guests are uniquely provided for. But if the mother of the bride feels slighted because I didn't treat her the way she expected to be treated (i.e., as the etiquette rules say you should treat the mother of the bride), then I haven't really responded to her in a caring manner.

One might argue here that meeting some expressed needs might violate the moral minimums in our society. I am willing to grant that this can happen. If it does, we must remember that the rules do not have a life of their own, but are guides. They help us to formulate a caring response because they speak to us of what most of us would want as a caring response in a similar situation. If the one needing care does not want the response suggested by the appropriate rule, we should listen to them very carefully and be willing to ignore the rule. For example, suppose someone wanted us to help him/her commit suicide. I suspect that ideally we could and should settle this kind of a case without appealing to rules. Instead, we should appeal to the facts of the case. Is the person terminally ill or merely depressed? These conditions require different remedies. In the first case, one might be doing the right thing to aid in the suicide. Here, one must count the cost to oneself, as well as the needs and desires of the one cared for. In the second case, we appeal beyond the expressed needs to the unexpressed needs. This person probably needs some other care. Here, we make every attempt to listen to this person, to understand his or her pain, but we also remind ourselves that suicide is the final option for dealing with pain. We make this decision, not by appeal to a rule, but by reminding ourselves of the times when we or someone we know came close to suicide. We remember how it felt and how it was resolved.

In some cases, though, I cannot respond as one caring. As I approach caring burnout, I can then appeal to rules and rights. I do not want my behavior to fall below some minimum standard, nor do I want the one in need of care to fall below some moral minimum.

In the ideal caring society with sufficient resources to meet needs and to provide for some sort of flourishing, each of us would spend roughly the same amount of time being cared for. We would experience this as children and as adults. Hence, we would be surrounded by a nexus of caring. We would be persons who cared for and were supported by a history of being cared for. We would be free, to some extent, to choose whom to care for because there would be others to provide for needs and for flourishing. We would not be totally free, because social roles would commit us to some responsibilities to care. It's not clear that rules and rights would play a very big part in this world, but this is certainly not the world in which we live.

The people in our world differ in their ability and their willingness to care for others. Since I am both a creature who can care and a creature who needs care, I would, if I were committed to caring, be faced with enormous needs for care while sometimes suffering from a lack of caring for myself. This is true even if we grant that the kind of caring (in particular, psychological caring) involved in reciprocal relationships sustains all parties in the relationship. But since such relationships don't come easily and naturally, I would have to spend some time and energy establishing a nexus of care to support myself. In creating and maintaining this nexus of care, I would be developing bonds and responsibilities of care.

But spending much of one's time getting one's own needs for care satisfied leaves little time for caring for others. At the same time, everyone else is in much the same boat. And the gross inequality in the distribution of resources means that many slip between the caring cracks and into dire need. This puts the caring person in a bind. Real need presents itself to a person who is often running a caring deficit of his or her own. Caring burnout results. The only way to effectively reduce caring burnout is to change cultural and social institutions toward a model of caring. This is not the path that our culture has taken. Instead we careen from me-firstisms to paroxysms of guilt about the tremendous needs that have resulted. We make renewed commitments to care which are rejected as softheaded a generation later.

What are caring persons to do? Caring persons should try to respond to need by caring for, but they must pay attention to their own needs for care. They must navigate through an uncaring world without falling into total caring burnout. They should work for institutions, cultures, and practices that would reduce subsistence needs by redistributing resources and increasing the supply of caretakers, and they should encourage social change toward a culture of reciprocity in meeting psychological needs. But while struggling in our pre-caring world, caring persons are not obligated to care until they slip into caring burnout. This denies their own status as persons who deserve care and is counterproductive. It diminishes, in the long run, the amount of care they can provide. As they approach caring burnout, they should refill their care tanks by taking care of their own needs. During this period of renewal, they are still required to respect the moral minimums represented by rules and rights.

I haven't talked about what the rules and rights should be. In drafting a set of rules and rights, I should be sensitive to two considerations. The first is that rules and rights provide a moral minimum. The second is that rules and rights reflect a consensus about moral minimums. In this sense, morality is the art of the possible.

The morally preferred way to live is to appeal to caring. This suggests that rules and rights should reflect a sense of what counts as need, and a conception of flourishing, and a recognition of what would usually be accepted, by the ones cared for, as appropriate ways of responding to need and providing for flourishing. Notions of need and flourishing ought to be sensitive to empirical considerations about human nature, interaction, social organization, and so on, but they also have an irreducibly normative component. A defense of rules and rights would need to defend this normative component. We would also want rules and rights that would provide a climate for moral growth toward a caring society.

Rules and rights do play an important role in my ethics of caring, but we shouldn't forget that our primary responsibility is to care for. If this means that we are often unsure about just what to do, then we must live with this uncertainty. Discovering what to do requires that we listen carefully to the ones cared for. We should also recognize that it is often painful to be confronted by those in need, and even by those whom we could enrich. Appealing to rules provides a measure of security for ourselves, but we shouldn't allow it to distance us from the objects of care.

NOTES

1. I owe a special debt to Nel Noddings, whose powerful defense of caring inspired me to take caring seriously. *Caring: A Feminine Approach to Ethics and Moral Education* (Berkeley: University of California Press, 1984). I have also benefited from hearing talks given by Michelle Dumont, and by my many conversations about feminist ethics with her over the years. A special thank you to Dianne Romain, who has encouraged me in this project and given me much food for thought. Melissa Burchard, Michael Katz, and William Shaw gave me very useful comments on an earlier version of this paper.

2. Hume argued that the task of moral philosophy ought to be to look reflectively at actual moral practice. This conception also can be seen, though to a lesser extent, in Aristotle, and in Alasdair MacIntyre, *After Virtue* (South Bend, Ind: University of Notre Dame Press, 1981).

3. Annette Baier argues forcefully that we should pay exclusive attention to reforming current moral practices. See *Postures of the Mind: Essays on Mind and Morals*, especially chapters 11–15 (Minneapolis: University of Minnesota Press, 1985).

4. Carol Gilligan, *In a Different Voice* (Cambridge, Mass.: Harvard University Press, 1982).

5. Starhawk, *Dreaming the Dark* (Boston: Beacon Press, 1988), 44.

6. Dick Schubert, one of my creative and courageous colleagues, makes such assignments.

7. See my "The Random Collective as a Moral Agent" for a further discussion of collective action and obligation. *Social Theory and Practice* 11, no. 1 (Spring 1985), 97–105.

8. Alasdair MacIntyre, following Aristotle, made much of this notion of role-responsi-

bility. See *After Virtue*. See also Virginia Held, *Rights and Goods* (New York: The Free Press, 1984).

9. Noddings makes much of the requirement that caring demands an on-going relationship. It is on this basis that she denies that we can have an obligation to care for the starving children in Africa and animals. In an October 1988 talk to the Society for Women in Philosophy, she allowed that caring for does not exhaust our obligations so we could have other obligations to the starving children in Africa. I would prefer to say that we have obligations to care for the starving children and animals, but that not all caring obligations require direct care.

10. Peter Singer, *Practical Ethics* (Cambridge: Cambridge University Press, 1979), 168.

11. This analysis is from Milton Mayeroff, *On Caring* (New York: Harper & Row, 1971).

12. The inappropriateness of slavish caring has long been a theme in feminist thought. Betty Friedan called thinking that one's role in life requires such caring "the problem that has no name." See *The Feminine Mystique* (New York: Dell, 1963).

13. See Elizabeth Wolgast, *The Grammar of Justice* (Ithaca, N.Y.: Cornell University Press, 1987), chapter 3.

II. Comparisons across Theories

Harmonia and *Koinonia*: Moral Values for Pythagorean Women

JULIE K. WARD ███████████████████████████████

> They [women] must not destroy the reputation they had acquired through tradition
> and put the writers of myths in the wrong; on the grounds of their recognition
> of the justice of women—because they give away clothes and adornments when
> others have need of them without witnesses, and this trustfulness does not result
> in lawsuits and quarrels—because of this, poets created the myth that three women
> had but one eye between them, such was the concord among them. If one was
> to apply this to men and say that one who had first obtained something could
> easily part with it and even willingly added something of his own, no one would
> believe it. For it is not in the nature of men.
>
> (Iamblichus, *Vitae Pythagorica*, ch. 55)

I. INTRODUCTION

Since the publication of Carol Gilligan's research in 1982, feminist scholarship
on the topic of women and moral thinking has expanded greatly.[1] The responses
to Gilligan's writing have been not only numerous but broad in scope. Some
feminists have claimed that her research reveals the existence of a distinctively
female or feminine moral voice, characterized by an "ethic of care" (as opposed
to an ethic of justice); others have argued that the identification of a particular
way of thinking as "feminine" is problematic for various reasons.[2] In this essay I
have not entered into the debate of whether an ethic of care belongs exclusively
to women, or whether it can be coherently asserted apart from an ethic of justice.[3]
My conclusions as a historian of philosophy are more limited. Originally, I was
provoked by some new translations of ancient Greek writings attributed to women
Pythagoreans.[4] In examining them, it struck me, first, that many of the texts were
concerned with practical ethics, and second, that the letters (in particular) reflected
a certain perspective toward the concrete ethical problems taken up in the letters.
The characteristics of the content of the letters, especially those attributed to one
woman, Theano, led me to conclude that they were in fact written by women,
for they differed from letters of the same school attributed to men. The former

reflect an intimate knowledge of the conflicts within a household, and a particular concern for the preservation of personal relationships both within and outside of the family. Although it may be argued that Pythagorean teaching (about which I shall say more in a moment) requires that men and women strive equally to attain the ideals of social harmony and fellowship, it appears that women have interpreted these principles somewhat differently than men. In this respect, I suggest that an analogy can be drawn between these findings and those of recent feminists who claim that there exists a division of moral labor along the lines of gender.[5] Then, as now, regulating the public social order was largely in the hands of men, and regulating the private in the hands of women.[6] Consequently, although the moral ideals of Pythagoreanism were held to be equally binding on men and women, the interpretation and application of such ideals depended on their sphere of action.

II. THE PYTHAGOREAN TRADITION

The ancient Greek period is not known for its valuation of women and female pursuits: the historical record of women's accomplishments and activities is slight, and most of our information about women in that era comes to us through the eyes of male poets, playwrights, or philosophers. One exception is the writings belonging to the Pythagorean tradition.[7] We have today fragments of works, whole essays, and letters attributed to Pythagorean women, probably of the Hellenistic period. These texts are significant in that, if genuine, they constitute the only extant body of Greek prose by women in the pre-Christian period.[8] Although at present the dates of the writings and their attribution remain matters of scholarly debate, the most recent work does not dispute female authorship.[9] I shall proceed on the assumption that the texts, even if pseudonymous, were in fact written by women, and probably within the period between the fourth and first centuries B.C.[10] It is not improbable that writings by women should come down to us from the Pythagorean tradition since we know from various sources that this school had always encouraged women to join, in contrast to other ancient schools that discouraged them.[11] For example, Iamblichus, the doxographer of the fourth century A.D., lists seventeen names that he claims to be of famous Pythagorean women (V.P., 267). Unfortunately, either most of these women did not write anything, or most of their writing has been lost, for the texts we possess are attributed to only six: Aesara (or Aresas), Melissa, Myia, Periktione, Phintys and Theano.[12]

The issues raised in the writings by women are varied, including the nature of the soul, virtue, and wisdom, but common to all is a certain moral perspective that permeates their discussion. Such a stance is not surprising given the ethical aud religious orientation of Pythagorean thought. Basic to Pythagoreanism is the doctrine of the transmigration of souls, according to which the final aim of the soul is the liberation from the cycle of birth and death and its entrance into a state of unity with the divine.[13] Since the liberation of one's soul is achieved by virtuous conduct, the way in which one lives becomes a matter of serious consequence, and it is understandable that the Pythagoreans emphasize moral actions thought to promote the catharsis of the soul.[14] A further consequence of the transmigration doctrine is the notion that all living things are akin insofar as everything is equally an embodiment of a soul-daemon, from which Pythagoreanism comes to support certain social practices that are unconventional for the ancient period in Greece. First, the school admits women on an equal basis with men and accords women a position of dignity within the community; second, it prescribes the humane treatment of slaves; third, it cultivates friendship, even to the point of self-sacrifice.[15] Despite its unconventional attitudes, Pythagoreanism does not espouse an egalitarian social structure in which all individuals are able to pursue their chosen activities. Rather, the tradition holds that all of nature, including human society, consists in an ordered hierarchy that reflects the gradations realized by the psychic transmigration of all living things.[16] The fundamental principle underlying the order of nature according to the Pythagoreans is referred to as *harmonia* (harmony, concord), and this ideal is central to understanding the moral perspective reflected in the texts by Pythagorean women of the Hellenistic period.[17]

Broadly speaking, Pythagorean moral thinking is characterized by a concern with preserving social harmony, both at the level of the family and of the larger community, so as to contribute to a more perfect cosmos.[18] From what we know of the early Pythagorean communities, the individual is educated to act for the good of the whole community: individual autonomy is subordinated to collective good.[19] The way in which women understand this ideal is reflected in the content of their writings. The authors of these works concur that the basic duty of women is to preserve personal and familial relationships. Even the titles of the writings suggest their orientation, as, for example, Periktione's *On the Harmony of Women* or Phintys' *On the Moderation of Women*. In addition, various letters discuss topics such as the duties of women to family and the gods, the correct behavior of wives to unfaithful husbands, and the necessity of refraining from luxury.[20]

III. LATE PYTHAGOREAN WRITINGS BY WOMEN

The adherence to traditional roles for women as well as the reliance on Pythagorean moral beliefs are exemplified in the Hellenistic writings by women. Although they reflect similar ideals with the extant writings attributed to male Pythagoreans of the same period,[21] what is distinctive about the women's work is the nature and number of the preserved letters. Of sixteen extant letters by both women and men, ten are by women, and of these, eight are attributed to one woman, Theano.[22] Surveying the letters, one finds that the majority of women (six of ten) are concerned with giving personal advice of an ethical nature to the recipient, in each case a woman, whereas the letters by men do nothing of the sort.[23] This suggests that the letter format is used as a tool in the moral education of Pythagorean women. I have selected one letter by Theano which consists in giving moral advice to another woman, Eurydike, as a means of illustrating the way in which Theano uses Pythagorean beliefs to defuse a moral problem. One general hypothesis I suggest is that what marks certain of these extant works as of distinctively female authorship concerns the way in which the writers utilize these beliefs within the letter as a means of promoting social harmony. In addition, not only do women seem to use letter-writing as a form of moral education to other, perhaps younger, women,[24] but this practice may be seen as constituting a special kind of moral activity performed on the part of the female writers toward others, similar to that which has been described as "emotional work" by one recent feminist thinker, Cheshire Calhoun.[25] Clearly, an important kind of ethical activity is that in which one serves as a mediator between two parties in a moral conflict. In such a situation, one's function, in part, is to show compassion toward the aggrieved party and, by reasoning morally with that party, to reorient her understanding of the conflict so that she can regain her emotional and intellectual calm with which to act. On Calhoun's conception, the reality of moral activity is not adequately reflected in the typical model of the lone reasoner working out moral judgments by oneself, but is more properly seen as a cooperative venture in which we perform various kinds of emotional work for others and thereby empower them as moral agents. I suggest that something similar to this role of moral mediator is demonstrated within one of the letters by Theano, in this case to a friend, Eurydike, on which I shall focus.

IV. THEANO'S LETTER TO EURYDIKE[26]

Theano, a Pythagorean, writes to another Pythagorean woman, Eurydike:

> Theano to Eurydike, the admirable: "What pain possesses your soul? You are disheartened for nothing other than that he with whom you live together (*sunoikeo*: i.e., husband) has gone to a *hetaira* and takes physical pleasure with her. But you should not be in such a way, excellent among women. For, do you not see that when hearing becomes full of the pleasure of an instrument, and is filled with the music of choral singing, when it is satiated with this, then it loves [to hear] the flute and it listens with pleasure to the reed pipe? Indeed, is there not a kind of fellowship (*koinonia*) between the flute, the musical chords and the wondrous ringing of the instrument of most honey-sweet quality? It is thus for you alone, just as it is for the *hetaira* with whom your man keeps company (*sunoikeo*). For, your man gives heed to you in his habits, his nature, and his thought, but at some time when he receives his fill, he will in passing keep company with (*sunoikeo*) the *hetaira*, for, to those in whom corrupting juices are stored, there is a certain desire for nourishment not counted among good things. Live vigorously."[27]

As a preliminary note, we may point out that the problem of infidelity which Theano addresses is a familiar one for women generally in ancient Greece, and so also for Pythagorean women.[28] But it is more significant that the topic forms the nucleus of a letter between those women, and that it has been preserved. These two facts suggest that marital infidelity on the part of the husband was a matter of importance to the community, which squares with other doxographical evidence we have on the radical, revisionary ethical teaching Pythagoras was known for.[29] Of more interest, however, are various features of the letter itself. Consider the contextual background of the letter: Eurydike's husband has spent time with a *hetaira*, or female prostitute, and Eurydike is disheartened; perhaps she considers an emotional break with him. Theano responds by inviting Eurydike to consider the situation in a new light through the use of a musical analogy. (It may be significant to the use of a musical parallel that the mythical Eurydike, a nymph, was married to Orpheus, the Thracian hero of such musical renown that when he sang and played on the lyre even wild animals were said to become tame and follow him. Thus, by extension, the name Eurydike may become associated with music.) One may ask why Theano chooses to give her advice in the form of an image to begin with. After all, it would be more direct simply to state her opinion, rather than to engage in metaphor. On the contrary, Theano's use of an image reflects psychological astuteness in dealing with a delicate moral problem. Consider the difference in force between suggesting an image and reminding someone of a rule or stating a moral principle. The idea of using an image to convey meaning indirectly rather than giving an explicit piece of reasoning, or mentioning a moral principle, demonstrates not only a sensitivity to another's emotions, but an understanding of what kind of information is appropriate in a specific situation.[30] The function of the musical analogy within the letter is to provide a compelling mental image that, in vividly representing a parallel to the lived situation, redefines and relocates the situation so that Eurydike can see how she should act. In spite of Theano's clear disapproval of the husband's action in the final two lines of the letter, her moral direction to Eurydike is to preserve her relation with her husband, and not to bear ill will toward the other woman. This interest in maintaining the web of personal relations is demonstrated by the double references to musical concord and to fellowship. Taken together, the point of the musical analogy is to stress the similarities between the three persons involved (Eurydike, her husband, and the *hetaira*) by making reference to two central Pythagorean principles, fellowship (*koinonia*) and concord (*harmonia*). Theano uses these ideals in an inexplicit way: they serve as part of the commonly shared beliefs between the women which give significance to the analogy. To be in a position to appreciate the motivating force of the musical analogy, we need to know some background information, first, on Pythagorean ideas about kinds of music, and second, about the larger principles of fellowship and concord, to which I turn momentarily.

Pythagorean musical theory includes a consideration of the effect of musical scales and sounds of specific instruments on human passions. According to Iamblichus, Pythagoreans hold that certain rhythms and melodies have a healing effect on the character and the emotions (*V.P.*, 64), consequently, they favor these and not the others. For example, they do not recommend the sound of the flute, for it is supposed to cause *hybris*, whereas sung, or chanted music, accompanied by the lyre is thought to produce a cheerful mood and is typically used in the spring-time.[31] Important for our consideration of the letter is the notion that both the flute and the pipe are inappropriate instruments insofar as their music is thought to cause strong passions in the listener. And yet, surprisingly, Theano mentions both the flute and the pipe as capable of giving pleasure to the otherwise musically sated ear of the listener. What Theano claims—that someone may prefer the notes of the flute or pipe when the "proper" kind of music, that is, choral music, fails to please—suggests that she is subverting the traditional teaching to make her larger point about social concord. That this is indeed the central theme is borne out by the two central points of the analogy. First, that there exists a kind of fellowship, or *koinonia* (a "sharing in common"), between the flute, the musical chords, and the "instrument of honey-sweet sound," the reed pipe, and second, that the same situation that holds for Eurydike holds for the other woman, the *hetaira* ("just as it is for you alone, so, too, is it for the *hetaira* with whom your husband keeps company"). In this second point, Theano suggests that Eurydike and the *hetaira* are alike in depending on the husband for company. Theano even uses the same verb, *sunoikeo* ("to live together"), to express the relation of husband to wife and husband to *hetaira*. Then Theano goes on to remind Eurydike of her husband's usual consideration of her, that he "heeds [her] in his habits, his nature, and his thought," and thereby creates a balance among the relationships. Thus, the weight of the analogy depends, first, on the suggestion that even among what would be to a Pythagorean very disparate kinds of music—soothing choral music on the one hand and exciting flute or pipe music on the other—there exists a kind of communion (*koinonia*), and second, on the parallel between this "harmony" of instruments and that of persons. The implication of the analogy, as I read it, is that all three persons are parts, analogically speaking, of some larger concord. The reference to *koinonia* within the musical analogy points to certain Pythagorean notions concerning numerical proportion and the ordering of the cosmos.

It is well-attested by doxographers (Iamblichus, Diogenes Laertius, Stobaeus) that the Pythagoreans hold that number and concord (*harmonia*) are the primary principles of explanation in the universe.[32] Since the world is mathematically ordered, that is, based on numerical proportions, *harmonia* is considered not only a principle of music and of mathematics, but of moral conduct. For, when one understands the order of the cosmos to extend to all natural things, including persons, one takes as axiomatic a principle of unity that makes all things into a community (*koinonia*).[33] So, Pythagoreans maintain there exists a concord (*harmonia*) in society in the sense of a right moral ordering between human beings which is consistent with that of the natural world. As they see it, there is no gap between the physical laws that regulate the natural world of bodies (heavenly or otherwise) and the moral laws that regulate social interaction—and this specifically includes the interaction of those within the household as well as without. Stobaeus claims the Pythagoreans hold that the same concord (*harmonia*) that binds the activity of the heavenly bodies binds the members of society: "the ordinance of nature, indeed, orders each individual and the order of each individual perfects the group and so the whole *cosmos*" (*Flor.*, 103, 26). For the Pythagorean woman, then, there is an obligation to perfect herself so that she may contribute to the perfection of her *oikos*, then her city, and finally add to the perfection of the *cosmos*.

V. INNER AND OUTER HARMONIA

I have suggested that Theano's letter to Eurydike is based on the Pythagorean notion that each individual has an obligation to act so as to preserve, or promote, the concord of social relations, whether in the family or in the city. The general ethical principle represented by *harmonia* is further demonstrated in a fragment of a work by Aesara called *On Human Nature*, which argues that human nature provides a standard for right action both within the household (*oikos*) and in the city (*polis*).[34] The argument depends on the notion that the soul has three parts, which are not equal in function or nature. The "best" part of the soul is to lead and govern, the second part both governs and is governed, and the third, desire, is governed. Since the soul is a unity, not a multiplicity, she argues that its unity cannot arise from a random association of dissimilar things, but requires a principle of arrangement, such that the parts are "fitted together" (*sunarmosan*, like *harmonia*, from *harmozein* meaning "to fasten together," "to join"). She also argues that the parts can be "fitted together" only if they are unequal in certain respects. Although she does not make explicit the reason, I infer that the notion of "being fitted together" carries with it the idea of difference, just as the notion of musical harmony presupposes differences in tone that are proportional (*harmonia*). When the parts of the soul are properly arranged, she calls the arrangement a "sharing in," or fellowship (*koinonia*), and a good order, and she claims that the virtues of justice, friendship, love, and kindliness are engendered. Thus, Aesara's argument that the social virtues are possible only through the subordination of certain parts of the soul to others depends crucially on the same principle, that of *harmonia*, as does Theano's letter.

To see the way in which Aesara's abstract argument about psychic *harmonia* has concrete application for the lives of women, we look to a second fragment, attributed to Phintys, entitled *On the Moderation of Women*.[35] She writes:

> A woman must be altogether good and orderly; without excellence she would never become so. The excellence (*arete*) proper to each thing makes superior that which is receptive of it: the excellence proper to the eyes makes the eyes so, that proper to hearing, the faculty of hearing, that proper to a horse, a horse, that proper to a man, a man. The excellence proper to a woman is moderation (*sophrosune*). For, on account of this virtue, she will be able to love and honor her husband.

Phintys begins with the notion that different things have distinct natures, and so, different "excellences," or ways of functioning, that are especially suited to the

type of things they are. From this primary claim, she argues that whatever it is
that makes a woman excel *qua* woman is her particular virtue or excellence (*arete*),
and since the ability to honor and love her husband is particular to woman, the
virtue proper to such a being is moderation (*sophrosune*). A woman ought to fulfill
her excellence as this will make her better as the sort of thing she is. And how is
woman's nature determined? After noting which excellences are common to both
men and women (e.g., courage, justice, wisdom, health, strength, keenness of
perception, and beauty), Phintys distinguishes what is peculiar to men and to
women, what kinds of activities are performed by each. Peculiar to woman is
"staying at home and indoors and welcoming and serving her husband," and having
specified the functions belonging to woman as such, she goes on to explain what
particular duties the woman of moderation possesses. Of the five duties the woman
has, the most basic, she claims, is maintaining fidelity to her husband (a view
echoed by other Pythagorean women such as Periktione and Theano). By doing
so, a woman goes some way toward *sophrosune* by maintaining the orderly arrangement of the parts of her soul, household, and city; as a result, the Pythagorean
highest goods, the social values of concord, friendship, and kindliness come into
being.

VI. CONCLUSION

If we now return to Theano's letter, we can see that one part of Theano's advice
depends on the connection between *harmonia* and *sophrosune*, or moderation: she
suggests that Eurydike ought to act as moderation dictates in this situation, with
understanding both toward her husband and the other woman. Why? First, because
she will thereby preserve her own psychic balance, and second, she will add to
the preservation of concord both within the household and within the larger
society. Theano's suggestion that just as there exists a *koinonia*, or fellowship,
between the flute or pipe and choral music, so there exists a similar fellowship
between Eurydike and the other woman provides a bold and compelling image
with which to persuade Eurydike of the right choice. Theano uses the analogy to
present the situation as one in which familial *harmonia* should be preserved: she
conveys the notion of the value of preserving the "fellowship" between the three
principal actors. And, surely, any Pythagorean woman knows that her duty as a
wife is to preserve "oneness of mind" with her husband, even toward one in whom,
as Theano remarks, "corrupting juices are stored." But all this, what may be seen
as the moral ideals underlying the letter, Theano does not directly state, but alludes
to through the images of the letter. Theano's omission does not weaken the value
of the advice to Eurydike, as the latter already accepts the notions of concord and
fellowship. It is enough that Theano mentions certain concrete images that provide
the outlines of an ethic of virtue for her friend. The letter, then, accomplishes
two things: first, it emotionally relocates the situation for Eurydike by emphasizing
the similarity between herself and the *hetaira*, and by recalling her husband's usual

consideration of her. Second, it suggests that Eurydike ought to act so as to preserve the values of concord and fellowship in her relationships.

The application of the Pythagorean ideals of *harmonia* and *koinonia* to the community, specifically to the domain of women, the household, has certain positive effects on their place within the society. Since goodness in the household contributes just as much to the perfection of the order of nature as goodness in the public realm, women perceive themselves as being real contributors to the social and moral "concord," and this perception has a direct bearing on how they frame their moral choices. This effect explains, I believe, the frequency of subjects relating to the moderation of women and domestic harmony, subjects that have failed to stimulate scholarly comment, apparently for reason of being deemed unworthy of scholarly attention. Although the roles of women are not interchangeable with those of men, Pythagorean beliefs do not have the effect of marginalizing the domain of women from that of the community, which helps to explain why more women belonged to this school than to other ancient schools. I have suggested that Pythagorean society with its beliefs about mathematical proportion and the kinship of all nature presents a conceptual model in which belonging to the sphere of the household does not imply inferior status. In contrast to the contemporary Western or European political tradition in which the public domain has come to focus on the marketplace and to exclude the household, which is taken as representing the domain of reproduction, nurturing, and affective concerns, Pythagorean thinking reinforces the connections between the *oikos*, the domain of women, and the *polis*, the domain of men.[36] Yet, having said this, I wish to emphasize the particular way in which female writers interpreted the Pythagorean principles of *harmonia* and *koinonia*, namely, as means of preserving human relationships through understanding human needs and weaknesses, and forgiving them.[37]

NOTES

1. *In A Different Voice* (Cambridge, Mass.: Harvard University Press, 1982). Books and articles on the topic have become too numerous to name, but see, for example, Eva Feder Kittay and Diana Meyers, eds., *Women and Moral Theory* (Totowa, N.J.: Rowman & Littlefield, 1987); Nel Noddings, *Caring: A Feminine Approach to Ethics* (Berkeley, Calif.: University of California Press, 1984); Joyce Trebilcot, ed., *Mothering: Essays in Feminist Theory* (Totowa, N.J.: Rowman & Allanheld, 1983).

2. See, for example, Marilyn Friedman, "Beyond Caring: The De-moralization of Gender," in Marsha Hanen and Kai Nielsen, eds., *Science, Morality & Feminist Theory* (Calgary, Alberta: University of Calgary Press, 1987), 87–110; Alison Jaggar, "Sex Inequality and Bias in Sex Differences Research," in Hanen and Nielsen, 25–39; Jean Grimshaw, *Philosophy and Feminist Thinking* (Minneapolis: University of Minnesota Press, 1988), esp. chs. 7, 8; Patricia Ward Scaltsas, "Do Feminist Ethics Counter Feminist Aims?" (see this anthology).

3. For a discussion of whether "the perspective of care" as Gilligan outlines it represents

how women reason, see "On *In a Different Voice*: An Interdisciplinary Forum," *Signs* 11 (1986), 304–333. On the question of the relation between the care and justice perspectives, see Grimshaw, 198–226; Owen Flanagan and Kathryn Jackson, "Justice, Care and Gender: The Kohlberg-Gilligan Debate Revisited," *Ethics* 97 (1987), 622–637; Annette Baier, "The Need for More than Justice," in Hanen and Nielsen, 41–56.

4. By Vicki L. Harper in Mary E. Waithe, ed., *A History of Women Philosophers* (Dordrecht: Martinus Nijhoff, 1987).

5. For example, see Marilyn Friedman, in Hanen and Nielsen, 87–110, esp. 94–95; Linda Nicholson, "Women, Morality and History," *Social Research* 50 (1983), 514–536; and Nicholson, *Gender and History* (New York: Columbia University Press, 1986).

6. Cheshire Calhoun, in "Justice, Care, Gender Bias," *Journal of Philosophy* 85, no. 9 (1988): 454–455, points out that moral theorists have emphasized property rights and taken contractual relations as basic to moral relations largely because they were themselves property holders, and acted in the public, economic domain, while women, as non–property holders, have not shared the same moral concerns. See also Annette Baier, "Trust and Antitrust," *Ethics* 96 (1986): 231–260.

7. I am concerned with the later Pythagorean writings, included in Holger Thesleff, *The Pythagorean Texts of the Hellenistic Period* (Abo, Finland: Abo Akademi, 1965). I am aware that the precise connections between early and late Pythagoreanism have not been analyzed; however, I use the term "Pythagorean" to describe the later (Hellenistic) as well as the earlier writings of the tradition.

8. The writings attributed to women appear in Thesleff (1965). Sarah Pomeroy, *Women in Hellenistic Egypt* (New York: Schocken Books, 1984), 61–68, thinks that these writings are authored by women and that the names are authentic, not forgeries by men. Susan Cole, "Could Greek Women Read and Write?" *Women's Studies* 8 (1981): 129–155, argues that while the evidence for the literacy of women in the 5th–4th centuries B.C. is slight, by the 3rd century, subsidized education for both girls and boys is not uncommon.

9. Holger Thesleff, *An Introduction to the Pythagorean Writings of the Hellenistic Period* (Abo, Finland: Abo Akademi, 1961), 30–77, discusses the critical analyses concerning dating and authorship; he suggests that the works attributed to women are pseudonymous, whereas Pomeroy (1984), 65–68, disputes this claim, and also rejects the argument that the material must have been written by men as women were illiterate. Pomeroy elsewhere argues that since by the 4th–3rd centuries women (at least upper class) have access to education, it is not implausible that the Pythagorean writings in question are in fact authored by women: see her *"Technikai kai Mousikai," American Journal of Ancient History* 2 (1977), 51–68.

10. Following Thesleff (1961), 99, given his estimation of dating based on the dialect, style, etc., of the writings in question.

11. On the equality of men and women in Pythagorean thought, see C. J. de Vogel, *Pythagoras and Early Pythagoreanism* (Assen, the Netherlands: Van Gorcum Press, 1966), 238. Also, see Iamblichus, *Vita Pythagorica liber* (hereafter, *V.P.*), 267; Diogenes Laertius (hereafter, DL) 8.42–43; Porphyry, *Vita Pythagorica* (hereafter, *V.P.*) 4, 19.

12. Iamblichus' list does not include all the names for which we have extant writings: Aesara, Melissa, and Periktione do not appear on the list, which need not imply the inauthenticity of the texts for the list is said to be of sixteen of the most famous Pythagorean women. Compare Thesleff (1961), 74.

13. On the connections between Pythagoreanism and Orphism, see W. K. C. Guthrie, *Orpheus and Greek Religion* (London: Methuen, 1952), 216–221. Also, see Edward Zeller, *Outlines of a History of Greek Philosophy*, tr. L. Palmer (New York: Harcourt, Brace, 1931), 31 ff.

14. See Iamblichus, *V.P.* 96–100; Porphryry, *V.P.* 19; Zeller (1931), 32–34. Plato in *Phaedo* 62b ff. is purportedly giving an account of certain Pythagorean beliefs about the soul.

15. On the importance of friendship, see De Vogel, 150–159. Also, the story of Damon and Pinthias, Iamblichus, *VP* 234–237.

16. See Arthur Lovejoy, *The Great Chain of Being* (Cambridge, Mass.: Harvard University Press, 1957), on the development of the idea of the *scala naturae* in Greek thought, ch. 2, esp. 58–59.

17. *Harmonia* is derived from *harmozein* meaning "to fit together," " to join." The musical aspect is related to the Pythagorean doctrine of the harmony of the spheres, which is based on theories of numbers underlying musical chords; however, since everything can be understood through numerical relations, even abstract qualities, like justice, can be so expressed. See Guthrie (1962), 296–318; Zeller, 32–38.

18. See, e.g., Stobaeus, *Floregium* (hereafter, *Flor.*) 103, 26; Mario Meunier, *Femmes Pythagoriciennes, Fragments et Lettres* (Paris, 1932), 13 ff. The motivation to bring one's life into conformity with the laws of the *kosmos* seems to follow directly from their "discovery"; the principles of *harmonia* are then both descriptive and prescriptive. Compare Aristotle, *Metaphysics* 987b28.

19. The notion that the individual good is subordinate to that of the *polis* is present in Greek moral and political thought, including that of Plato and Aristotle. However, the Pythagorean tradition emphasizes the moral obligation of the individual to the community more than conventional beliefs: according to Stobaeus, they claim God does not preside over nature for His own good, nor for the good of nature, but for the common good (*Flor.* 85,18).

20. All letters in Thesleff (1965). Melissa's letter to Kleareta (115–116) concerns the range of a woman's duties, and the need to refrain from luxury; of Theano's letters, one to Eubule (195–197) concerns the need to avoid personal luxury, one to Eurydike (197) on the problem of an unfaithful spouse, one to Kallisto (197–198) on the humane treatment of slaves, and one to Nikostrate (198–200) on the correct behavior of a wife to an unfaithful spouse.

21. Thesleff (1961), 75–116, qualifies these writings as Hellenistic pseudepigrapha, distinguishing them both from early Pythagorean writings (prior to 4th century B.C.) and later nonpseudonymous writings (1st century B.C. onward).

22. See the conspectus by Thesleff (1961), 11–23. Of the letters, two are attributed to Archytus (are likely forgeries; compare Thesleff, 74), one to Lysis, two to Philalaos, one to Telauges, one to Melissa, one to Myia, and eight to Theano.

23. The subjects of the letters by men (contained in Thesleff [1965]) are: two by Archytus (45–46), one demanding the release of Plato and one on Okkelos' writings; one by Lysis (111–114) on Hipparchos' offense against secrecy; two by Philalaos (see Thesleff [1961],17), one praising the austere life of the philosopher, one praising the noble character of Anaximenes (to Anaximenes); one by Telauges (indirect account, see Thesleff [1961], 22) on Pythagorean contracts and the death of Empedocles.

24. For example, Theano's letter to Kallisto suggests that Kallisto is a younger woman to whom Theano is giving advice; see Vicki L. Harper's essay in Mary E. Waithe, ed., *A History of Women Philosophers* (Dordrecht: Martinus Nijhoff, 1987), 47–52.

25. Cheshire Calhoun, "Emotional Work" (see this anthology), argues that traditional agent-centered models of moral reasoning fail to provide a place for the type of activity in which we act as mediators in moral situations so as to help others "manage their agency." According to Calhoun, the fact that we perform such "emotional work" demonstrates the need for a new, mediator-centered conception of moral thinking.

26. Contained in Thesleff (1965), 197; also in Rudolf Hercher, *Epistolographi Graeci* (Pans, 1873), 606, 7, which has the ending salutation included here. Thesleff (1961), 113–114, places the probable date of Theano's writings (in Attic koine) as variable, perhaps as early as 4th–3rd century B.C. or later than the 2nd century B.C. Hence, she cannot be

identified with Pythagoras' wife; however, as it was customary to name children after famous persons of the school, this need not imply pseudonymous authorship. See Blaise Nagy, "The Naming of Athenian Girls," *Classical Journal* 74 (1979), 360–364; Pomeroy (1984), 66–68; Thesleff (1961), 73–76.

27. Note the use of *sunoikeo*, "to live with," to refer both to the relation between the wife and husband and between *hetaira* and husband, which emphasizes the similarity of the relations. On "fellowship" (*koinonia*), see Sextus Empiricus, *Adv. Math.* IX. 127.

28. See Sarah Pomeroy, *Goddesses, Whores, Wives and Slaves* (New York: Schocken Books, 1975), 86–92, on infidelity of men as the social norm: married men are allowed to have sex with prostitutes and female slaves in addition to their wives.

29. See C. J. De Vogel, 110–112, on the radical teachings of the importance of fidelity for both wives and husbands; certainly, such teachings go against the grain of the classical Greek tradition, aptly expressed by Demosthenes in the 4th century: "we have mistresses for physical pleasure, concubines to serve our person, and wives for the production of legitimate children" (Dem. 59.118–122).

30. Not only would an explicit argument be inappropriate in a letter to a friend, but as a form of information it fails to provide motivating force, whereas information given in images or metaphors is more powerful. See R. Nisbett and L. Ross, *Human Inference: Strategies of Social Judgment* (Englewood Cliffs, N.J.: Prentice-Hall, 1980).

31. See De Vogel, 162–166.

32. See Aristotle, *Meta.* 986a1, 987b28.

33. See Sextus Empiricus, *Adv. Math.*, IX. 127: "the followers of Pythagoras and Empedocles and most of the Italian philosophers say that there is a certain community (*tina koinonian*) uniting us not only with each other and with the gods, but even with the irrational animals. For, there is one spirit pervading the whole *kosmos*, like soul, and which makes us one with them."

34. Aesara's (or, Aresas, see Thesleff [1961], 74) fragment is included in Thesleff (1965), 48–50; 50 lines written in Doric prose, it is probably about 3rd century B.C., see Thesleff (1961), 114–115.

35. Phintys (possibly of Sparta, see Thesleff [1961], 76), is included in Thesleff (1965), 151–153; 80 lines written in Doric prose, it is also probably of the 3rd century B.C., see Thesleff (1961), 114–115. I follow Vicki L. Harper's translation: see Waithe (1987), 26–27.

36. See Iris Young's discussion of the opposition between reason and affectivity in "Impartiality and the Civic Public," 60–67, in S. Benhabib and D. Cornell, eds., *Feminism as Critique* (Cambridge: Polity Press, 1987).

37. I wish to thank Eve Browning Cole, Cheshire Calhoun, and Ezio Vailati for their comments, and Eve Browning Cole and Susan Coultrap-McQuin, the directors of the conference "Explorations in Feminist Ethics: Theory and Practice," held in Duluth, Minn., October 7–8, 1988, for the opportunity to present an earlier version of this essay.

Care and Respect

ROBIN S. DILLON ████████████████████████

It may seem obvious that caring for a person and respecting her are very different. Indeed, if we recall what Kant says about love and respect, the two might seem in tension, even at odds with one another: "The principle of *mutual love* admonishes men constantly to *come nearer* to each other; that of the *respect* which they owe each other, to keep themselves at a *distance* from one another."[1] The contrast that Carol Gilligan has drawn between two fundamentally distinct conceptions of morality also suggests that care and respect are quite different.[2] On the one hand, respect for persons and respect for the basic rights that every person possesses are central tenets in the "justice perspective" conception of morality; on the other hand, compassionate, responsive caring for particular interdependent individuals is the heart of the "care perspective" conception of morality.

Viewing care and respect as deeply dissimilar raises questions about the appropriate place of each in moral theory and moral life. We might regard each as having its own domain, with care belonging in the domain of intimate personal relationships and respect governing interactions in the public domain.[3] Or we might regard one or the other as the more fundamental basis for all interactions among people.[4] Kant, for example, views both love and respect as essential between friends, but he argues that friendship is insecure unless respect constrains and limits love, suggesting that even in intimate contexts respect has a kind of moral priority.[5]

Even though there is the appearance of contradistinction, an intriguing similarity between recent feminist explorations of care and some discussions of respect for persons suggests another way of understanding the two. I will argue that a closer consideration of respect shows that caring for another is a way of respecting her, but one that differs from the familiar Kantian view of respect. So, although it might now appear from the points of view of moral theory and moral life that we must either bind ourselves to an ethic of justice or an ethic of care, or view one or the other as morally fundamental, I believe that recognizing the connection between care and respect may provide the basis for a more integrative approach to morality.

I. THE NATURE OF RESPECT

To make this connection more perspicuous, let me begin with a general account of respect.[6] The word "respect," my dictionary tells me, comes from the Latin "respicere," which means "to look back at" or "to look at again." The idea of looking is carried through in many words used synonymously with "respect," for example, "regard" (from "to watch out for") and "consideration" (from "examine [the stars] carefully"). This suggests both that we re/spect things that are worth looking at again, and that in respecting something we pay careful attention to it. When we ignore or disregard something or dismiss it lightly, we are not respecting it.[7]

The looking metaphor does not capture all of the meaning of respect, for respecting also involves certain ways of acting in connection with an object; there are many different kinds of ways to respect. We respect things by showing consideration for them and taking them into account, by not violating or interfering with or intruding on them, by deferring to or obeying them, by acting courteously toward them, by keeping our distance from them and giving them room, by honoring, praising, and emulating them. If we violate or encroach on something, or despise, scorn, or condemn it, or act high-handedly or arrogantly or carelessly in connection with it, we are not respecting it.

These differences are significant, for as I will suggest they imply different kinds of respect. But it is worth asking what is common to these ways of acting, what makes them all *respect*. Most generally, respect is something we render; that is to say, when we respect something we accord it what it is due, what it calls for. Respect most centrally involves acknowledging and answering an object's claim to be entitled to or deserving of our attention and some further appropriate response.

This is a rather compressed explication of something that is in fact complex; let me tease out the central elements a bit further. First, as we have seen, respecting something involves paying attention to it, taking it seriously. Respect isn't merely *about* the object, it is *focused* on the object; and the focus is deliberate. Respecting is thus a matter of directed rather than grabbed attention, and of reflective consideration. In this way it differs from immediate attraction and fascination.

The attention is not only deliberate but also responsive: respect is something that an object claims from us, calls for, demands, elicits, commands, and so on. In this way respecting differs from liking, for example. When we respect something, we acknowledge its claim and so regard it as worth attending to. This sometimes means simply that it is worth it to us to take the object into consideration. But respect most centrally involves regarding the object as having worth; then, respect is a kind of valuing of the object: recognizing and responding to its value. In both cases, we view the object as worthy of consideration and regard it as a valid source of claims on our attention.

Not only our attention is called for, however; respect is not simply a matter of staring long and hard. Rather, we view the object as making valid claims on our subsequent conduct as well, so we regard a further response to the object to be deserved, due, owed, warranted, proper, fitting, appropriate. Thus, respect involves responding to the object in the appropriate fashion, which may involve certain ways of treating the object, certain patterns of conduct or behavior with regard to it, certain affective and attitudinal responses to it. It is important, however, that it is the nature of the object that determines what counts as an appropriate response; hence the need for careful attention. Moreover, the response, like the attention, is deliberate. That is, we do not find ourselves respecting something or discover by attending to our actions and feelings that we respect something; rather, respecting is something we decide to do and something we can choose not to do, even while recognizing that it is called for.

One element of this account deserves to be highlighted. Although we might like something for no reason, we cannot respect something for no reason nor for any old reason. Respecting something requires having a certain kind of reason, namely, that I believe that there is some feature or characteristic or some fact about it that makes it worthy or deserving of my attention and some further response. This fact or feature is the ground of respect: that in virtue of which it is worthy of respect.[8] Since respect is grounded in this way, what counts as respecting the object, acting respectfully, or responding appropriately out of respect is determined by the nature of the object and its respect-warranting fact or feature. There are many different kinds of things that call for different kinds of responses. Think of the differences among the following: (a) a mountain climber's respect for the elements; (b) respecting the terms of an agreement; (c) showing respect for a judge by rising as she enters her courtroom; (d) the equal respect owed all persons as such; (e) an environmentalist's deep respect for nature; and (f) having a great deal of respect for a person's character or little respect for wimps and scoundrels. I have argued elsewhere that an analysis of these cases reveals different varieties of respect.[9]

Consider the kind in (e). When we say, for example, that the way of life of the American Indians manifested their deep respect for nature, we mean that they regarded nature and natural things as having great value, as being fragile, and so as calling for special care. When we respect things that are regarded this way, we act or forbear acting out of benevolent concern for them. This kind of respect, then, involves cherishing; appropriate actions include protective ones, as a way of re/g(u)arding the object's special worth. I find this way of regarding and responding to something to be quite similar to the notion of care that informs discussions of the ethic of care. In the remainder of the essay I want to tease out the implications of this similarity for the concept of respect for persons.

II. RESPECTING PERSONS

An individual might properly be the object of several different kinds of respect. She might deserve, for example, the kind of respect for a person that involves the evaluative judgment that an individual has merit or that her character and conduct manifest her excellence as a person.[10] This kind of respect, which involves admiration and approval and is typically manifested in praising and emulating, is grounded in an individual's worthwhile qualities and moral excellences and is something that as a matter of fact not all persons deserve and that different individuals deserve in varying degrees: we might have a great deal of respect for Joanne but little respect, perhaps even contempt, for Denise.[11]

There is another kind of respect, however, which we are said to owe equally to all persons regardless of personal merit or moral excellence or lack thereof. Such respect is not a matter of appraising and admiring but of taking appropriate account of the fact that something is a person. Stephen Darwall has called this "recognition respect" for persons.[12] It involves (a) recognizing that something is a *person*, that is, a being with a certain moral worth and status, (b) understanding that the fact that something is a person constrains us morally to act only in certain ways in connection with her, and (c) acting (or being disposed to act) in those ways out of that recognition and understanding. When we respect a person in this sense, we treat her as it is appropriate to treat all persons simply because they are persons, and we comport ourselves in this manner out of our recognition of the kind of thing she is and of what is due all persons as such.

Now, as respect in general is grounded in those features of the object that make it worthy of consideration, so recognition respect for persons is grounded in what we might call the "morally significant features of persons": those features that make something a person and make persons things that must morally be taken account of. What constitutes an appropriate response to the fact that something is a person, then, depends on the nature of the morally significant features. Of course, how persons ought to be treated is a matter of dispute between various moral theories; but the idea of respect for persons as such is most commonly associated with Kant's conception of treating persons as ends in themselves: the end-in-itself formulation of the categorical imperative is widely regarded as the preeminent statement of the principle of respect for persons. On the Kantian account, it is the capacity for rationally autonomous moral agency that makes a being a person and makes persons matter morally. The fundamental moral task of each person is to develop and exercise this capacity; our moral task with regard to others is to let them do this. So it is that on this view recognition respect for persons most centrally involves, in Kant's words, keeping our distance from others: letting them be, refraining from hindering them in the pursuit of their ends, giving them room to realize and exercise their capacity to be rationally self-determining and responsible moral agents. Thus, as the Kantian view has been developed, respect for persons has come to be thought of primarily in terms of respecting each individual's equal basic human rights, the rights that protect the defining capacity of persons, and especially, respecting the fundamental right of each person to live her life as she sees fit.[13]

However, the Kantian conception is not the only way of conceiving of persons. Hence, the Kantian view of recognition respect is not the only way of taking appropriate account of the fact that something is a person.[14]

There is in the philosophical literature a variety of interconnected themes about persons and respect that is not captured by the Kantian conception.[15] This family of ideas about respect and what matters for and about being a person strikes a surprising chord, for it is structured by motifs that are central to various feminist accounts of the ethic of care, motifs such as the fundamental particularity of persons; attention and understanding as primary modes of moral response; insistence on active sympathetic concern for another's good.[16] When woven together, these themes form a pattern according to which we respect persons by caring for them as the particular concrete individuals they are. That is to say, these themes suggest that care is a kind of recognition respect for persons.

The themes include the following. (1) What matters about each of us is not (only) some abstract generic capacity but the fact that we are specific concrete individuals. So, respecting persons involves responding to others as the particular individuals they are. (2) It is a morally significant fact about us that we each have our own way of looking at ourselves and the world. So, respecting persons involves coming to know them in their self-defined specificity and trying to see the world from their point of view. (3) Another of our morally significant features is that we cannot be entirely independent and self-sufficient, for we have needs and wants that we cannot satisfy on our own. So, respecting persons involves more than refraining from interference; it requires caring for them in the sense of helping them to pursue their ends and to satisfy their wants and needs.

What emerges from these themes is an account of a kind of recognition respect that contrasts in important ways with the Kantian conception of respect for persons. In the spirit of integration that marks feminism in general and a feminist ethic of care in particular, I think it appropriate to call this "care respect."[17]

III. CONCRETE PARTICULARITY AS THE GROUND OF CARE RESPECT

A striking feature of the Kantian conception is that in viewing us as worthy of respect it abstracts from all particularities. The morally significant feature of persons on this view is something abstract and universal, not what distinguishes one individual from another, but what makes each equally and indistinguishably a person. Individual human beings are thus objects of respect only insofar as they are instances of the universal type "being with the capacity for rational moral agency."[18]

This aspect of Kantianism has drawn fire from a number of critics who contend that we are *essentially* fully specific and concretely particular individuals, each with our unique blend of needs, desires, abilities, and emotional constitution, our own peculiar histories, concerns, and projects, each with our own ways of viewing the world and our relationship to it.[19] These critics oppose what one has vividly described as "flensing the individual down to the bare bones of abstract person-hood."[20] Rather than disregard contingency and particularity, these critics contend, what we ought morally to take account of is precisely the contingencies that make me who I am. Thus, as one writer maintains, "respect for a person includes respect for this core of individuality . . . (and) appreciation of . . . the individual and human *me*."[21] On this view, then, to respect someone is to treat her not as a case of generic personhood, but as the whole fully specific person she is.[22]

This view of respect compares interestingly with Gilligan's description of the ethic of care as "grounded in specific context of the other";[23] with Nel Noddings's account of caring as "special regard for the particular person in a concrete situation";[24] with Seyla Benhabib's identification of the morality of care and responsibility with "the standpoint of the concrete other," which requires us to recognize and confirm the other as a concrete individual.[25] These accounts of care and respect, then, involve the same perception of their objects, suggesting that they are accounts of the same thing.

IV. CARE RESPECT AS RESPONDING TO PARTICULARITY

What constitutes taking appropriate account of persons conceived as specific concrete individuals? Drawing together the various themes about persons and respect, we can say that an appropriate response involves valuing an individual in her specificity, seeking to understand her in her own terms, and caring about and seeking to promote her well-being.

To take the first point, the care perspective suggests that each individual has intrinsic worth because she is the person she is. Thus, viewing others from the perspective of care respect requires attending to particularity not appraisingly or evaluatively but in the mode of appreciating and cherishing each person as an unrepeatable individual.[26] So care respect involves, as Elizabeth Maclaren puts it, valuing another in her "singular concreteness," as "irreplaceably himself or herself"; thus, "it is being-valued-as-irreplaceable which constitutes anyone's dignity."[27]

By contrast, although the Kantian formula of persons as ends in themselves is supposed to regard persons as irreplaceable,[28] there is a sense in which Kantian respect does in fact view persons as intersubstitutable, for it is blind to everything about an individual except her rational nature, which is what makes each of us indistinguishable from every other.[29] Thus in Kantian-respecting someone, there is a real sense in which we are not paying attention to *her*—it makes no difference to how we treat her that she is who she is and not some other individual. Kantian respect is thus not a "respecter of persons," in the sense that it does not discriminate or distinguish among persons. By contrast, care respect is a respecter of individuals. So, while Kantian respect requires treating all persons exactly the same, care respect may require treating different people differently.

This is not to say that care respect loses sight of the commonality of persons and of the reality of circumstances in which equivalent treatment is appropriate. What I find most powerful about the concept of care respect is that it manages to keep in sight both the fact that this person is a unique individual and that every other person is also a fully specific unrepeatable individual. That is, care respect has the resources to maintain a constructive tension between regarding each person as *just as valuable* as every other person and regarding this individual as *special*.[30]

V. CARE RESPECT AND UNDERSTANDING ANOTHER

A core theme of many feminist writings on morality is the way in which caring for another involves a certain kind of understanding of her.[31] Gilligan describes the care perspective as involving "the ability to perceive others on their own terms,"[32] while in Noddings's account, the fundamental aspect of caring is "engrossment," which is the apprehension of another's reality "from the inside."[33] Sara Ruddick reminds us of the centrality to caring relationships of what Iris Murdoch calls "loving attention," the "just and loving gaze directed upon an individual reality," which allows for the unimpeded, undistorted revelation of another person.[34] I hear echoes of this in certain discussions of respect.

Bernard Williams, for example, has argued that respecting a person involves what he calls "identification"; each person "is owed an effort at identification: that he should not be regarded as the surface to which a certain label can be applied, but that one should try to see the world (including the label) from his point of view."[35] Similarly, Elizabeth Spelman has suggested that respecting a person involves responding to her on the basis of her self-conception: "I treat you as the person you are just insofar as I recognize and respond to those features of you which are, in your view, necessary to who you are. We treat others as the persons they are just insofar as we try to respond to the way they choose to be seen, and not through our favored ways of seeing them."[36] This view of what constitutes an appropriate response to a person is, I want to suggest, capturable by the care respect model but not by Kantian respect. Care respect for another, then, involves trying to discover how she views herself and the world, trying to understand what it is like to be her living her life from her point of view.

We might wonder, however, why this kind of understanding is called for.[37] Let me suggest two important connections between understanding and appropriate response. First, there is the practical point. Since care respect involves promoting the other's good, then careful attention and clear-eyed perception of the other's particular needs, desires, and so on are certainly required. But equally important, if we are to have care *respect* and not just paternalistic taking care of, we have to promote what the other regards as important; or where that is not possible or where we cannot bring ourselves to do that, at least we have to take account of her conception of her own good.

The second point calls on a familiar idea, namely, that a person is a being who is reflectively conscious of herself and her situation. A person is the kind of being that not only lives her life and has certain purposes in living it, but also has a certain understanding of who she is and what she is doing that informs and structures her living. Moreover, she sees some of her characteristics and the characteristics of her situation as more crucial to her identity than others. This is not to say that a person and her life are nothing other than or different from what she takes them to be. But it does mean that taking such a being seriously requires trying to understand her consciousness of her own activities and purposes, trying to understand her in her own terms. In this way, identification is part of care respect and not simply a precondition for it. Moreover, this kind of attention and understanding of the whole specific individual that another takes herself to be requires sympathetic, concerned, involved interest and real effort, which are themselves expressions of our valuing of her and are thus constitutive of respect.

VI. CARE RESPECT AND PROMOTING THE OTHER'S GOOD

Cherishing and attentive understanding are not yet all that this particular individual calls for; respect requires not only a concerned focus but some further response as well. However, not just any response counts as respect. The knowledge gained through identification puts us in a better position to harm the individual; but harming is not an appropriate response. What is called for? The discussions of respect I am attending to suggest two modes of comportment as appropriate responses.

First, since we are to take seriously a person's self-conception and regard her as precious in her self-defined particularity (regardless of whether we admire or approve of every facet of it), then care respect not only requires, as Williams suggests, not suppressing or destroying an individual's reflective consciousness of herself and her situation;[38] it also requires us to take positive steps to protect and nurture its grounds, particularity, and self-definition.

Second, as the account of respect developed by R. S. Downie and Elizabeth Telfer suggests, appropriate treatment of an individual requires acting from sympathetic concern for her: caring for her and about her by caring for her interests, needs, projects, and passions as for one's own.[39] We are to cherish in a practical way another's concern for her happiness and her values,[40] by acting out of regard for her good and in order to promote her good. So, some philosophers have taken the principle of respect for persons to be an expression of the principle of Agape.[41]

These discussions of respect revolve around the idea that we are responsible for the well-being of others, responsible not simply not to degrade another's state of being but responsible for making a positive contribution to others' existence. Not only does this echo the emphasis in the ethic of care on responsibility and responding to others' real needs; it also respects an important fact about us, namely, that each of us at some points in our lives, particularly at the endpoints, needs to be *cared for*. But also, even when we are in our prime, none of us is as independent and self-sufficient as the Kantian conception of respect suggests. We need the help and support of others, and not just because the success of some of our projects requires teamwork. Taking an individual appropriately into account involves recognizing this fact of deep interdependence and the corresponding fact of mutual responsibility.

Thus, while Kantian respect might be thought to distance us from one another both in hiding our particular selves from one another and in erecting protective barriers of rights between persons, care respect can be seen as connecting individuals together in a community of mutual concern and mutual aid, through an appreciation of individuality and interdependence.

VII. CONCLUSION

Many discussions of care emphasize its home in the domain of close personal relationships and its essential connections with the emotions of affection and bonding love that are appropriate to such relationships. Care is thus not something that we could or probably even should extend to those outside our networks of personal relationships. But since care is not universalizable, we would be hard-pressed to regard it as the whole of morality or as the more fundamental basis for morality. The question then becomes how to integrate the demands of particularistic emotional connection and detached impartial universality.

I think the notion of care respect provides a means to approach that integration, for care respect is not restricted to the domain of personal relationships and it is not essentially connected with the emotions of love and affection, though it may involve sympathy and compassion. Not only is it properly extended to those whom we do not love, but it is, to adapt Noddings's phrase, how we are to meet *all* others morally.[42] Each of us is a fully particular and distinct individual, and that fact about us calls for recognition and response from each of us. But all of us also share a common humanity and warrant respect on that ground as well. What care respect enables us to do is to keep both these facts in sight, as it calls our attention both to the moral significance of the particularity of persons and to the moral significance of this fully particular, concrete individual.

One might object, however, that care respect as I have described it cannot be universalized as Kantian respect can, for it is just not humanly possible to meet everyone with the attention to detail, the valuing, the effort, the active promotion of their good, and so on, that care respect requires. Indeed, many of us barely manage to achieve this even with our closest loved ones.

What needs to be recognized here is that attention, understanding, responsiveness, promoting the other's good, and so on are all activities that admit of degree. Furthermore, pulling out all the stops for every individual one comes across is not only not humanly possible but may also be inappropriate for many individuals or in many situations. For instance, trying to apprehend the reality of another can be, for certain individuals and in certain circumstances, neither caring nor respectful but threatening in opening up the possibility for the exploitation of revealed vulnerabilities. But the inappropriateness and impossibility of pulling out all the stops for everyone does not mean that it would be either inappropriate or impossible to approach others generally with more constrained, context-sensitive expressions of care respect. One advantage of the idea of care respect is that it calls us to recognize that appreciation and reception of particular others cannot be restricted to the relative ease and safety of personal relationships, and it engages us in the task of trying to find ways to make both our encounters with others and the institutions within which we encounter them more fully and flexibly responsive. A further advantage is that it invites us to see care, care respect, and Kantian respect as arranged on a continuum of responsive stances toward other, rather than as competing and mutually exclusive. So, we might see Kantian respect as the minimal level of respect that care itself requires: I may not care about an individual and may be altogether unable to identify with her or to forge and sustain a relationship with her; but somebody might care for her, she is someone's daughter, friend, sister, and so she constrains my actions.[43]

I think a rich account of care respect can be developed. However, my aim in this essay has been the more limited one of calling attention to this notion and commending it for further pursuit as a promising way of responding to the challenge that feminist explorations of care have posed to the moral theoretic tradition.

NOTES

I am grateful to Annette Baier, Kurt Baier, Gordon Bearn, Janet Fleetwood, David Gauthier, John Hare, J. Ralph Lindgren, and Jean Rumsey for discussion and comments on earlier drafts.

1. Immanuel Kant, *The Doctrine of Virtue*, trans. Mary Gregor (Philadelphia: University of Pennsylvania Press, 1964), 116.

2. Carol Gilligan, *In a Different Voice: Psychological Theory and Women's Development* (Cambridge, Mass.: Harvard University Press, 1982); and "Moral Orientation and Moral Development," in Eva Feder Kittay and Diana T. Meyers, eds., *Women and Moral Theory* (Totowa, N.J.: Rowman & Littlefield, 1987), 19–33.

3. Such a view is suggested by, for example, Virginia Held, "Feminism and Moral Theory," in Kittay and Meyers, 111–128; Seyla Benhabib, "The Generalized and the Concrete Other: The Kohlberg-Gilligan Controversy and Moral Theory," in Kittay and Meyers, 154–177; Marilyn Friedman, "Beyond Caring: The De-Moralization of Gender," in Marsha Hanen and Kai Nielsen, eds., *Science, Morality and Feminist Theory, Canadian Journal of Philosophy* Supplementary Volume 13 (Calgary, Alberta: University of Calgary Press, 1987), 87–110. Lawrence Kohlberg also portrays care and respect as belonging to different domains in Kohlberg, Charles Levine, and Alexandra Hewer, *Moral Stages: A Current Formulation and a Response to Critics* (Basel: S. Karger, 1983), 20–21; but see note 4.

4. Kohlberg also argues that justice and respect are more fundamental than caring and particularistic relationship; see *Moral Stages*, 91–92. See Nel Noddings, *Caring: A Feminine Approach to Ethics and Moral Education* (Berkeley: University of California Press, 1984), for one who argues that caring is a morally superior way of relating to one another.

5. Immanuel Kant, "Conclusion of the Doctrine of Elements: The Union of Love and Respect in Friendship," *The Doctrine of Virtue*, 140–145.

6. In developing the ideas in this section, I am indebted to discussions with Annette Baier and to the insights of Lawrence A. Blum, "Compassion," in Robert B. Kruschwitz and Robert C. Roberts, eds., *The Virtues: Contemporary Essays on Moral Character* (Belmont, Calif.: Wadsworth, 1987); and *Friendship, Altruism and Morality* (London: Routledge and Kegan Paul, 1980).

7. There is an ambiguity lurking in the looking metaphor. For sometimes we look carefully at a thing in order to judge its quality, and sometimes we attend to it without evaluating it. This ambiguity is reflected in respect, as the discussion in section II below of two kinds of respect suggests.

8. Respect can thus be appropriate or inappropriate, properly grounded or unjustified. It is appropriate and justified when my attitude and conduct are directed to a worthy object, when my reason for respecting correctly picks out the ground in the object. But I can go wrong in respecting, for my respect can be misdirected, undeserved, ill-founded, as when I wrongly believe that the object has this feature or that having that feature makes an object worthy of respect. On this point, see Carl Cranor, "Toward a Theory of Respect for Persons," *American Philosophical Quarterly* 12 (October 1975): 309–319.

9. Robin S. Dillon, "Self-Respect and Justice," Ph.D. diss., University of Pittsburgh, 1987. See also Stephen Darwall, "Two Kinds of Respect," *Ethics* 88 (October 1977): 36–49; and Stephen Hudson, "The Nature of Respect," *Social Theory and Practice* 6 (Spring 1980): 69–90. The difference between (f) on the one hand and (a-e) on the other corresponds to the difference between the two kinds of looking mentioned in note 7 above and to the distinction Darwall draws between recognition respect and appraisal respect. Kinds (a-e) are, I have argued, all varieties of recognition respect.

10. Compare Darwall's appraisal respect and Hudson's evaluative respect.

11. I believe there are interesting connections between this kind of respect and care, but I leave them aside for the purposes of this essay. John Hare suggested to me that if I care about someone, I will have some evaluative respect for her or some of her qualities, because commitment produces loyalty and loyalty requires evaluative respect. Moreover, it seems psychologically impossible to care about someone whom you thoroughly despise, condemn, or deeply disapprove of. So it would seem that either care requires some minimal level of evaluative respect or care creates evaluative respect by finding something to praise.

12. Darwall, 38.

13. Kant's own account of respect for persons is more complex than this, for it involves more than one kind of respect and certainly requires more than respecting rights. I explain Kant's view of respect in "Kant on Respect, Self-Respect, and the Worth of Persons" (unpublished).

14. It should be clear from my discussion that Kantians have no privileged claim on the word "respect." Utilitarians, for example, can also rightly claim to respect persons by taking each into account in deciding how to produce the most good. However, Kantian respect and utilitarian respect are alike in viewing persons "thinly"; both thus contrast with the kind of respect I describe below, which views persons more "thickly." For a discussion of utilitarian respect, see Bart Gruzalski, "Two Accounts of Our Obligations to Respect Persons," in O. H. Green, ed., *Respect For Persons, Tulane Studies in Philosophy* 31 (New Orleans: Tulane University Press, 1982), 77–89.

15. I draw these elements primarily from the following: Bernard Williams, "The Idea of Equality," in Joel Feinberg, ed., *Moral Concepts* (New York: Oxford University Press, 1969), 153–171; Elizabeth Spelman, "On Treating Persons as Persons," *Ethics* 88 (1977): 150–161; R. S. Downie and Elizabeth Telfer, *Respect for Persons* (New York: Schocken Books, 1970); and Elizabeth Maclaren, "Dignity," *Journal of Medical Ethics* 3 (1977): 40–41.

16. I have relied primarily on the following discussions of care and a feminist ethics: Gilligan, *In A Different Voice*; Benhabib, "The Generalized and the Concrete Other"; Noddings, *Caring*; Virginia Held, "Feminism and Moral Theory"; Sara Ruddick, "Maternal

Thinking," in Marilyn Pearsall, ed., *Women and Values* (Belmont, Calif.: Wadsworth, 1986), 340–351; and Margaret Urban Walker, "Moral Understandings: Alternative 'Epistemology' for a Feminist Ethics," *Hypatia*, 1989.

17. On integration and feminism, see Marsha Hanen, "Introduction: Toward Integration," in Hanen and Nielsen, 1–21.

18. David Richards goes so far as to claim that the object of respect is not the person but the defining capacity itself: "respect is for an idealized capacity which, if appropriately treated, people can realize." Richards, "Rights and Autonomy," *Ethics* 92 (October 1981): 16. Compare this with the wording of the categorical imperative: "Act so that you treat humanity, whether in your own person or in that of another, always as an end and never as a means only." The wording suggests that it is "humanity in us," i.e., the defining capacity, that is the object of respect.

19. In addition to those mentioned in note 15 above, see also Bernard Williams, "Persons, Character, and Morality," in Amelie Oksenberg Rorty, ed., *The Identities of Persons* (Berkeley: University of California Press, 1976), 197–216; Alasdair MacIntyre, *After Virtue* (Notre Dame, Ind.: Notre Dame University Press, 1981); Robert Paul Wolff, "There's Nobody Here But Us Persons," in Carol Gould and Marx Wartofsky, eds., *Women and Philosophy: Toward a Theory of Liberation* (New York: Perigee/Putnam, 1976), 128–144; Edward Johnson, "Ignoring Persons," in *Respect for Persons, Tulane Studies in Philosophy* 31, 91–105; Michael Sandel, *Liberalism and the Limits of Justice* (Cambridge: Cambridge University Press, 1982).

20. Johnson, 93.

21. Melvin Rader, *Ethics and the Human Community* (New York: Holt, Rinehart, and Winston, 1964), 157; quoted in John E. Atwell, "Kant's Notion of Respect for Persons," in *Respect for Persons, Tulane Studies in Philosophy* 31 (1982), 22.

22. The phrase "treating a person as the person she is" comes from Spelman, "On Treating Persons."

23. Gilligan, "The Conquistador and the Dark Continent: Reflections on the Psychology of Love," *Daedalus* 113 (Summer 1984): 77.

24. Noddings, 24.

25. Benhabib, 164.

26. In this, care respect differs from the evaluative kind of respect mentioned in Section II. Evaluative respect is also responsive to particularity, but care respect involves an acceptance of the differences of the other that goes beyond toleration, even when her distinctive qualities are not intrinsically good or admirable.

27. Maclaren, 41.

28. See Kant's discussion of dignity and irreplaceability in *Groundwork of the Metaphysic of Morals*, trans. H. J. Paton (New York: Harper and Row, 1964), 102–103.

29. Friedman also makes this point in "Beyond Caring," 108.

30. The possibility of gracefully maintaining this tension may be seen in the way some parents of more than one child manage to see each child at the same time both as special and as equally important as the others.

31. For a useful discussion, see Walker.

32. Gilligan, "Conquistador," 77.

33. Noddings, 14.

34. Iris Murdoch, *The Sovereignty of Good* (London: Routledge and Kegan Paul, 1970), 34; Ruddick, 347–348.

35. Williams, "Idea of Equality," 159.

36. Spelman, 151.

37. We may wonder this, for in the everyday sense of caring, caring for someone and knowing all about her do not necessarily entail one another. On the one hand, I can identify with another in order to discover her weaknesses and so destroy or exploit her; and on the other, we are often content to let those we love remain enigmas to us. However, the

insistence on understanding that we find, for example, in Murdoch makes it clear that the latter is as much a moral failure as the former.

38. Williams, 161.

39. Downie and Telfer, 28.

40. See W. G. Maclagan, "Respect for Persons as a Moral Principle—I," *Philosophy* 35 (July 1960): 193–217; and "Respect for Persons as a Moral Principle—II," *Philosophy* 35 (October 1960): 289–305.

41. Compare Maclagan, Downie and Telfer, and Alan Donagan, *The Theory of Morality* (Chicago: University of Chicago Press, 1977).

42. Noddings, 4.

43. I owe this point, and this way of expressing it, to J. Ralph Lindgren.

Beyond Either/Or: Justice and Care in the Ethics of Albert Camus

ELIZABETH ANN BARTLETT ████████████████

Due to Carol Gilligan's ground-breaking study of women's moral development, the debate, which some claim to be an old one, over the ethic of care versus the ethic of justice has reemerged in recent years.[1] This debate has been useful in clarifying the differences and assessing the relative strengths and weaknesses of the two ethics. However, in serving more to set up a competition between the two ethics than to inform us of the possibilities that emerge from the conjunction of the two, the debate has reached a dead end. A more fruitful endeavor, I suggest, is to examine the possibilities of the relationship between justice and care. One way to do so is to examine an existing ethic that draws on both ethics. Albert Camus's ethic of "rebellion" is such an ethic. This ethic, discussed in this essay, shows how the ethics of care and justice must work in conjunction to secure their mutual goals of the respect of human dignity.

Before beginning a discussion of Camus's ethic, I will give a quick overview of the care versus justice debate. Briefly, the ethic of justice stresses the importance of the dignity of the individual and its expression in personal liberty, as well as the idea of justice as fairness in the application of universal principles of justice equally to all. The ethic of care emphasizes the importance of compassion, empathy, and the nurturance and growth of personal relationships.

Several critics have argued that "care" does not provide an adequate basis for sound moral and political practice. Broughton has argued that the inability of "caring" to transcend a parochial association with family and friends to extend to questions of citizen responsibility limits it as an ethical orientation.[2] He has also warned of the total lack of any mention of liberty in the ethic of care. Similarly, Mary Dietz has criticized the ethic of care and "maternal thinking" as inappropriate bases for political practice because of their necessary link with personal relationship rather than more abstract relations of citizenship.[3] She, like Broughton, has raised concern that an ethic based in "love" does not adequately address the reality of freedom and oppression, claiming that "not the language of love and compassion, but only the language of freedom and equality, citizenship and justice, will challenge nondemocratic and oppressive political institutions."[4] Tronto has questioned the adequacy of the ethic of care on grounds that it is both "strategically dangerous" (in that its assertion in a context that defines male as normal contains an implication of female inferiority) and "philosophically stultifying" (in that women may find themselves trapped by the necessity to defend "women's morality").[5]

Others, however, have questioned the adequacy of the ethic of justice, suggesting that the ethic of care provides a corrective to traditional moral theories. Adler has argued that the stringent consistency of principle demanded by the ethic of justice can serve to undermine a person's morality, while the emphasis found in the ethic of care on including the context of our moral choice in our reasoning about those choices serves to enhance our morality.[6] Similarly, Friedman has argued that an adequate basis for moral choice must include the rich knowledge of the context of the choice. Further, she has challenged what she sees to be the assumption implicit in the ethic of justice that the public world of government and the marketplace is of greater importance than the world of personal relationships, family, and friends.[7] Indeed, many of those who embrace the ethic of care have argued that it should be used to inform our political theory and practice precisely because of the priority it gives to concrete loving relationships.[8] Such a priority would result in a more life-affirming and creative politics.

Gilligan herself has claimed that she is interested only in elucidating the two different moral orientations, without establishing a hierarchy between them.[9] However, she has presented them as mutually exclusive. She has suggested that the two ethics are akin to the perceptual paradoxes of the bird and the rabbit, or the vase and the two women's faces. We can see one, and then the other, but we cannot perceive nor can we act on both simultaneously. The perception and enactment of one necessarily precludes the perception and enactment of the other.[10]

In making this suggestion, Gilligan sets up a dualism between the two ethics, which is troubling for two reasons. First, as Walker has argued, in an ethic with a duality of fundamental ethical principles, it is too easy, despite our best intentions, to establish a hierarchy in which one overrides the other.[11] Second, even if we could sustain a "separate but equal" positioning of these two ethics, as previously suggested, the dualism maintains an opposition between them which inhibits any examination of the possibilities of relations between justice and care.

As Tronto has suggested, when placed in the context of political theory and practice, such an examination of the proper relationship between care and justice becomes necessary and important.[12] She believes that we need to ask what is the place of caring in a just society, and I would add, what is the place of justice in a caring society. Charlotte Bunch has reiterated this concern, saying, "It's not a question of whether justice or caring is more important. It's a question of whether we can create a new relationship between these possible ethics. That's where the real challenge lies."[13]

It is precisely this challenge which I intend to address here by exploring three premises of Albert Camus's ethic of "rebellion," which suggest ways in which justice and care can, and indeed must, fruitfully interrelate: (1) justice and rights claims originate in caring; (2) both justice and compassion, as defined by the ethic of "rebellion," imply a moral and political community; and (3) caring places ethical and practical limits on justice and rights claims. I examine each of these three points in turn, using examples from Camus's novel *The Plague* to illustrate each point.

Before presenting my argument, a brief definition of Camus's concept of "rebellion" is in order. "Rebellion" is an action that simultaneously rejects injustice and oppression and affirms human dignity. It is a claim for justice based not in resentment of the privileges one does not have, but rather in the affirmation of who one is. (Because Camus does not use the term "rebellion" in its usual sense, I will keep it in quotations throughout. It is to remind, rather than distract, the reader.)

JUSTICE ORIGINATES FROM CARE

Locke, Kant, and others claimed to arrive at their universal principles of justice through the application of a disinterested and impartial reason. Rawls set up his "veil of ignorance" to ensure that our interests, our passions, our caring, do not interfere with our ability clearly to perceive and derive principles of fairness.[14] Not so for Camus, who would argue that we demand justice, and clearly perceive its incumbent rights claims precisely because we care. In Camus's ethic of "rebellion," justice and rights originate from a passionate and compassionate concern for oneself and for others.

Camus gave the example of a slave who refuses enslavement, even though risking his or her life. The slave does so not because he or she has rationally set out to prove the existence of a natural right to be free, but rather because she passionately feels that she is valuable. She knows and affirms her self-worth. At that moment of clear-sighted passion, the slave discovers the right to human dignity.[15]

Camus argued that the demand for justice arises not only out of affirmation and care for one's own dignity, but arises as well from compassionately witnessing the oppression of others.[16] Certainly we have all felt outrage at other women's accounts of abuse and battering, or at the spectacle of police brutality, or at the misshapen bodies of children suffering from malnutrition. It is these moments of compassionate recognition of human dignity, not a dispassionate calculation of rights, which give rise to the demand for justice.

In *The Plague*, Dr. Rieux, witnessing the torturous death of a child, is moved to "mad revolt" against the injustice of disease and death. The scene is the hospital ward, where many are dying, including a small child.[17]

> In the small face, rigid as a mask of grayish clay, slowly the lips parted and from them rose a long, incessant scream, . . . filling the ward with a fierce, indignant protest, so little childish that it seemed like a collective voice issuing from all the sufferers there . . . it was over.

The doctor begins to walk out in weariness and anger, but the priest stops him.

"Why was there that anger in your voice just now? . . . "
"There are times when the only feeling I have is one of mad revolt. . . . "
  And until my dying day I shall refuse to love a scheme of things in which
children are put to torture."

Here the witnessing of the suffering and injustice of others moves the doctor to
revolt, to act for justice, the concrete well-being of people.

BOTH "JUSTICE" AND "CARE"
IMPLY COMMUNITY

The ethic of "rebellion" addresses concerns on both sides of the debate regarding
the extension of moral claims to the community; that is, concern that (1) "justice"
ignores the reality of human relationship; and (2) "care" ignores the significance
of political obligation. Justice, as defined by the ethic of "rebellion," is based not
on the assumption of individuals, autonomous and separate from each other, but
rather on human relatedness. As Camus put it, "I rebel, therefore we exist."[18] The
fact of human connectedness and concern lies implicit in every rights claim.
  Camus made this point in two ways. First, he argued that whenever persons risk
their lives or well-being in their acts of "rebellion," that risk implies that these
claims for which they rebel must extend beyond the individual to the common
good.[19] Second, Camus argued that every ethic based on the solitary individual
implies an exercise of power.[20]
  An individual claiming a right without recognition of the extension of that right
to all makes a demand for inequality which implies the dominance of some and
the oppression of others. To claim a right for oneself and not for others is to act
oppressively. Yet, as we have already seen, the act of "rebellion" is a rejection of
oppression of oneself and/or of others. Thus, claiming a right implies the extension
of that right to all, thereby confirming human interrelatedness. (This second point
challenges Dietz's assumption that "care" is separate and distinct from discussions
of equality.[21] Rather it implies that the movement toward equal rights is based on
the human interconnections emphasized in the ethic of care.)
  By the same token, acts of true compassion—voluntary and self-affirming choices
to "suffer with" others[22]—transcend individual concerns and build political community. Indeed, actions based on compassion may provide a more sound foundation
for political obligation than do those obligations based on contract, which may be
performed resentfully out of a sense of duty or fear of repercussion.
  Camus made this point in The Plague through the character of Rambert, a
reporter from Paris, who is trapped by quarantine in the plague-stricken town of
Oran. Rambert believes he has every right to break the quarantine and return to
Paris. He has no ties to the people of Oran, and makes every effort to buy, beg,

or steal his way out of town. More than a year has passed when he finally gets a forged pass through the black market. In the end, however, he chooses not to use it. By this time he is no longer a solitary individual claiming his right above all others to leave. He has worked many months, day and night, side by side with other townspeople to heal the sick, bury the dead, and rid Oran of the plague. His solitary victory, without the liberation of his friends, would be meaningless to him. " 'Until now I always felt a stranger in this town, and that I'd no concern with you people. But now what I've seen, I know that I belong here whether I want it or not. This business is everybody's business.' "[23]

Thus, it is because of his caring and compassion that Rambert recognizes an obligation to the community that transcends his "parochial associations." It is because he experiences friendship in a concrete way that he can extend the obligations of friendship to the community in a meaningful way.

CARE DEFINES JUSTICE

Finally, according to Camus, only those actions which retain the impulse and commitment to care serve justice. As Camus put it, "rebellion" that is forgetful of its origins (these being care and compassion) negates itself.

Camus's work *The Rebel* is replete with examples of demands for justice which became acts of oppression because they abandoned "care." Camus examined ideologies and political regimes that arose from compassion for oppressed peoples but forgot their origins and destroyed the lives of the people they had hoped to save. He pointed, for example, to the French Revolution, which in the name of justice, deified Reason, and brought a reign of terror on all those who did not conform to its laws.[24] Similarly, he pointed to the Russian Revolution and regime of Stalin, which in the name of a justice in a far-off golden age, justified the sacrifice of the lives and liberties of the people they sought to liberate. Both the French and the Russian Revolutions began as compassionate refusals of oppression for people, which ended by placing principles above people, and thus became vehicles of oppression. In each instance, the claim for justice became more important than the people who were to be served.[25]

Camus refused a dogmatic adherence to a "justice" to which anything and everything, including friendship, must be sacrificed. He could find no justification for placing principles before particular friendships. "If anyone," he wrote regarding the Algerian revolts, " . . . still thinks heroically that one's brother must die rather than one's principles, I shall go no farther than to admire him from a distance. I am not of his stamp."[26] He could justify only those acts of "rebellion" which remained faithful to their origins in care and friendship. Justice not grounded in the care and friendship of particular persons too easily becomes abstract. The monologue of dictators or lawyers replaces the dialogue of friends. Principles replace persons. Justice, losing touch with humanity, becomes unjust.

Thus, Camus argued that it is the element of caring which defines the boundary between those actions which are just and those which are unjust. Justice that abandons care self-destructs. If justice becomes a devotion to the ideal of justice in and of itself, rather than a caring for particular persons, it becomes a tool of oppression. If "the long demand for justice exhausts even the love that gave it birth,"[27] the plague of oppression and injustice has won.

A scene in The Plague, with the doctor and his friend, Tarrou, illustrates this last point. After months of being locked in the town, battling the plague, the two friends decide to break quarantine and go for a swim, " ' . . . for friendship's sake. . . . Go for a swim. It's one of those harmless pleasures. . . . Really, it's too damn silly living only in and for the plague. Of course, a man should fight for the victims, but if he ceases caring for anything outside that, what's the use of his fighting?' "[28] What's the use? Isn't the point of fighting the plague (read: injustice) the fact that we value each other, that we care? Yet if we get so caught up in our struggle, so consumed by "justice" at all costs, that we no longer care, then we simply perpetuate oppression.

CONCLUSION

Camus's ethic of "rebellion" does provide us with a model of an ethic that embraces the relationship, rather than the opposition, of justice and care. This model suggests that at the core of both the ethic of care and the ethic of justice lies a deep and passionate concern for human dignity, for respect of that in us which cannot be reduced to abstract principles. Camus's concern is not for an eternal idea of justice, or for caring that is entirely self-serving, but rather for a justice and care that can be realized on this earth through honest dialogue, compassionate response, and mutual understanding.[29] Justice, for Camus, must be embedded in particular persons, their passions, their friendships, their concrete realities. Justice divorced from these is meaningless. Caring must move beyond the servicing of individual interests to an inordinate concern for the dignity of each and all of us. Far from being separate ethics, Camus would argue that it is only in the context of justice that caring moves from self-service to compassionate service and that it is only in the context of caring that the claim for justice is born and sustains meaning.

NOTES

1. On women's moral development, see Carol Gilligan, In a Different Voice: Psychological Theory and Women's Moral Development (Cambridge, Mass.: Harvard University Press,

1982). On the justice/care debate, see Jean C. Tronto, "Beyond Gender Difference to a Theory of Care," in *Signs* 12 (1987), 644–663.

2. John M. Broughton, "Women's Rationality and Men's Virtues: A Critique of Gender Dualism in Gilligan's Theory of Moral Development," in *Social Research* 50 (1983), 597–642.

3. Mary J. Dietz, "Citizenship with a Feminist Face: The Problem with Maternal Thinking," in *Political Theory* 13 (1985), 19–37.

4. Dietz, "Citizenship," p. 34.

5. Tronto, "Beyond Gender."

6. Jonathan E. Adler, "Moral Development and the Personal Point of View," in *Women and Moral Theory*, ed. Eva Feder Kittay and Diana T. Meyers (Totowa, N.J.: Rowman and Littlefield, 1987).

7. Marilyn Friedman, "Care and Context in Moral Reasoning," in *Women and Moral Theory*.

8. Sara Ruddick, "Remarks on the Sexual Politics of Reason," in *Women and Moral Theory*. See also Jean Bethke Elshtain, "Reflections on War and Political Discourse: Realism, Just War, and Feminism in a Nuclear Age," in *Political Theory* 13 (1985), 39–57.

9. Linda K. Kerber et al., "On *In a Different Voice*: An Interdisciplinary Forum," in *Signs* 11 (1986), 304–333.

10. Carol Gilligan, "Moral Orientation and Moral Development," in *Women and Moral Theory*.

11. James C. Walker, "In a Different Voice: Cryptoseparatist Analysis of Female Moral Development," in *Social Research* 50 (1983), 665–695.

12. Jean C. Tronto, "Political Science and Caring: Or, the Perils of Balkanized Social Science," in *Women and Moral Politics* 7 (1987), 85–98.

13. Charlotte Bunch, "A Global Perspective on Feminist Ethics and Diversity," in this volume.

14. John Rawls, *A Theory of Justice* (Cambridge, Mass.: Harvard University Press, 1971).

15. Albert Camus, *The Rebel: An Essay on Man in Revolt*, trans. Anthony Bower (New York: Random House, 1956), 14–15.

16. Ibid., 16–17.

17. Albert Camus, *The Plague*, trans. Stuart Gilbert (New York: Modern Library, 1948).

18. Camus, *The Rebel*, 22.

19. Ibid., 15.

20. Ibid., 36.

21. Mary J. Dietz, "Citizenship with a Feminist Face," 34.

22. Compassion means, literally, "suffering with." In her discussion of suffering, Eleanora Patterson distinguishes common suffering which is involuntary and/or based in denial and degradation of self-worth, from compassionate suffering, which is voluntary and based in affirmation of self-worth. See her "Suffering," in Pam McAllister, ed., *Re-Weaving the Web of Life* (Philadelphia: New Society Publishers, 1982).

23. Camus, *The Plague*, 188.

24. Camus, *The Rebel*, 115–130.

25. Ibid., 161.

26. Camus, *Resistance, Rebellion, and Death*, trans. Justin O'Brien (New York: Vintage Books, 1974).

27. Camus, "Return to Tipasa," in *Lyrical and Critical Essays*, ed. Philip Thody, trans. Ellen Conroy Kenny (New York: Vintage, 1953), 168.

28. Camus, *The Plague*, 231.

29. Camus, *The Rebel*, 283.

Feminism and Modern Friendship: Dislocating the Community

MARILYN FRIEDMAN ■■■■■■■■■■■■■■■■■

INTRODUCTION

Abstract individualism considers individual human beings as social atoms, abstracted from their social contexts, and disregards the role of social relationships and human community in constituting the very identity and nature of individual human beings.[1] Against this abstractive individualist view of the self, many feminists have asserted a conception of what might be called the "social self."[2] This conception acknowledges the fundamental role of social relationships and human community in constituting both self-identity and the nature and meaning of the particulars of individual lives.[3]

Some of these anti-individualist developments emerging from feminist thought are strikingly similar to other theoretical developments that are not specifically feminist. Thus, the "new communitarians," to borrow Amy Gutmann's term,[4] have also reacted critically to abstract individualism. The communitarian self, or subject, is also not a social atom but is instead a being constituted and defined by its communal attachments and historical context.

However, communitarian philosophy as a whole is a perilous ally for feminists. Communitarians invoke a model of community focused particularly on families, neighborhoods, and nations. These sorts of communities harbor social roles and structures that have been highly oppressive for women. But communitarians seem oblivious to those difficulties and manifest a troubling complacency about the moral authority claimed or presupposed by these communities in regard to their members.

This essay is an effort to reorient communitarian thought in a more feminist direction. In the first part, I develop three criticisms of communitarian philosophy as it is found in writings by Michael Sandel[5] and Alasdair MacIntyre.[6] In the second, I suggest that certain types of community and social relationship, which communitarians generally disregard, can help to counterbalance the communitarian emphasis on family, neighborhood, and nation. With that alternative model in view, we can begin to transform the communitarian vision of self and community into a more congenial ally of feminist theory.

I. THE SOCIAL SELF, IN
COMMUNITARIAN PERSPECTIVE

In contrast to the atomistic self of classical liberalism,[7] the new communitarians posit the conception of a self whose identity and nature are defined by her contingent and particular social relationships—relationships that communitarians generally extol. Thus, Michael Sandel speaks warmly of "those loyalties and convictions whose moral force consists partly in the fact that living by them is inseparable from understanding ourselves as the particular persons we are—as members of this family or community or nation or people, as bearers of this history, as sons and daughters of that revolution, as citizens of this republic."[8] Voicing similar sentiments, Alasdair MacIntyre writes:

> We all approach our own circumstances as bearers of a particular social identity.
> I am someone's son or daughter, someone else's cousin or uncle; I am a citizen
> of this or that city, a member of this or that guild or profession; I belong to this
> clan, that tribe, this nation. Hence what is good for me has to be the good for
> one who inhabits these roles. As such, I inherit from the past of my family, my
> city, my tribe, my nation, a variety of debts, inheritances, rightful expectations
> and obligations. These constitute the given of my life, my moral starting point.
> This is in part what gives my life its own moral particularity.[9]

For communitarians, social relationships and communities have a kind of normative legitimacy; they define the "moral starting points," to use MacIntyre's phrase, of each individual life. The traditions, practices, and conventions of our communities have at least a prima facie moral claim on us.

I will discuss three features of the communitarian notions of self and social relationships which are troubling from a feminist standpoint. First, the communitarian's metaphysical conception of an inherently social self has little usefulness for normative analysis; in particular, it will not support a specifically feminist critique of individualistic personality or its associated attributes: the avoidance of intimacy, nonnurturance, social distancing, aggression, or violence. A metaphysical view that *all* human selves are constituted by their social and communal relationships does not itself entail a *critique* of highly individualistic selves, or yield any indication of what degree of *psychological* attachment to others is desirable. On metaphysical grounds alone, there is no reason to suppose that caring, nurturant, relational, sociable selves are *better* than more autonomous, individualistic, and independent selves. All would be equivalently socially constituted at a metaphysical level. Thus, the communitarian's metaphysical conception of the social self appears *irrelevant* to feminist theorists seeking a *normative* account of what might be wrong or excessive about competitive self-seeking behaviors or other individualistic traits or dispositions.

My second concern about communitarian philosophy has to do with the legitimacy of the communal norms and traditions that are supposed to define the moral starting points of community members. As a matter of moral psychology, it is common for persons to *regard* the norms, traditions, and practices of their communities as legitimate; however, this point about moral psychology does not entail that these norms really *are* legitimate. Unfortunately, the new communitarians seem to regard the moral norms and traditions of communities as having a real, morally binding force over their members, at least as "moral starting points." MacIntyre refers to the "debts, inheritances, *rightful* expectations and obligations"[10] which we "inherit" from family, nation, and so forth.

But this normative complacency is very troubling. Many communities practice the exclusion and suppression of non-group members, especially outsiders defined by ethnicity and sexuality.[11] Are there no "rightful expectations and obligations" *across* community lines? Don't whites, for example, have obligations of respect and fair treatment toward blacks, Hispanics, and Native Americans? Didn't Jews, Gypsies, Poles, Czechoslovakians, and others have "rightful expectations" that Germany would not practice military conquest and unimaginable genocide? If there are such *inter*-community obligations which *override* communal norms and practices, then moral particularity is hardly explicated by communal norms and practices alone.

Besides excluding or suppressing outsiders, the practices and traditions of numerous communities are exploitative and oppressive toward many of their own members, particularly women. In general, to evaluate the moral identities conferred by communities on their members, we need a *theory* of communities, of their interrelationships, of the structures of power, dominance, and oppression within and among them. Only such a theory would allow us to assess the *legitimacy* of a community's norms, traditions, and practices.

A third problem with communitarian philosophy has to do with the *sorts* of communities evidently endorsed by communitarian theorists. The substantive examples of community listed by MacIntyre and Sandel fall largely into two groups. First, governmental communities constitute our civic and national identities in a public world of nation-states. Thus, Sandel writes of "nation or people, . . . bearers of this history, . . . sons and daughters of that revolution, . . . citizens of this republic."[12] Second, local communities center on family and neighborhood; some sociologists call these "communities of place."[13]

But where, one might ask, is the International Ladies Garment Workers' Union or the Committee in Solidarity with the People of El Salvador? Although MacIntyre does mention professions and, rather archaically, "guilds,"[14] these references are anomalous in his work, which, for the most part, ignores such communities as trade unions, political action groups, and so forth.

Communities of government form a particularly suspect category for feminist analysis. We all recall how governing communities have, until only recently, *excluded* the legitimate participation of women. It would seem to follow that they have accordingly *not* historically constituted the identities of women in profound ways. As "daughters" of an American revolution spawned parthenogenically by the "fathers of our country," we find our communities of government to have denied us the self-identifying heritage of our political *mothers*. In general, the contribution made to the identities of various groups of people by governing communities is quite uneven, given that they are communities to which many are *subject*, but in which far fewer actively *participate*.

There is an underlying commonality to most of the communities that MacIntyre and Sandel actually cite as constitutive of self-identity and definitive of our moral starting points. Sandel himself explicates this commonality when he writes that, for people "bound by a sense of community," the notion of community describes *"not a relationship they choose (as in a voluntary association) but an attachment they discover*, not merely an attribute but a constituent of their identity."[15] It is the communities to which we are *involuntarily* bound to which Sandel accords metaphysical pride of place in the constitution of subjectivity. In Sandel's view, these communities " . . . describe a form of life in which the members find themselves commonly situated 'to begin with', their commonality consisting less in relationships they have entered than in attachments they have found."[16] Thus, the social relationships one finds, the attachments discovered and not chosen, become the points of reference for self-definition by the communitarian subject.

For the child maturing to self-consciousness in her community of origin, typically a complex of family-neighborhood-school-church, it seems uncontroversial that "the" community is found, not entered, discovered, created. But this need not be true of an adult's communities of mature self-identification. Many of these adult communities are, for at least some of their members, communities of *choice* to a significant extent: labor unions, philanthropic associations, political coalitions, and, if one has ever moved or migrated, even the communities of neighborhood, church, city, or nation-state might have been chosen to an important extent. One need not have simply discovered oneself to be embedded in them in order that one's identity or the moral particulars of one's life be defined by them. Sandel is right to indicate the role of found communities in constituting the unreflective, "given" identity that the self discovers when *first* beginning to reflect on itself. But for *mature* self-identity, we should also recognize a legitimate role for *communities of choice*, supplementing, if not displacing, the communities and attachments that are merely found.

Moreover, the discovered identity constituted by one's original community of place might be fraught with ambivalences and ambiguities. Our communities of origin do not necessarily constitute us as selves who *agree or comply* with the norms that unify those communities. Some of us are constituted as deviants and resisters by our communities of origin. Thus, Adrienne Rich writes about her experiences growing up with a Christian mother, a Jewish father who suppressed his ethnicity, and a family that taught Rich contempt for all that was identified with Jewishness. In 1946, while still a high school student, Rich saw for the first time a film about the Allied liberation of Nazi concentration camps. Writing about this experience in 1982, she brooded, "I feel belated rage that I was so impoverished by the family and social worlds I lived in, that I had to try to figure out by myself what this did indeed mean for me. That I had never been taught about resistance, only about passing. That I had no language for anti-Semitism itself."[17]

As a student at Radcliffe in the late 1940s, Rich met "real" Jewish women who inducted her into the lore of Jewish background and customs, holidays and foods, names and noses. She plunged in with trepidation: "I felt I was testing a forbidden current, that there was danger in these revelations. I bought a reproduction of a Chagall portrait of a rabbi in striped prayer shawl and hung it on the wall of my room. I was admittedly young and trying to educate myself, but I was also doing something that *is* dangerous: I was flirting with identity."[18]

One of Rich's projects throughout her life, so evidently *not* inspired by her community of origin alone, was to explore and reconstruct the identity found in that original unchosen context. The communitarian view that *found* communities and social attachments constitute self-identity does not, by itself, explicate the source of such a quest. It seems more illuminating to say that Rich's identity became, in part, "chosen," that it had to do with social relationships and attachments that she sought out, rather than merely found, created as well as discovered.

Thus, the commitments and loyalties of our found communities, our communities of origin, may harbor ambiguities, ambivalences, contradictions, and oppressions that *complicate* as well as *constitute* identity, and that have to be sorted out, critically scrutinized. In these undertakings, we are likely to utilize resources and skills derived from various communities and relationships, not merely those which we found or discovered. The whole tenor of communitarian thinking would change once we opened up the conception of the social self to encompass *chosen* communities, especially those which lie beyond the typical original community of family-neighborhood-school-church and nation. No longer would communitarian thought present a seemingly conservative complacency about the private and local communities of place which have so effectively circumscribed women's lives.

In the second part of this essay, I will explore more fully the role of communities and relationships of "choice," which point the way toward a notion of community more congenial to feminist aspirations.

II. MODERN FRIENDSHIP, URBAN COMMUNITY, AND BEYOND

Modern friendships and many urban communities share an important feature that is either neglected or deliberately disregarded by communitarians: these relationships are based partly on choice. I believe that friendship and urban community can offer us crucial insights into the social nature of the modern self.

Let's first consider friendship as it is understood in this culture. Friends are supposed to be people whom one chooses on one's own to share activities and intimacies. No particular people are assigned by custom or tradition to be a person's friends. No consanguineal or legal connections establish or maintain ties of friendship. As this relationship is widely understood in our culture, its basis lies partly in voluntary choice.

In this context, "voluntary choice" refers to motivations arising out of one's own needs, desires, interests, values, and attractions, *rather than* motivations arising from what is socially assigned, ascribed, expected, or demanded. This means that friendship, unlike the relationships of family, neighborhood, and so on, is more likely to be grounded and sustained by shared interests and values, mutual affection, and reciprocal esteem.

Friendship is more likely than many other close personal relationships to provide social support for people who are idiosyncratic, whose unconventional values and deviant life-styles make them victims of intolerance from family members and others who are unwillingly related to them. In this regard, friendship has socially disruptive possibilities, for out of the unconventional living that it helps to sustain, influential forces for social change may arise. Friendship has had an obvious importance to feminist aspirations as the basis of the bond which is (ironically) called "sisterhood."[19] Friendship among women has been the cement not only of the various historical waves of the feminist movement, but also of numerous communities of women throughout history who defied the local conventions for their gender and lived lives of creative disorder.[20] In all these cases, women moved out of their given or found communities into new attachments with other women by their own choice, that is, motivated by their own needs, desires, values, and attractions, rather than, and often *in opposition to*, the expectations and ascribed roles of their found communities.

Like friendship, many *urban* relationships are also based to an important extent on choice. Much evidence suggests that urban settings do not, as commonly stereotyped, promote only alienation, isolation, and psychic breakdown. The communities available to urban dwellers are different from those available to nonurban dwellers, but are not necessarily less gratifying or fulfilling.[21] Sociological research has shown that urban dwellers tend to form their social networks, their communities, out of people who are brought together for reasons other than geographic proximity. Communities of place, centered on family-neighborhood-church-school, are more likely, for urban dwellers, to be *supplanted* by other sorts of communities, resulting in what the sociologist Melvin Webber has called "community without propinquity."[22] Voluntary associations, such as political action groups, support groups, and so on, are a common part of modern urban life, with its large population centers and the greater availability of critical masses of people with special interests or needs. As the sociologist Claude Fischer has stated, in urban areas, "population concentration stimulates allegiances to subcultures based on more significant social traits" than common locality or neighborhood.[23]

Literature reveals that women writers have been both repelled and inspired by urban communities. The city, as a concentrated center of male political and economic power, seems to exclude women altogether.[24] However, as literary critic Susan Merrill Squier points out, the city can provide women with jobs, education, and the cultural tools with which to escape imposed familial demands; the city can also *bring women together*, in work or in leisure, and lay the basis for bonds of sisterhood.[25] The quests of women who journey to cities leaving behind men, home, and family are subversive, writes literary critic Blanche Gelfant, and may well be perceived by others "as assaults upon society."[26] Thus, urban communities of choice can provide the resources for women to surmount the moral particularities of family and place which define and limit their moral starting points.

Perhaps it is more illuminating to say that communities of choice foster not so much the *constitution* of subjects but their *reconstitution*. We seek out communities of choice as contexts in which to *relocate* and *renegotiate* the various constituents of our identities, as Adrienne Rich sought out Jewish community in her college years. A community of choice might be a community of people who share a common oppression. This is particularly critical in those instances in which the shared oppression is not concentrated within certain communities of place, but, rather, is distributed throughout social and ethnic groupings. Thus, unlike ethnic minorities, women are a paradigm example of such a *distributed* group and do not comprise a traditional community of place. Women's communities are seldom the original, nonvoluntary, found communities of their members.

To be sure, nonvoluntary communities of place are influential and not entirely without value. Most lives contain mixtures of relationships and communities, some which are given/found/discovered, and others which are chosen/created. Most people probably are, to *some* extent, ineradicably constituted by their original communities of place, their original families, neighborhoods, schools, churches, or nations. It is noteworthy that dependent children, elderly persons, and all other individuals who are at great risk, need the *support* of communities whose *other* members do not or cannot choose arbitrarily to *leave*. Recent philosophical study of communities and relationships *not* founded or sustained by choice has brought out the importance of these social networks for the very constitution of social life.[27] But these insights should not obscure the additional need for communities of choice to *counter* the oppressive and abusive relational structures in those nonvoluntary communities.

Thus, the uncritically assumed communities of place invoked by the communitarians appear deeply problematic. We can concede the influence of those communities without having to endorse it. We must develop communitarian thought *beyond* its complacent regard for the communities in which we have merely found ourselves toward an awareness of the crucial importance of *dislocated* communities, communities of *choice*.[28]

NOTES

An earlier version of this essay was published in *Ethics* 99, no. 2 (January 1989): 275–290, © 1989 by the University of Chicago Press, reprinted by permission.

    1. Critiques of this view may be found in many feminist writings. Compare Carole Pateman, *The Problem of Political Obligation: A Critique of Liberal Theory* (Berkeley: University

of California Press, 1979); Zillah Eisenstein, *The Radical Future of Liberal Feminism* (New York: Longman, 1981); Nancy C. M. Hartsock, *Money, Sex, and Power* (Boston: Northeastern University Press, 1983); Alison M. Jaggar, *Feminist Politics and Human Nature* (Totowa, N.J.: Rowman & Allanheld, 1983); Naomi Scheman, "Individualism and the Objects of Psychology," in Sandra Harding and Merrill B. Hintikka, eds., *Discovering Reality* (Dordrecht: D. Reidel, 1983), 225–244; Jane Flax, "Political Philosophy and the Patriarchal Unconscious: A Psychoanalytic Perspective on Epistemology and Metaphysics," in Harding and Hintikka, 245–281; and Seyla Benhabib, "The Generalized and the Concrete Other: The Kohlberg-Gilligan Controversy and Moral Theory," in Eva Feder Kittay and Diana T. Meyers, eds., *Women and Moral Theory* (Totowa, N.J.: Rowman and Littlefield, 1987), 154–177.

2. Compare my "Autonomy in Social Context," in James Sterba and Creighton Peden, eds., *Freedom, Equality, and Social Change: Problems in Social Philosophy Today* (Lewiston, N.Y.: Edwin Mellen Press, 1990).

3. For feminist discussions of the need for social and moral theory to take better account of the fundamental role of social relationships and community, see Carol Gilligan, *In a Different Voice* (Cambridge, Mass.: Harvard University Press, 1982); Drucilla Cornell, "Toward a Modern/Postmodern Reconstruction of Ethics," *University of Pennsylvania Law Review* 133, no. 2 (January 1985), 291–380; Annette Baier, "Trust and Antitrust," *Ethics* 96, no. 2 (1986), 231–260; Owen Flanagan and Kathryn Jackson, "Justice, Care, and Gender: The Kohlberg-Gilligan Debate Revisited," *Ethics* 97, no. 3 (1987), 622–637; Hartsock, 41–42; and Virginia Held, "Non-Contractual Society," in Marsha Hanen and Kai Nielsen, eds., *Science, Morality and Feminist Theory* in *The Canadian Journal of Philosophy*, Supplementary Vol. 13 (1987), 111–138.

4. "Communitarian Critics of Liberalism," *Philosophy and Public Affairs* 14, no. 3 (Summer 1985), 308–322.

5. In particular, Sandel, *Liberalism and the Limits of Justice* (Cambridge: Cambridge University Press, 1982).

6. In particular, MacIntyre, *After Virtue* (Notre Dame, Ind.: Univ. of Notre Dame Press, 1981).

7. Contemporary liberals do not regard the communitarians' metaphysical claims as a threat to liberal theory. The liberal concept of the self as abstracted from social relationships and historical context is now treated not as a metaphysical presupposition, but, rather, as a vehicle for evoking a pluralistic political society whose members disagree about the good for human life. With this device, liberalism seeks a theory of political process which aims to avoid relying on any human particularities that might presuppose parochial human goods or purposes. See John Rawls, "Justice as Fairness: Political Not Metaphysical," *Philosophy & Public Affairs* 14, no. 3 (1985), 223–251, and Joel Feinberg, "Liberalism, Community, and Tradition," in *The Moral Limits of the Criminal Law* 4 (Oxford University Press, 1988).

8. Sandel, 179.

9. MacIntyre, 204–205.

10. MacIntyre, 205; my italics.

11. A similar point is made by Iris Young, "The Ideal of Community and the Politics of Difference," *Social Theory and Practice* 12, no. 1 (Spring 1986), 12–13.

12. Sandel, 179.

13. Young, 12, notes that these are the social networks that people tend to think of when they think of "community."

14. MacIntyre, 204.

15. Sandel, 150; my italics.

16. Ibid., 151–152.

17. Adrienne Rich, "Split at the Root: An Essay on Jewish Identity," in *Blood, Bread, and Poetry* (New York: W. W. Norton, 1986), 107; reprinted in Evelyn Torton Beck, ed., *Nice Jewish Girls: A Lesbian Anthology* (Trumansburg, N.Y.: Crossing Press, 1982), 67–84.

18. Rich, 108.

19. Martha Ackelsberg points out the ironic and misleading nature of this use of the term "sisterhood" in " 'Sisters' or 'Comrades'? The Politics of Friends and Families," in Irene Diamond, ed., *Families, Politics, and Public Policy* (New York: Longman, 1983), 339–356.

20. Compare Janice Raymond, *A Passion for Friends* (Boston: Beacon Press, 1986), esp. chaps. 2 and 3.

21. Claude Fischer, *To Dwell among Friends* (Chicago: University of Chicago Press, 1982), 193–232.

22. Melvin Webber, "Order in Diversity: Community without Propinquity," in R. Gutman and D. Popenoe, eds., *Neighborhood, City and Metropolis* (New York: Random House, 1970), 792–811.

23. Fischer, 273.

24. Compare the essays in Catherine Stimpson, et al., eds., *Women and the American City* (Chicago: University of Chicago Press, 1980, 1981); and the special issue on "Women in the City," *Urban Resources* 3, no. 2 (Winter 1986).

25. "Introduction" to Susan Merrill Squier, ed., *Women Writers and the City* (Knoxville: University of Tennessee Press, 1984), 3–10.

26. Blanche Gelfant, "Sister to Faust: The City's 'Hungry' Woman as Heroine," in Squier, 267.

27. Compare Baier, Held, and Pateman.

28. I am grateful to Cass Sunstein and the editors of *Ethics* for helpful comments on an earlier version of this essay. This essay was written with the support of a National Endowment for the Humanities Summer Stipend and a grant from the Faculty Research Committee of Bowling Green State University.

III. Constructing an Ethical Life ■■■■■■

Ethics and Self-knowing: The Satisfaction of Desire

WINNIE TOMM ███████████████████████████████

I. DESIRE AS POWER

An underlying assumption in this essay is that personal desire is the basic motivator of social action. I assume that individual agency and social constructionism are mutually influencing determinants in human interaction. I believe that the particular mode of individual agency is shaped by each person's desire(s). The implication of these assumptions and beliefs for the discussion of ethics which follows is: desire is the instigator of all ethical conduct. I have argued this extensively elsewhere.[1]

The question here is: Is there a desire which, if revealed, might open up possibilities for more women to claim their moral agency through expression of that desire? Jessica Benjamin provides an important framework in which to answer the question of women's desire(s).[2] She develops a spatial metaphor for desire: a desire for space which allows for separation and connection. Benjamin claims that the desire for separation and connection is integral to human consciousness. The two tendencies mutually construct each other. Inner space is necessary for an agent to interact with another; otherwise it is mere reaction, without any subjective power. The impetus for action is seen to come from the co-creational activity of subjects through intersubjectivity.

Carol Christ speaks to intersubjectivity from the perspective of women-identified imagery and language that reflects one's inner space.[3] It is impossible, from Christ's point of view, for women to relate as agents when they (we) are required to fit sidewise into the linguistically constructed reality that is derived largely from men's inner subjectivity and corresponding imagery. Christ rightfully claims that women need to draw on images and symbols of female power that acknowledge the "legitimacy of female power as a beneficent and independent power."[4] We need a language that affirms "female power, the female body, the female will, and women's bonds and heritage."[5] In agreement with Benjamin and Christ, I believe that ethics is a matter of acting out our desire for inner space—where one's subjective power is grounded—while at the same time living through that power in relation to other subjects.

Ethical conduct is seen by both Benjamin and Christ as the manifestation of each person living inside her/his own space while, simultaneously, co-constructing each other through transforming connectiveness. Because of the widespread social pressure on women to conform to the desires of others, it is important for women to know their own desire(s) and act accordingly. I support Benjamin and Christ's assumption that knowing one's desire is a prerequisite for self-determination and, coextensively, for ethical conduct. This view of ethics is not, of course, restricted to feminist ethics. The feminist component is the attention to women as moral or ethical agents in light of widespread socialization of women to be "soluble" selves (dissolve into the realities of separate selves). In contrast, the self as "permeable" or "connective," as described by Catherine Keller, is a useful paradigm with which to work.[6] The view of self as permeable, that is both self-determined and socially constructed, is adopted in this essay.

I shall explore the relation between ethics and self-knowing from the point of view of satisfying the desire for separation and connection in self-determination and social relations. The notion "self-knowing" rather than "self-knowledge" is used in order to emphasize the inclusive relation between knowing and acting. Ethical conduct, that is, humane action, is seen to be concomitant with knowing oneself and others to be both self-legislating and socially connected subjects. As Murdoch describes, the social good arises in the same manner as the personal good: paying attention to the realities of subjects as both independent and connective selves.[7]

Self-knowing includes awareness of the wholly subjective component of self, that is, feeling states, as well as the reflective dimension of giving meaning to felt awareness. Both dimensions of knowing (feeling states and reflection) include intersubjectivity. They are determined by the manner of interaction between subjects. Ways of knowing oneself are inseparable from ways of knowing others and being known by them. Ann Belford Ulanov helpfully describes this process of intersubjectivity in terms of receptivity: receiving oneself, receiving the other, and being received by the other.[8] In part II of this essay, I shall discuss the intersubjective nature of ethics with reference to respect, sympathy, and autonomy. A basis for the intersubjective model of self-knowing and ethical conduct is explored in part III, where I develop a view of knowing oneself as a transformative process of becoming connected to one's own agency and that of others in ethical encounters.

In the view presented here, receptivity of one's own power disposes one toward receiving the power of others. An encounter between subjects who are wholly receptive and responsive to each other's presence constitutes the profound I–Thou ethical experience. Constructive energy enters the social domain through such encounters and opens space for different ways of knowing and, accordingly, different ways of being. The I–Thou encounter is the prototype for the I–You type of less intimate relations. It reduces the tendency toward the I–It relation of depersonalizing domination.[9]

A concern in feminist ethics is to emphasize responsibility, both personally and socially. That concern is closely associated with the issue of self-identity, that is, of both individuation and relatedness. How do we develop our desire for self-determination while, at the same time, paying attention to the determination of others? Excessive emphasis on individuation turns relationships into I–It dyads, while too much inclusiveness may necessarily entail the presence of a soluble self, in which one subject becomes the inessential other.

The model of the I–Thou relation provides the ideal for personal encounter in a momentary sense. Through loss of individual boundaries, we are able to glimpse our ontological connectedness to the other in a profound way that informs less enlightened moments and minimizes the probability of falling irrevocably into oppositional I–It relations. A danger of emulating the I–Thou encounter is the possibility of despair during its absence. Its enlivening effect may lead one to experience all other relations as less than satisfactory. The search for the ultimate inclusive encounter might make one insensitive to the value of more accessible I–You relations, which are characterized more by mutual respect of individual boundaries within the context of sympathetic response to the other. Because of the drive toward self-determination and the need to preserve an inner space in which one lives within one's privateness, the inclusiveness of the I–Thou encounter is not satisfactory as a general way of interpersonal encounter. It is necessary to live with others in a way that allows inner space to exist separate from interpersonal space.

In contrast to the I–Thou encounter, the I–You manner of relating permits a continuum between private and shared experience, without including an oppositional stance between self and other that characterizes the I–It relation in its objectification of the other. In the I–You relation, the interactive process between self and other is one of enlivenment rather than self-loss. Both subjects are able to maintain an integrity between inner felt awareness and outer, shared expression. Satisfaction of the desire for self-expression depends on respecting individual autonomy as well as interdependency.

Such moral sensitivity is both self-regarding and other-regarding. Because self-expression is possible only within the context of satisfactory interpersonal relations, lack of respect toward either self or other leads to dissatisfaction of self-expression and, coextensively, social injustice. Benevolence and self-love are two dimensions of the same phenomenon, namely, moral agency. When self and other are experienced as interacting aspects of a continuous process, sympathy with the well-being of the other coexists with self-interest. Moral agency is understood in this essay to be integrally connected to knowing the self as ontologically connected to the other. Self-knowing includes knowing that one's self-determination is inextricably tied to that of the other. Social justice depends on such self-knowing.

Ethical theory, moral agency, and political action are given greater coherency when contextualized within a theory of human nature.[10] A person's ways of being in the world correlate with her or his ways of giving meaning to experiences. Meaning-giving depends on prior assumptions regarding purposes and values. These are invariably self-referential. Personal values are associated with what one perceives to be one's purpose or lack of purpose. Social values are coextensive with personal values. A theory or set of assumptions about the nature of reality and one's place in it affects the ways in which an individual participates in a society. Conversely, social realities shape one's consciousness of human nature. It is well known that a circular relation characterizes material determinism and personal consciousness. In this essay, I hope to indicate the continuity between self-expression and social realities.

Part II of the essay is about the role of respect, sympathy, and autonomy in the satisfaction of personal desire in ethical theory, agency, and political action. Justice is discussed in light of those three notions.

Part 3 develops an account of self-knowing. It is a theory of human nature which includes views about metaphysics, epistemology, motivation for action, and freedom. Ethics is explained in terms of ways of interacting, based on ways of knowing oneself in the context of interrelatedness. Satisfaction of the basic desire for personal power is required for social justice.

II. ETHICS

Respect. I see ethics to be largely about respect within a context of human interdependency. It is respect for the inner space of personal location as well as for interpersonal dialogical space. Respect for disparate interests is a matter of justice. Justice in patriarchal judicial systems is invariably problematic for women.

Justice is determined by societally defined principles of fairness. In patriarchal judicial systems principles of so-called fairness have entailed discrimination against women and have tyrannized women in the name of justice. Tyrannical legal systems evolve because of built-in biases about the rights of certain privileged persons over the rights of others. In such systems, justice privileges the authors of justice. A striking example of that fact is justice with regard to rape. The treatment of a rape victim in the courts most often depends on her respectablility as defined by male authors of social morality. A woman's respectability derives largely from her marital status, indicating that her sexuality is the responsibility of her husband and is therefore to be controlled by him. A "loose woman" is one whose sexuality is not legitimized by a particular man and who is therefore perceived as a threat to the moral fiber of the society. Accordingly, "she deserves what she gets." The term "loose woman" would have no coinage in a society that was not male-centered. If women had political control over their bodies, male morality would not define the good and bad girls. Men's morality has been adopted by the majority of women in patriarchal societies. Envy among women largely revolves around their alignments with men, the moral legislators of women's sexuality. Good and bad women are so defined with reference to male ownership interests, primarily with regard to family name and wealth. Women's sexuality is generally circumscribed by those interests. If we reject men's ownership over our sexuality and take personal responsibility for it (as the "loose woman" does), we cannot assume protection in the patriarchal system of justice.

If ethics were to be defined in terms of respect for persons, including respect for women's responsibility for our own sexuality, and justice is defined as the protection of personal respect (rather than the protection of property), then an ethics of justice is continuous with an ethics of care. The rationale for emphasizing an ethics of care is that it brings forth the importance of responsiveness and receptivity to particular individuals. To treat a person with respect is to pay attention to that person's needs and desires. To act morally is not, as Kant argued, to ignore personal interests for the sake of treating another as a sovereign subject. One's own personal interests as well as those of the other are part of the relationship between two subjects. Objective indifference toward personal subjectivity is inconsistent with interaction between subjects. The presence of one person to another requires that each person projects inner subjectivity into the field of interpersonal creativity. Moral agency is the expression of inner power in response to the inner power of another.

The basic desire that underscores moral agency is that of creating inner space in which one's power of projecting oneself forth in relation to others is made possible.[11] Inner space is relational: it exists within the context of interconnecting circles of self, home, and community. A theory of ethics must take into account the interconnecting circles of a person's existence. Recognizing self, home, and community as interacting networks means acknowledging the interweaving strands of societal and personal rights and responsibilities. Justice and caring derive from the common source of the desire to express one's power—a desire that is satisfied only through the creation and maintenance of private and interpersonal space. Inner space is the location of self-respect; intersubjective space is where mutual respect of interacting subjects is expressed. Justice reflects the more abstract concern to protect the right of self-expression in the face of conflicting expressions. One aspect of caring is opening up space for solitude, both for oneself and others. The other aspect is to move toward the other from one's own center with respect for the privacy of the other. Receptivity and responsiveness to another can be described as sympathy.

Sympathy. Sympathy is shared awareness. It motivates ethical conduct. Sympathy (moral sensitivity) with the expression of others is very often undermined by selfishness, a lack of sympathy with others (moral callousness).[12] Injustice occurs when there is a lack of sympathy toward the other. Lack of sympathy is not merely indifference, it entails ignorance, fear, and hostility. Where there is no sympathy there is ignorance of (no way of knowing) the other. Hostility is the reaction of fear of the unknown. Ignorance, fear, and hostility are fundamental to injustice or selfishness. They are intrinsic to the desire to dominate others in I–It relations. Patriarchal ethics are grounded in injustice toward women. Men's ignorance and fear of women's sexual power largely form the basis for their hostility toward women. Patriarchal morality is based on the desire for power over the other, beginning with sexual power over women and extending to political power over nations. The politics of sex has the same source as the politics of wars: ignorance, fear, and hostility toward the other.

Autonomy. Most often the authors of justice have been men who have given priority to invisible ideologies over visible networks of enmeshment. The interests of nations, for example, have been elevated and disentangled from the interests of the family and personal relations. Maternal nurturing has supported an evolutionary process dominated by a war mentality. Yet, the two domains of activity— private and public—have been regarded largely as disconnected from each other. That separation is closely connected to belief in disinterested autonomy with its implication of detachment from emotional bias. To be a sovereign or free person, in the patriarchal view, means ignoring emotional entanglement in concrete situations of relatedness for the sake of impersonal principles of justice. It means closing off the inner space of one's subjectivity and ignoring it in others, thereby eliminating the possibility for constructive, integrative interaction. This form of self-loss and alienation corresponds with the desire to conquer, to replace self-loss with possession of the other. The desire for integration disappears when the inner space is occluded. Access to the most important dimension of one's consciousness is obstructed, causing one to be out of touch with one's own power of relationality—the source of sympathy and, therefore, of justice. The possibility for creating intersubjective space in which selves are revealed and known to each other is thereby excluded.

An example of this form of alienation, resulting in the treatment of women as nonautonomous beings, can be found in the use of reproductive technology. Although some women benefit from reproductive technology, the increasing, lucrative business of manipulating women's reproductive capacities reduces women to mechanistic means of production. Separation of the functions of the womb from other aspects of a woman's ways of knowing herself eliminates the possibility for her to experience personal, integrative power. This form of fragmentation prohibits the existence of a centered self. The absence of centeredness of self entails lack of self-respect, which corresponds with the lack of ability to relate to another person in a responsive, sympathetic way. It constitutes self and social alienation.

If, however, one respects the existence of subjective and intersubjective spaces, metaphorically alluded to as places where one encounters oneself and others, promotion of self-alienation and insensitivity toward the other is less likely. The self is contextualized within the web of interdependent relations. The notion of disinterested autonomy never arises in an account of self as relational existence. The focus becomes one of interconnectedness rather than disconnectedness.

III. SELF-KNOWING

Metaphysics. The assumption of interacting spatial domains depends on the prior assumption that self-expression is more adequately defined in terms of relationality than individuation. That assumption is supported by still another prior assumption: that relationality characterizes the basic nature of reality.

By metaphysics I mean theories about the nature of what there is. I have elaborated on this elsewhere (Tomm 1984, 1987a, 1987b, 1988) and will only briefly outline here why I believe metaphysics is important to ethics.[13] I am advocating a metaphysics of interrelatedness, not a metaphysics of separateness, as in Kant, for example.[14] It is a theory of continuously emerging patterns of interaction or different forms of structural coupling, as described by Maturana and Varela.[15] Structural coupling refers to the ways in which structures (in this case, selves as structured organizational systems) are connected with each other and, thereby, determine the reality of each other. The self, as a process, evolves in a structurally determined way, invariably in relation to other emerging phenomena. Development of self into person is a process of emergence according to patterns of interconnectedness. As self-consciousness (i.e., reflection about one's experiences) develops, one interacts with the conditions of one's context according to one's way of experiencing oneself. Self-knowing is the process of giving meaning to the relations between oneself and the context in which one is evolving. The process of self-evolution is a process of drift, given direction by the intentionality of interacting subjects. Intentionality is determined according to desires as well as beliefs about the satisfaction of desires. Structural determinism is the process in which each subject of the drift contributes to the relations of interaction, thereby determining the nature of participating subjects. The nature of reality supposed here is a process of drift, characterized by interacting, emerging processes, and directed by degrees of awareness of the origin, nature, and desired destiny of the interactive process. One's way of knowing about oneself is coextensive with one's way of knowing about one's participation in the process of drift.

Epistemology. A theory of knowledge in which autonomy and interdependency are inseparably connected is fundamental to an explanation of knowing authoritatively. There has been a predominance of epistemologies that have assumed the independence of the cognitive activity of the sovereign, objective "I" and the feeling, subjective "me." In the reconstitution of knowledge, as espoused by feminists, the emotive dimension of knowing is recognized to be constitutive of consciousness.[16] While the affirmation of universal, emotively toned knowing did not originate with feminism, it has been highlighted by feminists and has revolutionized epistemology. We no longer accept that knowledge is constituted by clear and distinct ideas, independent of emotional persuasions. At the center of knowledge are the heartfelt interests, attitudes, and values of the knower. It is more accurate to speak of ways of knowing than of *having* knowledge.[17] The ideal of feminist epistemology is contextualized ways of knowing in which one knows through emotional and discursive connectedness to others. Self-emergence (autonomy) occurs through experiencing the supportive power of another as one lives in one's own subjective power. The "I" of discourse reflects the "me" of subjective, felt experience. It is when the "me" is revealed through discourse that the "I" is known to the other. The transcending "I" (i.e., person-in-relation) is continuous with the immanent "me" (i.e., the wholly subjective). Knowing oneself, knowing another, or knowing an object requires connectedness between subjective awareness and reflective description of the knower. It also requires partial revelation of the subjectivity of the known. Attention to the revelations of the other constitutes caring for the other. Knowing, in this sense, is a form of caring. Abstract knowing is not possible in the context of concrete relationality.

Abstract principles, however, are relevant to feminist ethics. For example, a metaphysics of interrelatedness provides an orientation that disposes one toward an epistemology of contextualized knowledge. Contextualized knowledge is constituted by the interplay of one's own subjectivity with that of another as they are known to each other through discourse. Abstract principles of human nature are derived from concrete experiences. They, in turn, contextualize particular encounters or political platforms, giving them greater meaning and direction than they otherwise would have. Contextualized ways of knowing include both concrete sympathetic encounters and abstracted interpretations.

Contextualized knowing should not be construed as complete relativism. Apart from the illogicalness of complete relativism, there is an additional problem with it. Complete relativism would privilege men in a male-dominated society where men's ways of knowing are given more credence than women's. If all knowledge is relative to the context, and the context favors male authority, then women's knowledge would be relatively less important. Accordingly, it is not in women's interest to argue for complete relativism. A form of mitigated relativism (or mitigated realism, whichever way one is disposed to think) is required, in which authoritative knowing is acknowledged according to reasonable evidence and not merely on the basis of personal bias.[18] Reasonable evidence includes subjective, felt experience as well as linguistic, analytical interpretation. Discourse includes the chaotic influence of subjectivity on the formalized, structured presentation through language.

Motivation for action. We are motivated to act according to the ways in which we experience our interconnectedness, or lack of it. If we assume that the basic desire is to create a "room of one's own" in which a person is able to feel full in one's aloneness with oneself and thereby move into fullness of relation with another, then we would conclude that the ultimate goal of human endeavor is to experience the greatest possible fullness of being. Because the basic ontology is assumed to be a process of emerging patterns of interconnectedness, fullness of being would consist in experiencing the highest degree of interrelatedness. Increasing awareness of oneself as an aspect of that process is consistent with compassion for others, just as it is consistent with concern for ecology.

Moral agency is experiencing oneself as a contributor in the structurally determined process of evolution toward greater autonomy and connectedness. Self-responsibility within the context of structural determinism is located at every moment during the interactive drift. The ways in which a person receives and responds to other persons, animals, and things determines the evolution of self into person. A person can only be person-in-relation, based on the drive for self-preservation in the process of evolutionary drift. The self is the process of going forth in the world.

The person is the process of self meeting other selves in mutually influencing interactions. Self evolves into person according to the degree to which the drive for autonomy and connectedness is satisfied. The evolution of women as persons has, in general, been inhibited because women's desires for their own spaces have not been satisfied.

Freedom. Autonomy is achieved when one's power of self-expression is realized through the creation of space in which self-determination can occur. The goal of a just society would be the facilitation of personal autonomy within the context of interpersonal connectedness. The process of achieving that goal would be based on an ethics of sympathy or moral sensitivity. Sociopolitical action depends on moral agency—recognition of oneself as responsible for contributing to an evolutionary drift toward integration rather than separation. Freedom is having the inner space from which to go forward in the move toward integration and participate as a subject in dialectic creativity. Justice is respect for and protection of that freedom.

IV. CONCLUSION

Ethics is about personal and social, integrative power. Feminist ethics focuses on women's power, a power that has been denied in patriarchy. Feminist consciousness of the desire for "a space of one's own" is central to the current reformulation of ethical theory, moral agency, and political action agendas. Personal autonomy requires an unobstructed inner source of subjective power. Such space is required for self-knowing. To experience oneself as autonomous is to give one's own meaning to one's experiences. This form of self-knowing is a form of self-respect and is fundamental to a respectful disposition toward others. When self is experienced as an aspect of the process of interacting selves, self-knowing includes respecting the self-knowing of others. Moral agency is identical with self-knowing which, in turn, is the same as experiencing oneself in a process of interdependence. The social expression of personal power, as I have been discussing it, is political action aimed at changing the social structure from its present organization based on an ethics of exclusion to one governed by an ethics of sympathy (shared awareness). Self, home, and community are seen as interacting domains with shared purposes and values through which the desire for the power of self-expression is to be satisfied.

Notes

1. Winnie Tomm, *Spinoza, Hume, and Vasubandhu: The Relation between Reason and Emotion in Self-Development* (Ph.D. diss., University of Calgary, Alberta.)
2. Jessica Benjamin, "A Desire of One's Own: Psychoanalytic Feminism and Intersub-

jective Space," in Teresa de Lauretis, ed., *Feminist Studies/Critical Studies* (Bloomington: Indiana University Press, 1986), 78–101.

3. Carol Christ, *Laughter of Aphrodite: Reflections on a Journey to the Goddess* (San Francisco: Harper & Row, 1987), and "Toward a Paradigm Shift in the Academy and in Religious Studies," in Christie Farnham, ed., *The Impact of Feminist Research in the Academy* (Bloomington: Indiana University Press, 1987), 53–76.

4. Carol Christ, *Laughter of Aphrodite*, 121.

5. Ibid., 120.

6. Catherine Keller, *From a Broken Web: Separation, Sexism, and Self* (Boston: Beacon Press, 1986).

7. Iris Murdoch, *The Sovereignty of Good* (London: Ark, 1985).

8. Ann Belford Ulanov, *Receiving Woman: Studies in the Psychology and Theology of the Feminine* (Philadelphia: Westminster, 1981).

9. John Macquarrie, *In Search of Humanity: A Theological and Philosophical Approach* (New York: Crossroads, 1983).

10. Debra Shogan, "Categories of Feminist Ethics," *Canadian Journal of Feminist Ethics* 1 (1986), 4–13.

11. Jessica Benjamin, "*A Desire of One's Own.*"

12. Mary Pellauer, "Moral Callousness and Moral Sensitivity: Violence Against Women," in Barbara Hilkert Andolsen, Christine E. Gudorf, and Mary D. Pellauer, eds., *Women's Consciousness, Women's Conscience* (San Francisco: Harper & Row, 1987), 33–50.

13. See also Winnie Tomm, "Autonomy and Interrelatedness: Spinoza, Hume, and Vasubandhu," in *Zygon: Journal of Religion and Science* 22 (1987), 459–478; "Gender Factor or Metaphysics in a Discussion of Ethics," in *Explorations: A Journal for Adventurous Thought* 6 (1987), 5–24; and "Sexuality, Rationality, and Spirituality," forthcoming in *Zygon: Journal of Religion and Science.*

14. Sources for the metaphysic of interrelatedness are Mary Daly, *Gyn/Ecology: The Metaethics of Radical Feminism* (Boston: Beacon, 1978), and *Pure Lust: Elemental Feminist Philosophy* (Boston: Beacon, 1984); Catherine Keller, *From a Broken Web*; John Macquarrie, *In Search of Humanity*; Rosemary Radford Ruether, *New Woman, New Earth: Sexist Ideologies and Human Liberation* (New York: Seabury, 1983).

15. Humberto R. Maturana and Francisco J. Varela, *The Tree of Knowledge: The Biological Roots of Human Understanding* (Boston: Shambala, 1987).

16. See Lorraine Code, *Epistemic Responsibility* (Hanover: University Press of New England, 1987); Marsha Hanen and Kai Nielsen, eds., *Science, Morality, and Feminist Theory*, Supplementary Vol. 13, *Canadian Journal of Philosophy* (1987); Genevieve Lloyd, "Feminist Philosophy and the Idea of the Feminine," paper presented at annual meeting of the Canadian Society for Women in Philosophy, Dalhousie University, Halifax, Nova Scotia, September 1986; Andrea Nye, "Woman Clothed with the Sun: Julia Kristeva and the Escape from/to Language," in *Signs* 12 (1987); Petra von Morstein, "Epistemology and Women in Philosohy: Feminism is a Humanism," in W. Tomm and G. Hamilton, eds., *Gender Bias in Scholarship: The Pervasive Prejudice* (Waterloo, Ontario: Wilfrid Laurier University, 1988).

17. Mary Field Belenky et al., *Women's Ways of Knowing: The Development of Self, Voice, and Mind* (New York: Basic Books, 1986).

18. Lorraine Code, *Epistemic Responsibility*; Thelma McCormack, "Feminism and the New Crisis in Methodology," in Winnie Tomm, ed., *The Impact of Feminism on Research Methodologies*, forthcoming, Waterloo, Ontario, Canada, Wilfrid Laurier University.

Seeing through Women's Eyes:
The Role of Vision in Women's Moral Theory

ELLEN L. FOX ████████████████████████

One of the most fascinating and suggestive elements of recent moral philosophy written by women is the recurring theme of *vision* as crucial to a full understanding of morality. To see and to be seen clearly, with sensitivity to rich detail and subtle moral nuance, has been identified by women from different traditions as profoundly important to a well-lived life. In this essay I will first briefly explore this metaphor in the works of several important writers; then I will point to an area of concern, namely, the appropriate role of the viewing self in relation to that which is viewed. Some writers have suggested that some form of self-transcendence is required for proper seeing; others have argued strongly that self-transcendence is too much like self-abnegation, a process that is profoundly dangerous for women. By viewing these perspectives synoptically, I hope to facilitate future thinking and research in the direction of the place of vision and the viewing self in morality. In particular, I believe that many moral problems of special interest to feminists can be effectively reconceived using the metaphor of vision. I will address some of these possibilities in my concluding remarks.

Some of the most widely read writers who have had something to say about proper seeing include Simone Weil, Iris Murdoch, Martha Nussbaum, Sara Ruddick, Marilyn Frye, and Maria Lugones. It is obvious from this list that a variety of traditions and perspectives is represented; the first three women do not explicitly identify themselves as feminist theorists, and although the latter three do, they are each representative of different strains of feminist theory. I wish there were space enough in this essay to consider all these writers, since each has outlined the problem in an original and suggestive way, and each highlights different aspects of the tension between the self and that which is beheld. Certain strains of thought can be traced through the writings of one to another. Weil, for example, profoundly influenced Murdoch, both of whom in turn influenced Nussbaum and Ruddick. Lugones addresses herself directly to Frye, and is explicitly modifying Frye's arguments to fit her own theoretical needs. Thus, starting with Weil and following out her influence on Murdoch and then on to Frye and Lugones should help to provide us with an understanding of the metaphor of vision in its historical development.

Simone Weil's too often underrated contribution to twentieth-century philosophy is noted by her readers for both its richness and its obscurity. Within the present constraints, we can do little more than glance at her thought as developed in a particularly relevant essay, "Reflections on the Right Use of School Studies with a View to the Love of God."[1] As the title suggests, Weil argues that one of the most important reasons for learning to concentrate on one's studies is that such concentration aids in developing the concentration needed for prayer. And prayer, for Weil, is a certain form of extremely pure attention, or attentive seeing. In a telling passage, she writes,

> The love of our neighbor in all its fullness simply means being able to say to him: "What are you going through?" It is a recognition that the sufferer exists, not only as a unit in a collection, or a specimen from the social category labeled "unfortunate," but as a man, exactly like us, who was one day stamped with a special mark by affliction. For this reason it is enough, but it is indispensable, to know how to look at him in a certain way. . . . This way of looking is first of all attentive. The soul empties itself of all its own contents in order to receive into itself the being it is looking at, just as he is, in all his truth.[2]

For Weil, the foremost reason for learning to see rightly is that it is our only means of finding God. Weil's mystical Christian perspective is evident in the passage above as it is in most of her later writings. She has no qualms at all about the soul "emptying itself of all its own contents" since she has confidence that God will fill her being with his presence and truth. For Weil, proper attention does not mean active searching; she argues that attention really consists of a kind of open, receptive waiting, where the self does not intrude or try to take a more forceful, participatory role in the pursuit of God. We must simply set our hearts on God, or the truth, and then wait: "There is a way of giving our attention to the data of a problem in geometry without trying to find the solution . . . a way of waiting, when we are writing, for the right word to come of itself at the end of our pen, while we merely reject all inadequate words."[3]

Weil explicitly identifies this attention as appropriate behavior for a slave. She writes,

> May each loving adolescent, as he works at his Latin prose, hope through this prose to come a little nearer to the instant when he will really be the slave— faithfully waiting while the master is absent, watching and listening—ready to open the door to him as soon as he knocks. The master will then make his slave sit down and himself serve him with meat.[4]

It is fairly clear why no contemporary feminist should be willing to accept Weil's notion of attention without some important modifications. The posture of the attentive slave *might* work when directed toward God, or the truth, but when directed toward other human beings, it is a recipe for disaster. Particularly when practiced by women toward men, it has not, historically, produced the reversal described by Weil in which the master serves the slave with meat. Thus, though Weil's development of and emphasis on the notion of attention and attentive seeing are powerful and evocative, the notion needs to be reworked for secular use.

The first pass at secularizing the idea of attention comes from Iris Murdoch. Murdoch's work in this area can be seen as an attempt to retain as much of Weil's insight as possible while eliminating God from the picture. Nevertheless, Murdoch's approach retains much of the mystical tone of Weil's writing; for Murdoch we must simply focus our attention on Good instead of God. Murdoch also retains Weil's emphasis on selflessness in seeing. She writes, "I would suggest that the authority of the Good seems to us something necessary because the realism (ability to perceive reality) required for goodness is a kind of intellectual ability to perceive what is true, which is automatically at the same time a suppression of the self."[5]

She speaks elsewhere of the need to overcome the promptings of the "fat, relentless ego" in our search for reality. But Murdoch's position is a subtle one. She is not merely endorsing the abject selflessness of the slave; rather, she is concerned to advise us not to be greedy and consuming in our attention. She often seems to be intent on preventing us from "grafting the substance of the other" to ourselves, to use Marilyn Frye's terminology. Murdoch's particular project is to show us the deep similarities between art and morality, and to show that we must not allow our fantasies, fears, and needs to get in the way of clear, loving attention to art and to human beings.

Given this project, she tends to emphasize selflessness in a way that can seem excessive to a reader who is sensitive to feminist concern that women's selves not be diminished or denied, as they have been historically. The injunctions to "forget the self," liberally scattered throughout her essays, are frightening to one who has only just recently learned to claim her self for herself. But if we consider that Murdoch's intended audience was doubtless primarily composed of traditional moral philosophers rather than feminists, we can see why her tone would be different from the tone of a feminist theorist whose intended audience would be mostly other educated women who would share an understanding of feminist problematics.

Sensitivity to feminist priorities characterizes Marilyn Frye's observations on the nature of correct seeing. Like both Weil and Murdoch, Frye identifies correct perception with loving perception. But where Weil and Murdoch suggest that unloving (self-concerned) perception will simply fail to benefit the viewer, Frye urges that unloving, or arrogant, perception will harm the person or object that is beheld. For Frye, arrogant seeing is a more profoundly other-regarding enterprise than it is for either Murdoch or Weil, and thus on Frye's analysis vision has a firmer place in the realm of the moral; there is a greater urgency to her message. Harming ourselves is bad enough; the possibility that we are harming others as well transforms the situation into one of immediate concern.

In this contrast between concern for the viewer and concern for the viewed, we can see an important point of divergence between Frye's analysis of seeing and that of Murdoch and Weil. For Weil in particular, and also in large part for Murdoch, seeing is a passive enterprise; we simply rid our egos of their greediness and their distorting fears, and allow reality to present itself to us in its true form. But for Frye, seeing is a much more active endeavor. We do not simply submit to reality; we participate in creating it. That is why incorrect seeing is a matter for immediate moral attention. If we incorrectly construct an object with our perception, that will be a relatively minor problem; but if we incorrectly construct another human being, we can do her very severe damage indeed.

Frye is consciously aware that there can be a grave problem in determining the role of the viewing self in relation to that which is viewed. She observes,

> The loving eye is one that pays a certain sort of attention. This attention can require a discipline but *not* a self-denial. The discipline is one of self-knowledge, knowledge of the scope and boundary of the self. What is required is that one know what are one's interests, desires and loathings, one's projects, hungers, fears and wishes, and that one know what is and what is not determined by these. In particular, it is a matter of being able to tell one's own interests from those of others and knowing where one's self leaves off and another begins.[6]

Frye further notes that this is no easy task; identifying one's own boundaries and focusing awareness on those "contents of the soul" which might interfere with loving perception requires discipline and practice. On this point all the writers under discussion agree.

Murdoch has observed, "It is always a significant question to ask about any philosopher: what is he afraid of?"[7] If we ask this question of Frye, we will find that she is afraid of the metaphysical cannibalism that men have traditionally performed on women. Her emphasis on the separateness of the self from the beheld is in part a response to her concern that too much merging, too much intermingling of boundaries will not merely distort the viewer's perception but can have dire consequences for the beheld. The beheld can lose her own selfhood and become grafted to the viewer in a pernicious way. If we ask the same question of Maria Lugones, however, we find that Lugones fears the arrogant refusal to see as much as, or more than, the arrogant grafting of one's substance to another. Lugones and Frye are not really in disagreement with each other. Indeed, Lugones gratefully draws on Frye's work and acknowledges its importance to her. But their writing is divergent in that Lugones's concerns are, as noted, different from Frye's. Lugones writes,

> Frye also says that the loving eye is 'the eye of one who knows that to know the seen, one must consult something other than one's own will and interests and fears and imagination.' This is much more helpful to me so long as I do not understand Frye to mean that I should not consult my own interests nor that I should exclude the possibility that my self and the self of the one I love may be importantly tied to each other in many complicated ways.[8]

Lugones emphasizes the importance of seeing through the other's eyes, of sharing another's construction of the world in order to know both it and the other. She notes that this is something that those who are not in a position of power must constantly do in order to survive. The powerless must learn how the powerful construct the world in order to avoid being damaged or destroyed by some un-anticipated jagged edge in the world of the powerful. Lugones shares with Frye the sense that viewing is an active, participatory practice. She also knows the injury that can be done to the beheld if the beheld is not viewed with love. She writes movingly,

> White/Anglo women are independent from me, I am independent from them, I am independent from my mother, she is independent from me, and none of us loves each other in this independence. . . . I am incomplete and unreal without other women. I am profoundly dependent on others without having to be their subordinate, their slave, their servant.[9]

This passage is a clear articulation of the hope that there can be some kind of interdependence between two viewing subjects which cherishes and does not harm or diminish either one. Frye echoes this sentiment. Experience, however, bears out the truth of the reflection, common to all the writers, that loving interdependence takes discipline, concentration, and work. And some of that work must address some very difficult questions. These include: What are the boundaries of the self? Can these boundaries be crossed without damage to either individual? Which particular contents of the soul, which elements of the fat, relentless ego, must be dispensed with for the sake of loving vision and which must be retained in order for there to be a self that views? How active is the work of the viewer? All the writers I have discussed here, and others as well, have briefly addressed these problems, but the subject remains profoundly underdeveloped.

That we should develop this line of moral inquiry becomes clear when we see the ways in which it can help us to articulate and resolve certain troubling moral problems. If we really take the vision metaphor seriously, we have new grounds for the moral evaluation of many subjects that have been of interest to feminists in particular as well as reflective moral philosophers in general. The example of pornography is just one area that can be effectively reconceived from the perspective of vision. From this perspective, the feminist critique can be seen to be that pornography is a way of perceiving women which is arrogant (on Frye's theory) or not true to reality (Murdoch). An objection often made by liberals is that pornography does not actually harm anyone, unless the particular models involved were actively coerced; and much of the feminist reply has focused on showing that pornography does harm women even when liberal conditions for harm are not met. But there has not been a shared framework for discussing the nature of harm which would enable feminist writers to engage with sincere, conscientious writers in other traditions. Vision, taken seriously, can provide such a framework and would allow an articulation of the concept of harm which would be widely comprehensible.

The metaphor of vision can also help us to discuss aspects of our moral experience which are presently difficult to express adequately. To use an example from Murdoch, if a mother-in-law perceives her daughter-in-law as coarse and common rather than as simple, spontaneous, and gay, we know that the mother-in-law has done both herself and her daughter-in-law some harm; but it is very difficult to really capture the harm in the language of traditional moral discourse.

The vision metaphor captures the problem perfectly. If we develop Frye's line of thought, we can see that the mother-in-law has participated in constructing her daughter-in-law along lines that diminish her, and are not consonant with the kind of loving reality that all these writers, and many of the rest of us as well, see as far preferable to the frequently battering and hurtful reality that is often constructed all around us.

Thus, the debt we owe to all these theorists is considerable. If we can, as I urge, try to take the notion of moral vision seriously, we may have a means of expressing profound truths about the human condition which were previously difficult to formulate. The women who have contributed to this perspective should be seen with grateful and appreciative eyes.

Notes

1. Simone Weil, "Reflections on the Right Use of School Studies with a View to the Love of God," *Waiting for God*, trans. by Emma Craufurd (New York: G. P. Putnam's Sons, 1951).

2. Ibid., 115.

3. Ibid., 113.

4. Ibid.

5. Iris Murdoch, "On 'God' and 'Good'," *The Sovereignty of Good* (London: Ark Paperbacks, 1970), 66.

6. Marilyn Frye, *The Politics of Reality: Essays in Feminist Theory* (Trumansburg, N.Y.: The Crossing Press, 1983), 75.

7. Murdoch, 72.

8. Maria Lugones, "Playfulness, 'World'-Traveling, and Loving Perception," *Hypatia* 2, no. 2 (Summer 1987), 8.

9. Ibid.

Emotional Work

CHESHIRE CALHOUN

In thinking about our own moral experience, whether we do this in philosophic theories or sermons, solitary reflection or gossip, we stylize our experience. Each of us stretches the moral experiences occurring in our own lives on a common frame of concepts (agency, personal responsibility), images (self-mastery), and stock examples (keeping promises, being a good Samaritan). This common frame creates a homogeneity in the moral narratives that get told; what we say/think about morality repeatedly invokes these stock concepts, images, examples. The patterns of moral thinking thus stylize moral experience by determining what we notice or overlook, remember or forget, take as important or trivial about our moral life so that moral thinking only partially captures the completeness of experience.[1] Stylizing moral experience is not in itself objectionable. It becomes so when the terms of moral thinking—its images and concepts—jar with those that frame other significant experiences. For women, the terms of an ethics of justice—autonomy, mastering self-interest, rights of noninterference—may grate against the terms that frame their lives as women. Thus the different terms of an ethics of care may more comfortably and coherently style the same moral activities that were once jarringly thought of in terms of justice. But moral thinking may not only objectionably misstyle moral activities, it may also render invisible, unspeakable, or trivial routine moral activities that we sense (even if we cannot say) are central to goodness. My own sense is that this is what has happened to emotional work. "Emotional work" names something that feels familiar, that my moral aspirations call me to do and demand from others. Yet I find myself speechless, unable to think the activity and its moral dimensions. What is emotional work? Why does it elude moral thinking? How might we rethink morality?

Arlie Russell Hochschild coined the term "emotional work."[2] For her, it named our efforts to conform our emotions to what we believe we ought to feel. "The party goer," she says, "summons up a gaiety owed to the host, the mourner summons up a proper sadness for a funeral. Each offers up feeling as a momentary contribution to the collective good."[3] Her idea that emotions are prescribed—we *ought* to feel one way rather than another—comes out of a social constructionist view of emotion. Emotions do not lie beyond the pale of social life (being brute, perhaps biological, givens). They are tied to a society's meaning and value system and are subject to social and moral regulation. "Feeling rules" prescribe when, where, how much, how long, about what, and toward whom different emotions should be felt. Such rules prescribe not only emotional expression, but subjective experience. Hence the need to do emotional work on ourselves.

This understanding of "emotional work"—giving others their emotional due— does not elude moral thinking. For Aristotle, the virtuous person has his [sic] emotional house so well ordered that feeling the right emotions in the right ways is second nature. The religious possibility of sinning in one's heart or being pure of heart presupposes emotional obligations. Recently, Marcia Baron has argued that Kantian moral duties include emotional duties, since merely going through the motions is often less than what duty requires.[4] And in daily life, we pass moral judgment on heartlessness, selfish jealousy, sullenness, and self-pity. Moral thinking accustoms us to measuring moral track records not only by the yardstick of correct action, but also by that of correct emotion.

But what attracted some feminists, including myself, to the term "emotional work" was not this ordering of our emotional households. "Emotional work" names something else, a work women do and are expected to do, especially in managing the domestic household. It names a familiar moral activity that nevertheless escapes moral recollection and reflection. "Emotional work" names the management of *others'* emotions—soothing tempers, boosting confidence, fueling pride, preventing frictions, and mending ego wounds. Taking care of others, creating domestic harmony, and caring about how others fare morally calls for work on others' emotions. *This* emotional work eludes moral thinking. It falls outside our paradigms for moral activity.

Why does emotional work done on ourselves show up in moral thinking while emotional work done on others does not? Moral thinking tends to be dyadic and agent-centered. We think in terms of I, the agent, acting toward or on you, the patient. Given this emphasis on agency, we think that there are two morally assessable roles open to us. We can be (good or bad) moral *agents*, worrying about what we ought to do or give to others. We can also be (good or bad) moral *judges*, witnessing an agent–patient dyad and critically assessing what the agent ought to have done or given. In either case, we locate moral activity, responsibility, and praise- or blameworthiness exclusively in the agent. The patients are merely passive beneficiaries or victims of our agency, and the judges merely spectators. The moral individualism of this style of thinking makes it natural for us, when we think about moral activity, to think about *our own* moral activity. We understand our moral task to be putting our own moral households in order. We may turn a judicial eye on others' moral households, but governing their households is their affair, not ours. The link forged between moral activity and self-management is particularly strong in the more Kantian strain of our thinking. That strain equates managing others' moral activity with immoral disrespect for others' agency.

This picture of moral thinking explains the visibility of emotional work done on self and the invisibility of emotional work done on others. In evoking morally prescribed emotions in ourselves, we worry about managing the self, tidying our own moral households, looking outward only to judge others' emotional work. Emotional work on self is required lest others become victims of our mismanaged emotions. This fits a dyadic, agent-centered picture of moral activity. By contrast, managing *others'* emotions smacks of disrespectful manipulation of others' agency. In taking on the burden of managing others' emotions, we step beyond the moral roles "agent" and "judge." Thus emotional work on others becomes invisible to moral thinking.

Dyadic, agent-centered moral thinking may adequately trace the contours of some of our moral experience, but it lacks universal applicability. Emotional work on others, moral education, and moral counseling elude dyadic, agent-centered moral thinking. Because moral education and counseling often are emotional work, I want to start by exploring this more familiar territory and its proper style of moral thinking.

As parents, we assume the task of morally educating our children. In times of changing morals, we may also assume the task of educating fellow adults. Throughout our lives we find ourselves called on to provide moral counseling to those who ask "What should I do?" Moral education and counseling both involve more than teaching or applying moral standards. They involve teaching others how to interpret moral situations. A friend who asks "What should I do?" asks neither for a pronouncement nor a list of rules. She asks for help in putting her situation into perspective, finding some interpretation of her circumstances that will make one course of action clearly preferable.

Moral education and counseling elude dyadic, agent-centered thinking because the moral educator/counselor is neither agent (*her* actions are not the central issue) nor specular judge. Instead, she *mediates* between agent and patient, thus operating within an essentially triadic and mediator-centered moral relation. When, for example, I counsel a friend dissatisfied with her marriage and considering an affair, I mediate between her prospective agency and the prospective patients of her action (her husband, child, potential lover, and also herself). As mediators, our moral task is not self-management, but management of another. It is not our own moral household, but another's that needs ordering and for whose eventual order or disorder mediators assume partial responsibility. This participation in another's agency is partly what makes moral individualism strikingly out of place in mediator-centered moral thinking. Partly, too, in recognizing how our own moral households were constructed through moral education and are continuously refurbished through moral counseling, our moral debt to the mediating work of others becomes visible.

Placing moral mediation, not moral agency, at the center of moral thinking shifts our understanding of morality away from individual task to cooperative venture. This is not, however, the contractarian's tepid cooperative morality where each agrees to play by the rules and properly manage the self. It is a deeply cooperative morality in which agency itself is doubly open to management by others. First, moral reasoning preceding action paradigmatically occurs between people, not in private deliberation. Even if we sometimes reason in private, we do so only by interiorizing the dialogue through which we first learned morality and through which we ongoingly update and correct our moral thinking. In daily life, we rely on others not merely to manage their own agency, but to help us manage ours by listening and dialogue. Listening invites us to bring to mind and speech our interpretations of moral situations and our judgments about what would be best to do.[5] Dialogue shows us alternative interpretations and judgments—that agency is open to management by others means, second, that immoral action (the abuse of agency) is open to intervention by all those positioned to mediate. In daily life we do not see ourselves alone in a moral wilderness. We rely on others to intervene and protect us when we are about to be victimized; we rely on others to call offenders to task and to help us recuperate from or to mitigate the harm done by others' misuse of their agency.

Emotional work is the work of a moral mediator. It is part and parcel of moral counseling and educative moral dialogue. Because what we feel is tied to how we interpret situations, helping others get the right moral perspective cannot be detached from working to correct their emotional attitudes. I think of times, for example, when after a class on sexual harassment, a student has come to me with her story about a teacher or employer. Her emotional reaction to harassment concerns her. Even though intellectually she condemns harassment, she doesn't know how to feel its wrongness in her experience. She doesn't know how to feel angry, or if she does, she doesn't know how to accept the legitimacy of her anger. Self-doubts, self-criticisms, and respect for authority clutter her perceptions. So we tell a story about her experience that enables and legitimates anger. We talk about the unfairness of what happened to her, about how it undermined her achievement, about the contempt shown her as a woman, about her worthiness. This is emotional work—enabling someone to feel what, intellectually, she knows to be true. This is also emotional work on a grand scale, the kind that transforms emotional structure, making anger at harassment possible for the first time. This transformation of emotional structure goes hand in hand with a transformation in the moral belief system that defines the proper objects of anger, guilt, contempt, and so on. Emotional work is critical to successfully transforming a moral belief system, since only the emotional enlivening of moral beliefs allows them to have moral force.

Some emotional work more simply aims to correct inappropriate emotions founded on misinterpretations. In emotions of self-assessment (guilt, shame), other-assessment (anger, contempt), and wounding (feeling betrayed, let down, excluded, hurt), we sometimes get it wrong, laying blame or fault or bad intentions where they don't belong. Doing emotional work, then, is a matter of telling the story differently: "She didn't mean to dismiss your point. She thinks very highly of you. Remember how she usually appeals to you for confirmation." Or "You know your father wasn't really angry at you. He just wants to get his project finished without interruption. Maybe he'll do something with you later." A lot, though not all, of this emotional work not only mediates by shaping the person's moral interpretation of others, but also mediates between persons by creating understanding between them that at least permits forgiveness if not a retraction of blame. Telling stories about other people correctly, and thus doing emotional work well, draws on capacities of psychological acumen: the ability to hear between the lines, to read body language, to interpret inflection and tone, to add up behavior into a psychological profile. It also draws on a general understanding of human psychology as well as detailed understandings of particular persons and personality types.

Emotional work is also part and parcel of mediating intervention in the immoral exercise of agency. That is, caring about how others fare morally, and being willing to do emotional work, is not just a matter of caring that others get the right moral interpretations and thus that their emotional attitudes and moral actions are well-informed. In caring about how others fare morally, we also care about how they fare as patients of others' moral agency. The moral wound inflicted by abused agency goes beyond mere violation of rights or disrespect. It is also an emotional wound: hurt, resentment, humiliation; a feeling of being betrayed, let down, disregarded, shamed, isolated, counted for less. Although helpless to prevent emotional wounding, we may still be called on to do emotional work as a way of making the best of a morally bad situation. I recall being a new member in a department and unwittingly violating department policy for handling course overrides. When I was viciously tongue-lashed in front of my office mate, he intervened with humor, quipping, "Don't we wish there were hordes of students beating down the doors to our classes!" He turned what would have been, without moral support, a deeply wounding and possibly explosive situation into one of mild affront. This, too, is emotional work—taking the emotional sting out of moral abuse with humor, commiseration, compensation, or psychological explanations that make abuse forgivable.

But we are not always helplessly positioned where remedial emotional work is our only option. Emotions motivate action, and we may sometimes be morally called on to reroute others' actions by managing their emotions. Women who live with abusive men learn well the strategies that deflect anger from its path toward themselves or their children. They live walking on eggs, finely tuned to their men's emotions. But daily life is also strewn with eggs and the need to manage both individuals' emotions and emotional atmospheres in ways that will bring out the best in others and prevent the worst.

Both rerouting others' actions by managing their emotions and taking the emotional sting out of moral abuse are morally risky forms of emotional work. In protecting people from moral abuse or from its emotional sting once it happens, we may simultaneously be protecting from moral reproach and from being taken to moral task those who perhaps need it most. Virtuous emotional work must tread the fine line between protecting the deserving from harm and refusing to protect the undeserving from reproach.

I want to close with a note about benevolence. Fearing that managing others' interior (their emotions, needs, patterns of interpretation) would undermine or intrude on autonomy, agent-centered moral thinking thinks that benevolence provides instrumental goods. Out of benevolence, I offer a hand, directions, food, housing. The good Samaritan offers others the instrumental goods and services needed for carrying out their preformed plans. But there is another kind of benevolence we may feel important, one that moves into the interior and mediates between a person and herself by managing her emotions. The emotional blows we suffer in daily life may stop us in our tracks, or make us hesitate, or set us off our path. It is not for lack of the right tools that we fail to go forward, but for lack of desire. Grief, disappointment, lack of confidence, lost pride, failed trust undermine our agency as surely as malnourishment or homelessness. What we may need most is a story, one that reconciles us to the past and reopens the doors to the future. The ear that listens to grief or the voice that reminds us of the good in us allows that story to be told. It can be told poorly, dismissing grief, creating false confidence, or mending trusts that are better left broken. But done well, emotional work is the virtue of benevolence.

NOTES

1. I am thinking here of Peter L. Berger's and Thomas Luckmann's remarks on the power of language in *The Social Construction of Reality* (New York: Doubleday, 1966).

2. Arlie Russell Hochschild, "The Sociology of Feeling and Emotion: Selected Possibilities," in Marcia Millman and Rosabeth Moss Kanter, eds., *Another Voice* (New York: Anchor Books, 1975); and *The Managed Heart: Commercialization of Human Feeling* (Berkeley: University of California Press, 1983).

3. Hochschild, *The Managed Heart*, 18.

4. Marcia Baron, "The Alleged Moral Repugnance of Acting from Duty," *Journal of Philosophy* 81 (1984), 197–220.

5. I have in mind Nelle Morton's notion of "hearing to speech" in *The Journey Is Home* (Boston: Beacon Press, 1985). The presupposition underlying "hearing to speech" is that people often come to know their own minds first through dialogue. It is only the mistaken assumption that people are fully capable of knowing their own thoughts by themselves that leads to the view that helping people formulate their ideas is likely to be manipulative.

IV. Working within a Feminist Ethic

Feminist Ethics and Workplace Values

MARY C. RAUGUST ████████████████

A striking phenomenon in contemporary managerial and professional employment is the discontent of some notably talented and successful women employees. This discontent sometimes culminates in leaving a "good job" to search for a more satisfying career direction. The specific discontent at issue here arises from discomfort experienced in the values demonstrated in workplace arrangements.

Prevailing—and patriarchal—values of autonomy, rights, and individualistic justice are manifest in many or most workplace arrangements, in the ways that coworkers regard and relate to each other and in the ways that work products are measured and esteemed. In contrast, a feminist ethics based on cooperation, relationship, and interdependent nurturance may engender workplace arrangements that are more sustainable for women employees.

Three confluent streams lead to this discussion. Two streams arise within the field of ethics itself. The first is the growing tendency to impose an ethical analysis on "hard cases": commonly these are situations that appear to present mutually exclusive options, neither leading to a fully satisfactory outcome, the dilemma requiring resolution that will significantly affect individuals or groups. This tendency to search for and analyze ethical dilemmas reflects a growing acknowledgment that choices based on values surround and direct the course of our lives, and that ethical dilemmas are an inevitable characteristic of our choice-filled society.[1]

The second contemporary development that leads to this discussion is the elaboration of a "feminist" ethics, a formulation of ethical principles and process based on women's experience and on women's choices as demonstrated in behavioral and attitudinal study.[2] Feminist ethics, as it forms a basis for this consideration of workplace values, includes these assumptions:

- Traditional androcentric ethics has failed to take account of women's lives.
- Adding women's experience to androcentric philosophical theories is not sufficient; an alternative way of knowing is demanded.
- Feminist ethical discourse attends to values of cooperation, relationship, and interdependent nurturance.
- A feminist ethical epistemology is rooted in practical, everyday realities.

The third stream that feeds this discussion is the aforementioned discontent, on the part of some women, with patriarchal workplace arrangements. The second wave of feminism dovetailed with worldwide economic shifts in the 1960s and 1970s to produce a cadre of well-educated women ready to step into positions of status and control in the paid workforce. Many women planned to accept roles of power commensurate with their accomplishments; some even hoped to "feminize" those worlds of power by force of their womanly experience and values.

In fact, significant numbers of talented, well-educated, and energetic women have entered paid employment, and some have made their way to positions of substantive power. But many are restless and dissatisfied, and some are leaving their jobs, or even their chosen areas of concentration. They voice complaints that range from perceived demands that they sustain status quo and not rock any boats, to their exclusion from positions of real power, to the apparent likelihood that these worlds of power will continue to resist feminization.[3]

Many of those who are most discontent with their experience in paid employment remark that they are offended by the values and expectations embodied in the very fabric of the work environment. These workplace values are seen collectively as metaphor for broader assumptions about human nature, possible styles in relationships, and criteria for choices in behavior.

Workplace values, then, provide an illustrative frame of reference in which to examine the contemporary utility of ethical analyses, as well as the implications of competing ethical paradigms. This examination is speculative and meant to advance feminist assumptions about the intersections of ethics and everyday behavior.

It would be careless to oversimplify the reasons that talented, well-trained, and accomplished women resign from good jobs, abandon their professions, or leave the workforce altogether. Sexist discrimination is alive and well, and women walk away from jobs for a variety of reasons: inequities of pay and status, boredom and a lack of opportunity to learn new skills and to work at a variety of tasks, and myriad other discontents and desires. But here the focus is on that more narrowly defined group of women who find workplace environments to be so antithetic to their values that they come to believe that they must not continue to participate in the creation and maintenance of those environments.

The specific exemplars of this essay come from a three-year, foundation-funded demonstration project, the "Kennedy Aging Project,"[4] of which I was the (feminist) director. The project was charged with teaching health professionals about the problems and care of people who are both mentally retarded and old. All staff were selected by myself as director; as staffing proceeded, newly selected staff themselves collaborated in the ongoing selection process. Almost all staff members were harmonious in their philosophic and political outlooks, although there had been no explicitly feminist criteria utilized in the selection process.

The concept of "health" envisioned in the project was holistic; professional disciplines ranged from doctor and nurse to lawyer and social worker, to recreation therapist and spiritual counselor, among others. The project provided service as a first priority. Teaching was the second priority and research—the accumulation and analysis of data—was carried out only insofar as that work did not interfere with service or teaching.

The workplace arrangements of the project were chosen thoughtfully, deliberately, and cooperatively. Although our work with clients was imbued with ethical considerations from the beginning of the undertaking,[5] it was only toward the end of the three years of work that it became clear to us that our workplace itself could be seen as embodying certain ethical tenets, in fact, tenets of feminist ethics. This embodiment can be examined by pairing specific tenets of feminist ethics with certain domains of workplace values that appear to correspond, as an ethics-in-the-field.

The first tenet is that relationship with other beings, rather than the declaration, defense, and exercise of individual rights, is the central priority of ethical enactment. In the work described here, the participants (professional and nonprofessional, faculty and students) chose to work in service to people who were not only mentally retarded but also old, people who are doubly disparaged and neglected by most of the professional community. Our charge was to teach health professionals about these people as clients; the interdisciplinary team chose to do that teaching in a context of direct, face-to-face service. And while most medical personnel focus on the curable (the transformative) transaction, the staff of the Kennedy Aging Project, in contrast, accepted profound levels of disability and handicap as givens, and worked to better the day-to-day context of lives that we came to see as triumphs of a survival spirit.

A second tenet of feminist ethics is that the giving and receiving of care, appropriate to specific persons and their situations, is a principal measure of outcome for ethically determined behavior. By contrast, the patriarchal system of ethical measure looks to the autonomy and/or liberty of the singular individual. In the Kennedy Aging Project the central focus of our work was to take care of our clients—and their caregivers—and of each other. The office space was planned so that waiting clients and their caregivers would be amused and pleased. Waiting itself was kept to a minimum. Telephone contacts and opportunities of introduction were consciously courteous and welcoming. Our lunchtimes were deliberately social occasions, occasions for expression of a familial interest and concern. No effort was made to bolster a sense of the autonomy of individuals, except in our intent to respect the independent decision-making capacities of our clients. Work efforts of fellow workers were also respected, in the sense that each was an independent and self-regulating worker and no one was exclusively the waitperson for any other.

Third, feminist ethics emphasizes interdependence over individualism, and a mutuality of giving and receiving over entitlements to one-sided taking of nurture from others. The manifestation of these aspects of feminist ethics in a day-to-day work environment appears most consistently as a leveling of status. In the Kennedy Aging Project, every faculty person and administrator participated in direct, face-to-face contact with clients who were old and mentally retarded. Each was personally responsible for telephone calls to caregivers, contact agencies, and family members on behalf of clients, and for summary letters that described in detail the findings and recommendations of the interdisciplinary team. The interdisciplinary team itself played out the themes of interdependence and mutuality, as no one discipline was preeminent. Each representative of a distinct discipline (law, medicine, social work, ministry, nursing, psychology, rehabilitation medicine, and leisure) was responsible for teaching all other team members a rudimentary familiarity with their own special disciplinary language, concepts, and processes.

A fourth tenet of feminist ethics requires focus on a distinct and particular "other," in contrast to patriarchal ethics, which speaks of the "other" as generalized, faceless, and impersonal. The staff of the Kennedy Aging Project steadfastly refused to reduce the clients that we worked with to a statistically blended "population." In fact, one special gift that each of us took from our work in the project was a compendium of interviews, home visits, and accounts of life histories of intensely memorable individuals. The power of this experience would be reduced if it were to be leveled into impersonal generalities, as in the common manner of research.

Feminist ethics also counters the process by which patriarchal ethics proposes formulaic, deductive decisions. Instead, decisions that are rooted in context and are responsive to the particularities of the individual case are sought. In the Kennedy Aging Project this preference was played out in meticulous examination of the life circumstances of each client, with detailed examination of every aspect not only of dysfunction, disability, and handicap but also of resource and capability. We were helped, of course, by the fact that each case came to us because there were dilemmas of care, and required thoughtful brainstorming to search out all possible avenues of solution for finding needed services.

Sixth, the characteristic processes of feminist ethics are described as being circular rather than linear, atemporal rather than time-bound, and accepting rather than transformative. These characteristics of feminist process were played out at the Kennedy Aging Project in the establishment of rituals, repeated acts of mutual help, and social exchanges based on storytelling. For instance, a potluck party was held every three months, with ritualized formalities of invitation, decoration, and food specialties. Every Monday morning two or three of us brought freshly baked bread as part of team meeting. We served as an interdisciplinary clipping service for each other, bringing items of interest not only in direct relation to our shared work but also in response to personal interests such as quilting, backpacking, and cooking. And we told and retold stories of our families, especially our children, and our own hobbies and avocations, so that we all became observers of each other enmeshed in the small everyday details of our individual lives.

Finally, it is a tenet of feminist ethics that virtue is seen as the highest good—an emphasis that takes precedence over justice—and that at every juncture exploitation and hurt are to be avoided by vigorous intent and effort. I believe that this perspective was embodied in the work of the Kennedy Aging Project by our devoted attention to provision of the best possible service to our clients, and the best possible education for our "students," both those with whom we worked directly and those with whom we communicated by written materials. By this firm attention to service and education—the *content* of our appointed work—we de-emphasized any focus on power relations within our project or as we were embedded in a larger agency. We wasted little energy firming our position in the agency, and we did not need to maneuver for power with each other within the project.

The Kennedy Aging Project can be seen as a model of a workplace environment that instantiates many of the values of feminist ethics. The project offered all of us who identified with these values an environment that felt welcoming, appreciative, and appropriate.

These examples of work at the Kennedy Aging Project are cited as embodiments of feminist ethics. A certain correspondence of theoretical tenets and workplace arrangements is alleged. This correspondence is put forward as a (partial) solution to the problem of the voluntary attrition of talented and successful women from positions of managerial and professional responsibility. Women who leave their work because they are ill-at-ease about the value climate of the workplace, and discontent with the apparent bases of decision-making, are entitled to an alternative experience of workplace arrangements. A recurrent query from these women is whether they can find places to work "within the system," or whether they must occupy their hearts, minds, and energies in a separatist and therefore economically fragile alternative system.

The time seems right for the application of ethical analyses to the everyday arrangements that determine our everyday experiences at the workplace. The perspective offered by feminist ethics provides an alternative way of analyzing and deciding according to values that are harmonious with women's experience. Perhaps this insight into our need for a commensurate ethical framework will lead us to workplace values that can sustain our best efforts at meaningful work.

Notes

1. P. Singer, *Practical Ethics* (New York: Cambridge University Press, 1979); S. Spicker, S. Ingman, and I. Lawson, eds., *Ethical Dimensions of Geriatric Care* (Boston: Reidel, 1987).

2. E. Kittay and D. Meyers, eds., *Women and Moral Theory* (Totowa, N.J.: Rowman and Littlefield, 1987); S. Benhabib and D. Cornell, eds., *Feminism as Critique* (Minneapolis: University of Minnesota Press, 1987); C. Gilligan, *In a Different Voice: Psychological Theory and Women's Development* (Cambridge, Mass.: Harvard University Press, 1982).

3. M. Campbell, *Why Would a Girl Go into Medicine? Medical Education in the United States: A Guide for Women*, 2d ed. (Old Westbury, N.Y.: The Feminist Press, 1979).

4. M. Howell, D. Gavin, G. Cabrera, and H. Beyer, eds., *Serving the Underserved: Caring*

for *People Who Are Both Old and Mentally Retarded* (Boston: Exceptional Parent Press, 1989); M. Howell, T. Barbara, and R. Pitch, *Death and Dying: A Guide for Staff Serving Developmentally Disabled Adults* (Boston: Exceptional Parent Press, 1989); M. Howell and R. Pitch, *Ethical Dilemmas: A Guide for Staff Serving Developmentally Disabled Adults* (Boston: Exceptional Parent Press, 1989).

    5. Howell and Pitch.

Some Issues in the Ethics of Collaborative Work

CANADIAN FEMINIST ETHICS THEORY GROUP:
LORRAINE CODE
MAUREEN FORD
KATHLEEN MARTINDALE
SUSAN SHERWIN
DEBRA SHOGAN

Debra: In March of 1987, the Canadian Research Institute for the Advancement of Women (CRIAW) brought together approximately fifty women from across Canada to discuss issues relevant to feminist ethics. Our particular group arose as a result of some dissatisfaction with the tone of that conference with respect to the role philosophers might play in a project on feminist ethics. Although we are situated thousands of kilometers apart, we felt strongly enough about addressing theoretical questions about feminist ethics that we convinced CRIAW to help us to meet again, which they did in November of that year at their annual conference. Since that meeting, most of our work has been done by mail or computer. We did not have another opportunity to meet as a group until this September when we got together at the Canadian Society for Women in Philosophy's (CSWIP) annual conference in Edmonton, and we made our first presentation of our work. Although considerable material had passed back and forth across the country, none of us felt particularly confident about whether we would be able to consolidate this material into a satisfactory presentation for CSWIP. After a few hours of discussion, we felt that we could produce a coherent presentation that did justice to all our concerns. At the completion of the CSWIP conference we shared a feeling of excitement that collaborative work could be accomplished harmoniously even in the face of significant geographical and institutional obstacles. More recently, we have recognized, as many other feminist groups have learned, that the differences among us can also result in tension and dissonance—that we cannot always depend on our interactions to be harmonious. As a result, the task of finding ethical ways of accommodating these and other sorts of stresses has become all the more pressing to us.

From the beginning we recognized that this project would allow us the opportunity to write something substantive both about feminist ethics and about the ethical process of doing a collaborative project with other feminists. In our experience, these two parts of the project are intertwined, and we consider our process of doing a collaborative project to be a case study for the substantive aspects of theory which we are developing. Our approach in presentations has been to shift voices, each speaking in her own voice the sections that are of principal interest to her. Our style of presentation consciously reflects our attempts to understand how and why this particular group of women has been able to work as well together as we have, when some of our other experiences in collaborative work have often been unsuccessful and painful.

We are five Canadian women who are at quite different stages of our careers; we do not have the same access to resources; we have considerably different personal lives—some of us are lesbian, others are married. And as we have discovered, we are not always of a like mind on some of what we want to say about feminist ethics. This is our preliminary account of what we think to be ethical issues in our collaborative work.

Lorraine: One aspect of this project that constantly strikes us is its self-referentiality. Every point I make is itself caught up in innumerable ethical problems vis-à-vis the group: problems about how I can justify speaking as I do—or remaining silent, when I do. Questions arise having to do with who I am speaking for, and whether I should be speaking in this way—not to demonstrate that I have done my philosophical homework (both the reading and the thinking)—which is the issue I usually struggle with in my writing—but to demonstrate with each point I make that my commitment to the group is taken into account *at the same time and in the same way* as my commitment to getting the ideas to seem right.

One positive facet of this self-referentiality is the experience that every step we take in the construction of this community is also a step in the creation of our feminist ethical position. That part of it is gratifying, and often surprising. Another facet is more bewildering. It is the struggle to maintain a balance between acknowledging that I *know* what I am talking about because it's something I've worked on reasonably well for some time now, and not wanting to be authoritarian in presentation of it, even though I need to be authoritative, to an appropriate degree—nor wanting to implicate the group in something that may seem quite beside the point to most of the other members. All of this seems to be a self-referential problem about getting the context right. There is no stasis in the context from which we derive our perceptions of ourselves as persons in relation even when we are those persons. We are constantly reshaping it.

Kathleen: All of us have had previous experiences—positive and negative—of feminist collaboration. In the negative experiences, unresolvable ideological and temperamental differences produced unfruitful collaborations. Our project is different in significant ways from these other experiences—negative and positive.

First of all, it's reactive. We're doing it because "fear of theory" shut us out of a conference. Second, we had to organize and act in concert to get a hearing and a commitment from a national feminist research body. Third, in order to make an entry point for our positions as ethical theorists, we had to present our work in an explanatory way that might oversimplify it or otherwise make it misleading. Fourth, because of an ongoing struggle with the research body over the question of its commitment to us, we risk becoming paranoid. Now all these factors, which seem at first like obstacles or limitations, could be perceived as advantages. If we find creative ways not to be defensive, the very humbleness of the project—a mere work of translation for nonexperts—could be its strongest point. That is, by not setting out to make some theoretical coup, we might well be able to learn the most from each other and to advance our own self-understanding.

Susan: Collaborative research seems to be a field that amply demonstrates the wisdom of Annette Baier's suggestion that we focus on the significance of trust (and anti-trust) in ethics.[1] In considering the differences between our happy and unfortunate collaborative experiences, a key feature seems to be one of mutual trust. This statement seems to be so obvious as to be trivially, tautologically true; in fact, as Baier has argued, trust is not easy to come by or to maintain, and it is not appropriately offered in all collegial enterprises. It is a worthy project to investigate the conditions in which it can and should thrive. We have each experienced the particularly deep sense of betrayal that comes when things go awry in shared endeavors with other feminists. We have each learned, the hard way, that shared political values are not always adequate to protect relationships in the face of such unhappy realities as personal or institutionally imposed competition, unequal power, personal dislike, differing senses of responsibility, misunderstandings, jealousies, and even, occasionally, sheer cruelty. But without a certain degree of trust, it is difficult to make the necessary efforts and to expose our separate selves to the risks of exploitation, dismissal, or ridicule, even though such exposure is required if we are to have any product to show for the collaborative effort. When there have been disagreements among us, there has always been someone able to hear the positions of the disputants, so none of us has yet to feel isolated in a position tuned out by the rest. Best of all, we do not have a single person who has assumed the mediator or advocate role, but we have been able to rotate that responsibility to avoid typecasting—this allows each of us the freedom to disagree with any other. Five turns out to be a good number for this arrangement, since it means that there are enough of us to avoid roles; an odd number helps to protect against factions, and the group is not so large as to lose the necessary intimacy for effective communication.

Maureen: It seems to me that we acted as if the group was trustworthy even in advance of our having had enough interaction together to know this to be true. Individually, and as a group, we had entered the project *already committed* to the task of constructing a group dynamic that would promote trustworthiness. I feel that our success would not have come as quickly or as smoothly had we allowed defensiveness or skepticism to dominate our early interactions. In considering this further, I feel that the stance we adopted very much reflects the strategies that we have been trying to incorporate in our analysis of feminist ethics. The dynamics of that cooperative effort are familiar: encouraging participants to feel confident that their contributions will be respected, acting responsibly to ensure that one's own contributions were completed on time and were accessible to group participants, publicly acknowledging the efforts of other participants, publicly acknowledging groups who are not represented, reading and listening to other participants carefully, making every effort to understand the point of analysis as well as the progression of the argument so as to better join with the other participants in a cooperative search for understanding. The general direction of these strategies is clear: to listen for the voices of women as we attempt to articulate our own experiences from our own perspectives. These strategies are adopted out of our understanding that speaking and being heard are privileges not often accessible to women and they are skills that must be cultivated and nurtured. These commitments reflect our feminist consciousness, first, of the ways in which women have been silenced and continue to be silenced and, second, of the ways in which the political context of engaging in philosophical discourse makes such "pretrust" possible in some cases, and impossible or, at least, immoral in others. I doubt whether our group's success would have been as great or as quickly attained (to the extent that it has been attained) if we had not adopted a position of pretrust. I want to explore the intuition that this commitment is appropriate only within very limited political (moral and epistemological) contexts. I suspect that it is only our belief that we share a feminist consciousness that values the expression and exploration of women's experiences that makes such pretrust appropriate. The moral and political appropriateness of pretrust would be more restricted as the political differences between participants diverge. We are a group of white women in academia. The subject matter we have discussed thus far emphasizes our common experiences as women excluded from philosophy, as women interested in writing about feminist ethics. We have not even begun to deal with some of the substantive issues that might bring the contrasts in our experiences into focus. I think that we would have been less willing to proceed with pretrust if our group had included women who were disadvantaged in very different ways from us. I also believe that in these more complex situations, pretrust ought to be a carefully chosen strategy, which is tested by many of the sorts of questions Barbara Houston and Ann Diller ask in "Trusting Ourselves to Care."[2] Where the possible benefits to collaborative research of adopting a position of pretrust come into tension with political caution, pretrust is inappropriate.

Debra: Although we do share a number of common experiences, there are important differences among us (geographical, financial, in our credentials, scholarship, experiences in academia, other work experiences, age, childbearing, relationships to men, lesbian identities, and so on). It may be that our commonalities allow us to speak in a "modified, unified voice" in the theoretical part of our work and that our differences will make it necessary to speak with different voices when we begin to address some practical applications of our work. This is not to suggest that it will be difficult for our theoretical work to inform practice—just that we may differ about which are the most pressing problems for the application of our theoretical work as well as the implications to practice of what we agree on in theory. For example, we agree about dominance being fundamental to an understanding of gender but we may come to disagree about practical strategies to deal with this. We need at least to entertain the thought that mutual trust, taking turns, and having a sense of humor are all possible in this group because our collaboration to this point has not underlined any significant differences among us. A test of how successful we are as collaborators will occur when we attempt to write, in a unified voice, about something that makes us confront our differences. Speaking for myself, I am not sure about my willingness to collaborate, let alone in a unified voice, on ethical issues specific to the sexual lives of heterosexual women. I am aware that this admission risks disturbing our sense of mutuality.

Lorraine: One problem that arose out of our first collaborative presentation is that three of us tended to use "we," "us," and so on, whereas two of us said "I" in most of our remarks, and the others were not pleased. This experience is connected with the problem of whether we are speaking in a unified voice—and also, it would seem, with the question of individualism contrasted with individuality. My sense at this stage—speaking self-consciously in the first-person singular—is that there are aspects of this project which we contribute, initially, as I. My emphasis on the epistemological dimension of every problem is a relatively neutral example, but one that I see as my contribution—even though it is by no means immune to criticism, discussion, reinterpretation, and re-creation. There are counterparts of this issue for each of us, sometimes singly, sometimes in agreement with one or two others. When we write a final piece, these currently individualized contributions may coalesce so that we can often speak as "we"—but probably not always. Issues will remain which bear most directly on the experiences of one or just a few of us: issues that are so close to us that we will not want the others to speak for us, or to speak as though we were unified. If we refuse to speak except when we can do so in a unified voice, we will sidestep the really challenging aspect of this project: that of drawing on our sense of mutuality to enable us to address our differences.

Susan: For me, a very valuable aspect of this project has been the insight and confirmation I get from writing for a collaborative presentation. Each of us is normally isolated to varying degrees in our research; I personally feel enormously isolated most of the time, surrounded by antifeminist philosophical colleagues and antiphilosophical feminist colleagues. I have had my share of hostile, hurtful responses to my work, and despite also having my share of success, I still feel terrified to expose my work to others. In this group, I find the right balance of support and critical appraisal to make exposure comfortable. When others read my drafts with an awareness that they may be included in a publication/presentation bearing their names as well, I trust them to read each draft carefully and point out anything questionable; but I also trust them to offer those comments in a spirit of cooperation and not destruction or superiority, for they are as interested as I am in being able to keep this process going to its conclusion. I feel theoretical progress is made when we can agree (as far as possible) among ourselves about claims that merit the collective use of "we."

Kathleen: There is a continuum from monovocality to polyvocality in collaborative work. We seem to be heading for a middle path. I don't think we can write in a unified voice. I don't think we can say "we" about everything. Nor do I think we should or that we have to. But unless we see ourselves as proceeding like the supreme court with a majority and minority opinion, I'm not sure that we have to worry about setting up binary oppositions: winning/losing; dominant/subordinate discourse. As long as we stay committed to hearing each other's differences and not suppressing them in the name of party unity, it doesn't seem to matter. At the same time, I do recognize that the notion of polyvocality or the decision not to suppress differences seems an unusual way of writing ethics. It could also be seen as challenging the moral certainty of "the" feminist project. Can feminism risk relativism? Can feminism reject traditional epistemology as the "bourgeois trap of all traps" (Althusser)? From what materials and from what standpoint are we building feminist ethics? It might be nice to claim to be writing from a liberated zone, as Irigaray seems to do, but it's an impossible position at least at present and outside of science fiction or other utopian discourses. I'm also concerned that polite respect for difference might turn into liberal tolerance and the neutralizing of oppression. With all the feminist brouhaha about difference over the last ten years or so, the notion of oppression or exploitation seems to have been lost sight of. And yet, difference was brought to the attention of the more privileged theoreticians among ourselves not only by Derrida but by outraged, muted voices of lesbians, working-class women, women of color, and Jews. How we decide to proceed promises to be more exciting and revealing than the usual procedural questions.

Lorraine: In the abstract we sent to this conference, we began by stating that "feminist ethics requires a rethinking of the concept of a moral community, shaped by a repudiation of individualism in favor of a new kind of relational view of moral agents." My tentative view, at this stage in the process, is that we have been attempting in our associations with one another to live just those claims. We have been endeavoring to constitute a moral community among ourselves, where we try—not always successfully or with perfect agreement—but we try not to act primarily as individuals but as participants in a communal activity, where mutuality, wherever possible, overrides individualism (though not our individuality). The point we have reached at this stage in the process seems to be sensitive to the contextualized nature of our dialogue.

Our collaboration so far seems to recapitulate the history of the women's movement, at least in some of its aspects: first a recognition of commonality, and exhilaration at the very fact that we have so much in common; then a deepening of the discussion for our first presentation, resulting in a growth of trust and frankness, which amounts to an explicit affirmation of our commitment to the community. And now, perhaps the most difficult stage, we will have to see whether we have established enough cohesion to deal with our differences without fragmenting our still-fragile community.

Notes

1. Annette Baier, "Trust and Anti-Trust," *Ethics* 96 (1989), 231–260.
2. Ann Diller and Barbara Houston, "Trusting Ourselves to Care," *Resources for Feminist Research* 16 (1987), 35–38.

V. NEW DIRECTIONS IN THEORY

From Maternal Thinking to Peace Politics

SARA RUDDICK ███████████████

Mothering/nurturing is a vital force and process
establishing relationships through the universe.
Exploring and analyzing the nature of all components involved in a nurturing activity puts
one in touch with life extending itself. . . . We
can choose to be mothers, nurturing and transforming a new space for a new people in a new
time.

> Bernice Johnson Reagon

Peace the great meaning has not been defined.
When we say peace as a word, war
As a flare of fire leaps across our eyes.
We went to this school. Think war;
Cancel war, we were taught.
What is left is peace.
No, peace is not left, it is no cancelling;
The fierce and human peace is our deep power
Born to us of wish and responsibility.

> Muriel Rukeyser

In this essay I talk about a journey, a "progress," from a "womanly" practice and
way of knowing to a liberatory standpoint. Specifically, I plot a move from maternal
thinking to peace politics.

First, a word about "war" and "peace." No one can provide easy answers to
haunting questions about when and how to fight. I believe that violence is addictive,
that the effectiveness of violence is consistently exaggerated, and that the short-
and long-term costs of organized violence—economic, social, psychological, and
physical—are routinely underestimated. Meanwhile, the multiple rewards and effectiveness of "nonviolence" are underrated, misreported, and misunderstood. But
it is arrogant to urge nonviolent confrontation, let alone nonviolent reconciliation
and cooperation from a distance, whether in El Salvador, South Africa, Ireland,
or Palestine and Israel.

"War" is both the quintessential expression of violence and its most attractive representative. I believe that the ways of thinking that invalidate militarism will also undermine more covert and pervasive violence. "War" is familiar; the myriad forms of nonviolent confrontation, cooperation, and reconciliation that would be "peace" are still to be invented. I believe that to imagine forms of nonviolent resistance and cooperation is to imagine new personal and civic relationships to abuse and neglect. Hence in concentrating on the relationship of mothers to "war," I believe that I am also talking about less dramatic, maternal relationships to closer "enemies."

Although nonviolent action rarely succeeds without global outrage and resources, the conditions of peace and resistance are local. I speak as a citizen of the United States, a nation that, as I see it, frequently, even habitually, enters the social and natural world as an armed, invasive, exploitative conqueror. Within this nation, governments and communities "throw away," quarantine, track, and abuse their more vulnerable, assaulted, or troubled members. Whether moved by outright greed and racist bigotry or paralyzed by passivity, self-preoccupation, and despair, these governments and communities routinely fail to respond to the promise of birth, fail to provide the shelter, healing, and sustenance on which mothering depends. In the midst of this many-faceted violence, maternal thinkers and feminist ethicists can contribute in distinctive ways to imagining and creating "peace."

I begin with a question: How might it be possible to intensify the contradiction between mothering and violence and to articulate the connections between mothering and nonviolence so that mothers would be more apt to move from maternal thinking to peace politics?

The opposition between mothers and war is legendary. Mothering begins with birth and promises life; militaries require organized, deliberate killing. A mother preserves the bodies, nurtures the psychic growth, and disciplines the consciences of children; military enterprises deliberately endanger the bodies, psyches, and consciences that mothers protect. On the face of it, war and other organized violence threaten every aspect of mothering work—sheltering, protecting, attending, feeding, maintaining connections on which children depend. Understandably, the figure of the mater dolorosa—the mother of sorrows—is central to subversive war narrative. Just warriors know that war is hateful and cruel, but it is the mater dolorosa who refuses to subordinate the pain to a warrior's tale of just cause and victory. For her war remains a catastrophe that overshadows whatever purposes lie behind it. The mater dolorosa's vision of war as unredeemed suffering among the ruins takes on new poignancy as nuclear and advanced "conventional" weapons force us to imagine wars that threaten all human and global life.

If military endeavors seem a betrayal of maternal commitments, nonviolent action can seem their natural extension. Maternal "peacefulness" is not a sweet, appeasing gentleness but a way of living in which people demand a great deal of each other. When mothers fight with their children or on their behalf, when they teach their children ways of fighting safely without being trampled on or trampling on others, they engage in nonviolent action. Many individual mothers abuse their children; in most cultures children suffer from accepted but abusive practices; some cultures may legitimate systematic maternal abuse. Nonetheless, some maternal practices are sufficiently governed by principles of nonviolence to offer one model for nonviolent relationships. This does not mean that in these practices mothers achieve the nonviolence to which they aspire. Since children are vulnerable and the vulnerable are subject to abuse and neglect, mothers may be more than usually tempted by sadism, self-indulgent aggression, and self-protective indifference to the real needs of demanding children. It is maternal *commitment* to care for rather than assault or abandon children—whatever failure, guilt, and despair follows in that commitment's wake—that illuminates more public struggles to live nonviolently.

Yet mothers are not "peaceful." Wherever there are wars, mothers support and supply soldiers and, if encouraged, often become fierce and effective fighters themselves. Mothers are as apt as other people to welcome the excitements of violence, rewards of community solidarity, and promise of meaningful sacrifice. War also offers many mothers who suffer from discriminatory economic and social policies distinctive opportunities for adventure and material gain; "peace"-time military service often appears to provide their adolescent children with jobs, social discipline, education, and training that are unavailable or prohibitively expensive in civilian society.

Yet the myth of maternal peacefulness remains alluring. Mothers may be willing warriors, but war is their enemy, nonviolence often their practice. Precisely because mothers have played their supportive parts in military scripts, their refusal to perform might prompt a rewriting of the plot. Hence the urgency of my question: Can the contradictions between mothering and violence, the connections between mothering and nonviolence be made sufficiently visible, audible, disturbing, and promising to turn maternal thinking into an instrument of peace politics?

DIFFERENT VOICES, STANDPOINTS, AND "FEMINIST ETHICS"

My particular project, plotting a progress from maternal thinking to peace politics, is an instance of a more general transformative endeavor—namely, the transformation of "womanly" stances into feminist or liberatory standpoints. Several feminist philosophers have suggested that people who engage in "caring labor" acquire a distinctive epistemological stance, a "rationality of care."[1] Mothering is both an instance of caring labor and intertwined with many other kinds of caring such as homemaking, kin work,[2] nursing, tending the frail elderly, and teaching small children. Hence maternal thinking—a congeries of metaphysical attitudes, cognitive capacities, and values that arises from mothering—is one element of the "rationality of care."

Although societies differ in their ways of distributing the pleasures and burdens of mothering or caring labor, and although individual women and men are variously interested in and capable of these kinds of work, there is nothing distinctively feminine about mothering, nursing, or any other form of caretaking. There is, for example, no reason why men cannot engage in mothering, and many men already do. Nonetheless, maternal work, and more generally caring labor, have historically been the provenance of women. Maternal thinking and the rationality of care are therefore construed—and celebrated or minimized—as "womanly" achievements.

Accordingly, feminist psychologists and critics who identify values or ways of knowing associated with *women* typically attribute the differences they discover at least partly to the effect on women of the caring work they have undertaken. Conversely, certain feminists have cited the value of mothering and caretaking or of maternal thinking and the "rationality of care" in order to argue that women's perspectives offer a "standpoint" from which to criticize dominant values and invent new ones. At the least women's perspectives and voices should be included in any adequate moral or psychological theory. Many feminists make a stronger claim: the destructiveness and "perversion" of dominant values is intertwined with "abstract masculinity," while the values and relationships that would characterize more just and caring societies are intertwined with "caring femininity."[3]

But just as women (and men) who are mothers have not proved "peaceful," women generally have not reliably extended the domain of care beyond class, race, or neighborhood. Nor have they (we) consistently engaged in struggles for political liberty and economic and racial justice. (There are small, fluctuating "gender gaps" between women's and men's support of various progressive issues—perhaps especially peace and ecology. I am not, however, interested in women's possible, marginal superiority to men.) Nor are women's values and relationships reliably feminist. Women's work and stories are not only shaped by, but also often contribute to the exploitation of caretakers and the subordination of women. Women (as well as men) identify care with self-sacrifice, or responsiveness to need with pleasing others.[4] Despite the efforts of feminist and lesbian mothers, women (as well as men) embed the idea of maternity in a heterosexist, sexually conservative ideology. Women have to fight against women (as well as men) to acquire the power to refuse maternal work. If they become mothers, they have to resist women's (as well as men's) reductive definitions of their pleasures and needs as only maternal.[5] Any "feminine" standpoint that feminists might celebrate is yet to be achieved.

Nonetheless, "different voice" critics who set out to identify women's values and perspectives almost always[6] take themselves to be engaged in a feminist project. ("Different voice" theorists is a shorthand label for any critic, reader, or theorist who attempts to identify perspectives or ways of knowing associated with women. The label draws on Carol Gilligan's work *In a Different Voice* and was suggested by Nancy Goldberger, coauthor of *Women's Ways of Knowing*.) Most important, they normally aim to create a liberatory standpoint that at least is compatible with feminism and at best is an extension and expression of militant feminist vision.

Their effort to *transform* a "womanly" stance into a liberatory and feminist stand-point is an essay in "feminist ethics."[7]

Although different voice critics may find it impossible to separate their feminist commitments from their respect for women's voices, many of the actual voices currently dominant within North American feminism have serious misgivings about their transformative enterprise. These skeptical feminists claim that the idea of "womanly" difference will be used against women and is in any case empirically unfounded, exclusionary, ethnocentric, and sentimental. On their view "women" have been historically produced in asymmetrical opposition to a "masculinity" intertwined with racial privilege and defined in conjunction with Reason and Power. Nothing to these women can be named outside of oppressive patriarchal and ethnocentric definitions of "women"—no "womanly" work, "women's" op-pression, or female bodily experience. Women might speak and be spoken of once all hierarchical gender distinctions were laid to rest—but then "women's" different voices, if not "women" themselves, would be fading relics that should be buried not resurrected.

I do not directly address these feminist challenges here, but they have prompted me to review my particular project—plotting a progress from maternal thinking to peace politics—and to reread others' essays in transformative "feminist ethics" in order to get a clearer sense of what I (we?) have been about. In retrospect, I now discern three overlapping moments in the transformation of maternal thinking: heuristic representation of the "womanly" stance, which includes antiracist ele-ments; a diagnosis of flaws, including tendencies to racism, within, not apart from, the stance represented; and a transformative encounter with feminism and women's politics of resistance. I also see these moments in others' efforts to transform the "womanly" into the liberatory.

HEURISTIC REPRESENTATION: MATERNAL PEACEFULNESS

A "heuristic" representation serves both to discover and to reveal particular desirable aspects of the practices of thinking represented. Thus I represent maternal thinking *as if* it were already peaceful in order to discover and reveal the peacefulness I hope and believe to be there. It is not surprising that my rendition of maternal thinking contrasts in detail and as a whole with military thinking. For example, on my view, the attentive love of **mothering requires** concrete cognition, tolerance for ambivalence and ambiguity, receptiveness to change, and recognition of the limits of control. Mothers are apt to acquire a variegated concept of "nature" as at best beneficent, hospitable to goodness, and at worst a respected negotiating partner. These and many other capacities and attitudes provoked by mothering contrast with the abstractions and certainties of militarist thinking and with the exploitative attitudes toward human and nonhuman nature characteristic of militarism and the instrumental technocracy on which it depends.

More generally, I read—as I believe any antimilitarist could read—the "alternative epistemologies" that Margaret Urban Walker identifies in feminist ethics as opposed to militarism. "Attention to the particular," where attention is interlaced with disciplined caring, is inimical to the creation of "throwaway" people and "killable" enemies. Nonviolent activists have to construct morally relevant understandings that are "contextual and narrative"; just-war theorists rely on abstract causes, state boundaries, and rules of war. Military orders depend on both hierarchy and selfless bonding; nonviolent struggle envisions a future when moral deliberation will become "a site of expression and communication" where partners in conflict neither dominate nor submit.[8]

My articulations of maternal thinking and my readings of feminist ethics are not simply inventions. I try as best as I can to "cling" to the only data I have: honest memory, candid conversation, and the widest range of accurate reading and mother watching that I can manage. But no story of mothering is independent of the motives of the teller. I am obsessed with deliberate, organized, legitimate violence. I am determined to tell one story of maternal thinking that is ready to be turned into a story of peace.

I choose to look at mothering through the lens of nonviolence. I then "discover"—amid incontrovertible evidence of maternal abandonment and assault—a typical maternal struggle to create nonviolent forms of cooperation and conflict. I see women and men who are powerless, powerfully and passionately engaged with vulnerable and provocative children, making "peace." Resisting their own and others' violence, these mothers of both sexes sustain responsive relationships with their children despite disappointments, anger, and often radical differences in style and value.

In a similar vein I look for "sturdily antimilitarist" conceptions of bodies and bodily life that might be called forth both by working with children and by an appreciation of the giving of birth on which all mothering depends. Central to the antimilitarist conception of bodiliness I propose is a celebration of natality—the human activities of giving and receiving birth. I take the complex physical and social relations of birth giver and infant—the exquisite conjunction of radical interdependency and emergent individual separateness—as emblematic of the nonviolent connections through difference that mothers of both sexes struggle to sustain. Describing mothering as a sustained response to the promise of birth, I "see" mothers welcoming bodily life as a locus of pleasure and origin of will.

If my readings of mothering are sufficiently detailed and accurate, they should provoke in some other mothers a self-respecting, surprised recognition of antimilitarist tendencies and principles of nonviolence latent in their work and thought. Since mothers differ from each other in all the individual and social ways that people differ, it will take many versions of maternal thinking, some radically different from mine, to inspire among varieties of mothers the surprised recognition I aim for. Yet, granted the promise of that variety, it seems reasonable to hope that antimilitarist representations of maternal work and thinking will strengthen the "peacefulness" of individuals and contribute to the wider recognition of an active, unsentimental, civic, antimilitarist maternal identity.

DIAGNOSIS: MATERNAL MILITARISM

Heuristic representations of the sort I propose can seem perilously close to mystifying ideology. In order to ward off obfuscation and to insist on the need for change, I try to identify specific sources of maternal militarism within the practices of good enough, potentially peaceful mothers. For example, alongside a "sturdily antimilitarist" conception of bodily life I put a more familiar maternal conception of bodies which is incipiently militarist. A careful, caring welcome of bodily life and respect for bodily integrity is central to maternal nonviolence. Yet even the most benign mother may sometimes take her own and her children's "nature," their willful embodied being, as an enemy to be conquered. In times of rapid change or social crisis, a superstitious terror of the "stranger" can fuel an otherwise temperate mother's rage to control "disorderly," dirty, lustful, bodily life at home. Only in the most malignant forms of maternal thinking are children's bodies conceived as the site of pain and domination, the place where sadistic or terror-driven mothers enact their will. But many ordinary, good enough mothers struggle against their own compulsion for order and their drive to dominate unruly, "disobedient" children.

A maternal struggle to achieve a welcoming response to bodily life is emblematic of struggles to extend publicly maternal nonviolence. Just as mothers have to learn not to hurt or dominate what is strange and threatening in their own children, they also have to *strive* to respect and negotiate with alien and often frightening people outside their "own" circle. This is not surprising. Mothering typically begins with a passionate commitment to particular children and the particular people they live among. Although in a daily way mothers may try to create a peace worth keeping—one that is as free as possible from greed, domination, and injustice— domestic justice does not translate easily beyond the families and cultures in which it originates. Just because they hold themselves responsible for preserving the traditions and integrity, sometimes even the survival, of their social group, many mothers will fiercely support violence against the "enemy" (and therefore against the enemy's children) who seems to threaten their "ways," community, or state. At their not uncommon worst, parochial mothers engage in outright racist battle behind the shield of neighborhood and family.

Some mothers learn to hold their passionate loyalty to particular children in creative tension with a sympathy for other children, including those who are strange or strangers. Even these mothers may nonetheless counsel their children to embrace the violence that their state or political leaders tell them is necessary. Mothers train children in the ways of obedience that enable them at least to survive and at best to flourish—but also to "serve" when "called" by employers or governments.

Despite their responsibility for training, many mothers are expected to delegate "difficult" policy decisions to fathers and public officials. To the extent that they have complied with the deauthorization of their authority, they will be ill-prepared for independent-minded resistance to their government's or political group's militarist policies in a time of "emergency." By contrast, committed patriotic sacrifice to the whole nation, to all "our boys," can seem a generous extension of the parochial loyalties of most mothers' lives.

In *Lest Innocent Blood Be Shed*, an account of nonviolent resistance and rescue in a French village during the second world war, Phillip Hallie identified three habits of mind and will that enabled citizens of Le Chambon to appreciate and resist the evils of Nazi racism while many more of their well-intentioned compatriots refused to see or were unable to act. According to Hallie, "lucid knowledge, awareness of the pain of others, and stubborn decision dissipated for the Chambonnais the Night and Fog that inhabited the minds of so many people in Europe, and in the world at large, in 1942."[9] Conversely—adapting Hallie's praise to the purposes of diagnosis—maternal parochialism prevents many mothers from seeing, let alone caring about, the pain of distant or different others. Willingness to abdicate "difficult" decisions to public officials produces ignorance rather than "lucid knowledge" of the real character and motives of war-making and of the painful consequences for "others" of the policies of one's own government. A cultural expectation that mothers will weep for war but can do nothing to stop it makes "stubborn decisiveness" unlikely.

Maternal peacefulness is an empowering myth. At its center is the promise of birth: every body counts, every body is a testament of hope. To violate bodies—to starve, terrorize, mutilate, damage, or abandon them—is to violate birth's promise. At its best, mothering represents a disciplined commitment to the promise of birth and a sustained refusal to countenance its violation. But good enough mothers—like other, good enough women and men—protect themselves from lucidity and therefore from responsibility. The peacefulness of mothering as we know it is entwined with the abstract loyalties on which war depends, the racialism in which war flourishes, and the apolitical privacy that lets dominators and racists have their way. There is no sharp division between the Good Mother of Peace and her fearful, greedy, or dominating sister. The heuristic representation of mothers as peaceful is inseparable from the diagnosis of mothers as militarist. It is the same work, the same thinking, ready for and requiring transformation. It is precisely at the point of felt contradiction, at the intersection of the promise of birth and its violation, that a transformative encounter might occur.

TOWARD LUCIDITY, COMPASSION, AND DECISION

When I first began thinking about mothers, I was more concerned with what feminists could bring to maternal thinking than with what mothers could bring to the world. I construed mothering and feminism oppositionally. I wrote as a mother who believed that feminism trivialized or simplified the challenges of maternal work. But I also wrote as a feminist daughter who believed that feminism might manage to rescue a damaged and flawed maternity. As a feminist I wrote suspiciously of the very practices and thinking that as a mother I was determined to honor. Yet, so great (at that time) was some feminists' fear of—and other feminists' need of—a mother's voice, that my daughterly suspicion was barely heard.

I am no stranger to feminist fear of mothering. Of all the essentialist identities to which "women" have been subject, the conflation of "the female" with hetero-sexual (or lesbian?) mothering may well be the most fearsome. Given a sorry history in which so many women's bodies and dreams have been destroyed by enforced and repressive "motherhood," it is not surprising that feminists have not found it easy to hear, let alone to speak in, a maternal voice. Adrienne Rich may have been the first to name feminist matrophobia and the consequent feminist desire to perform "radical surgery" in order to cut oneself away from the mother who "stands for the victim, the unfree women."[10] Peace activist Ynestra King elaborates this feminist rejection: "Each of us is familiar as daughters with maternal practice, but most of us in becoming feminists have rejected the self-sacrificing, altruistic, infinitely forgiving, martyred unconditionally loving mother—for this is how I saw my mother—have rejected that mother in *ourselves* as the part of ourselves which is complicit in our own oppression."[11]

Feminists have good reason to reject a maternal identity that is still enmeshed in patriarchal and heterosexist institutions and that has often been legally, phys-ically, and psychologically forced on women who would otherwise reject it. This reasoned and conscious resistance to patriarchal institutions of motherhood is in-tertwined with less conscious fears. As we have learned from Dorothy Dinnerstein and other psychoanalytic feminists, in societies where almost all mothers are wo-men, few people overcome the fears and unfulfilled fantasies of Bad/Good, De-vouring/All Providing Maternal Creatures. If, as Marianne Hirsch[12] and others have argued, feminists are especially ambivalent about power, authority, conflict, and anger, they may also be especially liable to what Nancy Chodorow and Susan Contratto have called "The Fantasy of the Perfect Mother," with its attendant fear of maternal power and anger at maternal powerlessness.[13] Like Men of Reason, feminists who honor choice and control may be threatened by the unpredictability and vulnerability of children and by the stark physicality and radical dependencies of birth giving.

Yet, however grounded their (our) rejection or deep their (our) fears, feminists cannot afford to leave mothering alone. Just because "mother" has been a fearsome, crystallized female identity, mothering must be reconstituted as an enabling human work. Moreover, for many women mothering and giving birth are sex-expressive, sex-affirming constitutive identities. To the extent that feminists adopt an exclu-sively and excluding daughterly stance, these women will either reject feminism or accept their alienation as mothers within feminism just as they accepted their alienation as women within other movements and institutions that ignored or trivialized "womanly" experience.[14] By contrast, a mother-respecting feminism in which mothers (who are also daughter or sons) are speaking subjects, in which daughters (who are sometimes mothers) are attuned to maternal voices, can confront in the name of mothers the damages as well as the pleasures of mothering.

When I now imagine mothers' transformative encounter with feminism, feminism is mother-inclusive, and therefore the meeting is not intrinsically oppositional. A mother-inclusive feminism can avoid the arrogance of setting out to "rescue" militarist mothers from "their" insularity and denial. Various forms of peacefulness are at least as latent in mothering as in feminist practices. Both feminist and mothering practices are drawn to militarist power and domination; each practice has its resources for resisting its own and others' militarism. It is the conjunction of feminist and maternal consciousness, of maternal sympathies and feminist solidarity, that might shift the balance within maternal practices from denial to lucid knowledge, from parochialism to awareness of others' suffering, and from compliance to stubborn, decisive capacities to act.[15]

For example, women and men acquiring feminist consciousness tend to focus on the impact in their lives of norms of femininity and masculinity. They come to recognize that the stories they have been told and tell themselves about what it means to "be a woman" are mystifying and destructive. Central among these stories about women are various tales of female mothering: women are "naturally" suited for maternal work and men cannot be mothers; unless widowed, mothers should be married or at least heterosexual; mother love is free of anger and ambivalence; good mothers are unselfish; children's demands are consuming and therefore mothers shouldn't, and in a just world needn't, "work"; mothers can't pilot airplanes, don't like to sell or repair heavy machines, can't dedicate themselves to an art or command soldiers in combat . . . and on and on. In unraveling these and other stories, mothers acquiring feminist consciousness may well be prompted to explore undefensively their ambitions and sexual desires and in particular to describe realistically the angers and ambivalences of maternal love. As they ferret out the dominant myths of mothering, they may be able to confront the political conditions—what Adrienne Rich called the "institutions of motherhood"—that exact from them unnecessary sacrifices of pleasure and power.

Whatever the tensions and ambivalence of individual mothers acquiring feminist consciousness, a mother-respecting feminism brings a public and nearly inescapable lucidity to bear on its particular culture's mode of mothering. This feminist-inspired lucidity undercuts many kinds of violence in mothers' lives. Most obviously feminists name the abuses mothers suffer from lovers, employers, husbands, and strangers. Equally important, they recognize mothers' tendencies to "submit" or, even worse, to get their children to submit to or take the blame for the violence they suffer, perhaps especially when that violence is perpetrated by a father or a mother's lover. Feminists also look at *maternal* violence, and name the domineering or sadistic tendencies often barely concealed by the demands of discipline. But mother-respecting feminists look at mothers with a compassionate eye. They acknowledge the complex ambivalences of maternal passion, the poverty and desperation that often lie behind men's or women's maternal abuse or neglect, and the repressive and punitive control of female sexuality and birth giving that squander women's capacity to cherish their own or their children's bodily being. Most important, feminists move on from identifying and analyzing in order to create policies and spaces that offer mothers the minimal economic means and physical safety to take care of themselves and those they care for—to start again.

Mothers who "see" personal violences they previously denied, may find themselves seeing through the fantasies and moralities that justify organized public violence. Feminists have revealed the ways in which the "masculinity" for which men are rewarded is intertwined with the domination and violence that masculinity permits.[16] Militarist discourse is preeminent among the discourses of "masculinity"; as much as men have made war, war has made "men" as we know them. But if war is "manly," it is also "womanly." Many women are thrilled by the armed yet vulnerable Just Warrior who confronts Death on an illusory Battlefield. It is a feminine heroine "behind the lines" who keeps the "home fire burning" and with it the rare and increasingly outdated division between homes and battlefields, civilian and Soldier. A newly perceptive woman may suspect that myths of Heroic Deaths camouflage the realities of war's random, accidental, fratricidal killings as well as the cruelly vicious murder that making war permits. She may recognize that the fiction of a soldier's Battlefield is belied by the myriad soldier–civilian "relationships" created by distant bombings, fire torchings, search and destroy missions, forced relocations, prostitution, rape, torture, and pillage.

Mothers who begin to tease apart the fantasies of hero and battlefield that have buttressed their faith in war, are more likely to suspect the Men in Power and Defense Intellectuals in whom they have trusted. Evil Enemies, National interests, emergencies, conspiracies, and other worst-case scenarios are all vulnerable to the lucid, knowing gaze. When joined with a traditional commitment to protect, lucid knowledge may inspire mothers to protest policies that threaten their own children—thus adding distinctive maternal voices and energies to antinuclear and ecological politics. Increasing *habits* of lucidity might also enable mothers—against the odds of media distortion—to acknowledge the violence of their own government's military and economic policies.

But lucidity alone cannot inspire a maternal compassion that can undercut the ethnic rivalry or racist phobia that fuels violence. Mothers have to learn to apprehend, to appreciate, to identify with the suffering of "other" mothers and children if they are to act against the violence that "others" suffer or to fight the injustices to which violence is so often a response. Imaginative compassion is hard won. Differences among people—of race, class, wealth, gender, sexual preference, nationality, religion, and education—are typically more obvious and almost always more deeply felt than similarities. Of the many differences among people there may be none more painful than the difference between a mother who expects to be able to provide for her children's needs, share in their pleasures, and mitigate their unhappiness and a mother who expects that despite her efforts her children will be hungry, frightened, brutalized by bigotry, or humiliated and disabled by the hidden as well as the evident injuries of class. Moreover, mothers are committed to their children; every fragile, emerging, cross-cultural maternal identification is threatened by any division that sets one people and its children against another. We should read with astonishment the literary and historical record of maternal identification with "other" mothers and their children—including those of the "enemy." Despite the pull of parochial loyalty, fear, and distorting fantasy, at least some mothers can see in "other" and "enemy" mothers a real, particular, and variant form of the passionate attachments and connections that determine the shapes of their own lives.

Interpreted heuristically, cross-cultural maternal compassion[17] is evidence that the difficult discipline of attentive love central to maternal thinking can be tentatively if imperfectly extended. An attentive mother is pained by her children's pain but does not confuse the two separable sufferings or inflict on her child her own distinct, adult and motherly sorrow. She comforts her child and therefore *indirectly* herself. Similarly, cross-cultural mothers do not pretend that they share, or even fully understand, another's suffering. It is sufficient that they imaginatively apprehend another's pain as painful, that they are pained by the other's pain, and that they act to relieve the *other's* suffering and only indirectly their own. Although they may be prompted by shame or guilt, as well as by outrage and sorrow, they do not let their self-preoccupations hinder their power to act.

I believe that a feminist ideal of solidarity with women who struggle against violence can inform and strengthen existing yet fragile maternal compassion. A principal obstacle to compassion for the different "other" is that difference is so often created in a nexus of domination and oppression, outrage and shame. Sympathy is sabotaged by injustice; conversely, to adapt a phrase of Alice Walker's, only justice can stop the curse of mutual hate and fear.[18] Early feminist ideals of sisterhood that assumed a "common" oppression or experience of caretaking mystified real divisions among women and the damages of oppression.[19] A more recent feminist ideal of solidarity aims for a cross-cultural alliance among and identification with just those women who are resisting violence and abuse. Because ideals of solidarity are sex/gender-expressive, mothers would be inspired as women to identify with other women who, as mothers, strive to create for themselves and their children the conditions for dignified work, self-governance, effective love, and pleasure. (Men who are mothers take on themselves something of the feminine condition. See *Maternal Thinking*, chapter 2. They would therefore also identify to some extent with other women mothers.) Because these ideals legitimize women's struggle against specific injustices and abuse (as well as against more "natural" disaster), mothers moved by solidarity could be prompted to move beyond their shame, fear, or even their self-interest. A sex/gender-expressive extension of compassion and action will be more likely if there are actual existing struggles of women in resistance that can call forth and utilize acts of solidarity.

Fortunately in recent years, movements of women in resistance have developed in countries as different as South Africa, Chile, East Germany, England, Israel,

Palestine, and the United States.[20] A women's politics of resistance begins by affirming "womanly" obligations and then demands that governments or communities respect the conditions necessary for "womanly" work and love. For example, women are responsible for children's health; in the name of their maternal duty they call on their government to halt nuclear testing which, epitomizing its general unhealthiness, leaves strontium 90 in women's milk. Since women feed families, they "riot" for bread. Since (mostly) women actively nurse the sick, women organize not only for better pay but also for conditions that will allow them to do their work effectively. Since women are responsible for protective mothering, in Argentina, Chile and across Latin America, Madres publicly and dramatically protest the "disappearing"—the kidnapping, torturing, mutilating, and murdering—of their children.

Women in resistance create new values of activity and stubborn decisiveness. When women carry pictures of their loved ones in the public plazas of a police state, chain themselves to their capitol building's fence, put pillowcases and photographs up against the barbed-wire fences of missile bases, or create open alliances among "enemy" mothers, they translate the symbols of attachment into political speech. Insisting that their governors name and take responsibility for the injuries they risk and inflict, they speak a "woman's language" of loyalty, love and outrage; but they speak with a public anger in a public place in ways they were never meant to do. They are the heirs of the mater dolorosa, taking active, decisive, public responsibility for restoring a world in which their children can survive. As they fulfill expectations of femininity they also violate them, transforming, even as they act on the meanings of maternity and womanliness.

In a utopian mood I have envisioned a "feminist, maternal peace politics" made up of mothers, mother-inclusive feminists, and women in resistance. Feminist, maternal peacemakers draw on the history and traditions of women to create a *politics* of peace. They are inspired by the act and symbol of birth and by the passionate labor of women who throughout most of history have borne the primary responsibility for protection and care. Yet because they are feminists, these peacemakers subvert mythical divisions between women and men, private care and public justice, that hobble both mothering and peacemaking. Men become mothers and mothers invent new models and styles of public, nonviolent resistance and cooperation that are suitable to their particular temperament, personal history, social location, and economic resources.

The forms and ideologies of a feminist, maternal peace politics are various and just being invented. Yet even in its inchoate forms this politics is transforming the maternal imagination, creating in mothers new capacities to know, care, and act. This is not to say that feminist mothers or feminist and mother-identified men and women are the only or the loudest voices of peace. Many voices, wills, and projects are needed; there need be no competition for best peacemaker. It is enough that mothers who have hitherto played their parts in the scripts of the violent now move from maternal thinking to peace politics, thus contributing in their own

distinctively maternal ways to the many-faceted, polymorphous, collective effort
to make a peace worth keeping.

NOTES

1. For an excellent account of "standpoint" theories that rely on the idea of "caring
labor," see Sandra Harding, *The Science Question in Feminism* (Ithaca, N.Y.: Cornell University
Press, 1986). I rely especially on Nancy Hartsock, "The Feminist Standpoint: Developing
the Ground for a Specifically Feminist Historical Materialism," which is now the last chapter
of her *Money, Sex and Power* (New York: Longman, 1983). I have also used Hilary Rose,
"Hand, Brain and Heart," *Signs* 9.1 (1983), 73–91, and "Women's Work, Women's
Knowledge" in Ann Oakley and Juliet Mitchell, eds., *What is Feminism?* (New York: Pantheon, 1983), 161–184. There are many other accounts of the rationality of care with
differing emphases. Two more recent interesting articles are Patricia Hill Collins, "The Social
Construction of Black Feminist Thought," *Signs* 14, no. 4 (Spring 1989), and Joan Tronto,
"Beyond Gender Difference to a Theory of Care," *Signs* 12.4 (1987), 644–663. Drawing on
very different traditions and methodologies, Carol Gilligan and Nel Noddings also develop
"care" perspectives. For Gilligan and Gilligan et al., *In a Different Voice, Mapping the Moral
Domain*, and *Making Connections* (Cambridge, Mass.: Harvard University Press, 1982, 1989,
1990). For Nel Noddings see *Caring* and *Women and Evil* (Berkeley: University of California
Press, 1984, 1989).

2. Michaela de Leonardo, "The Female World of Cards and Holidays: Women, Families
and the Work of Kinship," *Signs* 12, no. 3 (1987), 440–453.

3. I am relying especially on Nancy Hartsock's language.

4. These examples are Carol Gilligan's, *In a Different Voice*.

5. See Barbara Christian: mothering offers "an insight into the preciousness of life,"
"because women are *reduced* to the function of mother, which often results in their loss of
a sense of self, the gift of seeing the world from [a maternal] angle is lost to them and their
communities"—"An Angle of Seeing Motherhood," in *Black Feminist Criticism* (New York:
Pergamon, 1985), 246.

6. A clear exception is Carol McMillan, *Women, Reason, and Nature* (Princeton, N.J.:
Princeton University Press, 1982). While a "partisan of women," McMillan is explicitly
antifeminist.

7. There are many other definitions and tasks of "feminist ethics," for example, elucidating feminist values or assessing moral concepts implied by or useful to feminist politics.

8. These phrases are from Margaret Urban Walker, this volume.

9. Phillip Hallie, *Lest Innocent Blood Be Shed* (New York: Harper & Row, 1979), 104.

10. Adrienne Rich, *Of Woman Born* (New York: Norton, 1978), 236.

11. Ynestra King, talk at the Columbia Seminar on Women and Society, Spring 1983.

12. Throughout these paragraphs I am relying extensively on the readings, analysis, and
political insights of Marianne Hirsch's *Mother-Daughter Plot: Narrative, Psychoanalysis, Feminism* (Bloomington: Indiana University Press, 1989), especially chapter five. This book
promises to create a new relationship, publicly and for me personally between mothering
and feminism (Bloomington: Indiana University Press, 1989).

13. Nancy Chodorow and Susan Contratto, "The Fantasy of the Perfect Mother" in
Barrie Thorne and Marilyn Yalon, eds., *Rethinking the Family* (New York: Longman, 1982).

14. According to Marianne Hirsch, a "daughterly-feminism" that casts mothers as object

or other can be subject to maternal critique of the sort that white feminists in the United States have been subjected to by women of color; Western feminists, by Third World women; and middle-class feminists, by working-class women.

15. Internationally and in the United States, feminism is a multifaceted social movement in the process of change and self-definition. I intend my remarks about feminism to be neutral and inclusive though I am sure they will seem ethnocentric or biased to some feminists. I hope that it is not necessary for my purposes to distinguish kinds of feminism: gynocentric, egalitarian, lesbian, individualist, relational, liberal, Third World, socialist, Marxist, radical, etc.

16. As Carol Cohn has pointed out: Feminists aim to "destabilize, delegitimize, and dismantle patriarchal discourses—to render their systems, methods, and presumptions unable to retain their dominance and power and thus to open spaces for other voices to be heard." "Emasculating America's Linguistic Deterrent" in Adrienne Harris and Ynestra King, eds., *Rocking the Ship of State* (Boulder: Westview Press, 1989), 155.

17. "Compassion" differs from "pity." The compassionate person does not feel superior to the sufferer for whom she has compassion. Nor does she separate herself from the sufferer's fate. On the other hand, compassion is not quite "empathy" or what Carol Gilligan and Grant Wiggins call "co-feeling." The compassionate person does not, and should not try to, actually share the others' suffering. Such appropriation almost always leads to misunderstanding and romantic, masochistic, or mystifying identifications. The compassionate person is pained by another's distinct and separate pain and acts to relieve both pains. On the importance of presumed equality to suffering see Simone Weil: "Whoever does not know just how far necessity and a fickle fortune hold the human soul under their domination cannot treat as his equals, nor love as himself, those whom chance has separated from him by an abyss. The diversity of the limitations to which men are subject creates the illusion that there are different species among them who cannot communicate with one another. Only he who knows the empire of might and knows how not to respect it is capable of love and justice." Simone Weil, "The *Iliad*, Poem of Might," in George A. Panichas, ed., *Simone Weil Reader* (Mt. Kisko, N.Y.: Moyer Bell Limited, 1977). See also Lawrence Blum on the importance of equality to compassion, on the dangers of the compassionate relationship, and on the necessity of sharing another's pleasures as well as pain. "Compassion," in Amelie Rorty, ed., *Explaining Emotions* (Berkeley: University of California Press, 1980). On the meaning and development of compassion, Carol Gilligan and Grant Wiggins, "The Origins of Morality and Early Childhood Relationships," in Carol Gilligan, Janie Victoria Ward, and Jill McLean Taylor, eds., *Remapping the Moral Domain* (Cambridge, Mass.: Harvard University Press, 1988) 11–140.

18. Alice Walker, "Only Justice Can Stop a Curse," in *Reweaving the Web of Life*, Pam McAllister, ed., (Philadelphia: New Society Publishers, 1982), 262–266.

19. In "Relating to Privilege," Aida Hurtado has spoken of a common oppression that women suffer but that takes different forms for white women and women of color. While white women are seduced by white men, women of color are rejected by them. But both are dominated and oppressed. Although this common identification may work cross racially for women's subordination to men, and although many mothers suffer as women in relation to men, mothers seem to me more ineradicably divided by differences in the violence they suffer or perpetrate and differences in the resources they have to resist violence and provide for their children. *Signs* 14.4, (1989), 833–855. Maureen Reddy has written of the ways in which, in some African American writing, maternal bonding creates a degree of alliance between Black and white women. "Reading White in Black: Biracial Relationships in several Black Women's Novels," manuscript, courtesy of the author.

20. For an interesting and different discussion of these movements see Ann Snitow, "A Gender Diary" in Adrienne Harris and Ynestra King, eds., *Rocking the Ship of State: Toward a Feminist Peace Politics* (Boulder, Colo.: Westview Press, 1989).

Lesbian Ethics and Female Agency

SARAH LUCIA HOAGLAND ▮▮▮▮▮▮▮▮▮▮▮▮▮

INTRODUCTION

It is possible to engage in moral revolution and change the values we affirm by
the choices we make. It is possible for lesbians to spin a revolution, for us to weave
a transformation of consciousness.[1]

My focus is lesbian for several reasons. A central element of lesbian oppression
has been and remains our erasure by the dominant society. If lesbians were truly
perceptible, then the idea that women can survive without men might work its
way into social reality. This suggests that lesbian existence is connected logically
or formally in certain ways with female agency: the conceptual possibility of female
agency not defined in terms of an other.

Besides a conceptual/material—that is, a logical—possibility, I find a more concrete possibility. By affirming our lesbianism, lesbians have questioned social knowledge at some level. In spite of our varied assimilation (including absorption of
dominant, oppressive values), through lesbian existence comes a certain ability to
resist and refocus, an ability that is crucial to the sort of moral change I think can
occur. Because of this my focus is lesbian.

I contrast lesbianism with heterosexualism. By "heterosexualism," I do not mean
simply the matter of men having procreative sex with women. I am talking about
an entire way of life promoted throughout the fathers' society from religion to
pornography to unpaid housework to medicine. Heterosexualism is men dominating
and de-skilling women in any of a number of forms, from outright attack to paternalistic care, and women devaluing (of necessity) female bonding. Heterosexualism is a way of living (which actual practitioners exhibit to a greater or lesser
degree) that normalizes the dominance of one person in a relationship and the
subordination of another. As a result it undermines female agency.[2]

In naming the work "lesbian" I invoke a lesbian context, and for this reason I
do not define the term. To define "lesbian" is to succumb to a context of
heterosexualism, to invoke a context in which it is not the norm. Further, I think
of lesbian context as a ground of lesbian be-ing, a ground of possibility, a context
in which we perceive each other essentially as lesbians, a context in which we
create lesbian meaning. (One devastating effect of heterosexualism on lesbians is
an erasure of lesbian meaning.) This context exists because we focus on each other
as lesbians.

In stressing a centered focus rather than one riveted outward, I do not intend to encourage a uniform perception. I mean to suggest that we perceive each other in all our aspects, from our varied backgrounds to our political differences. But I also mean to suggest that we move among each other as "lesbians," not as "women." Once it was enough to be a lesbian; now we know better. We know that at most it creates the possibility of a certain kind of female agency. That involves the area of ethics.

My overall thesis is that the foundation[3] of traditional ethics is dominance and subordination, that its function is social control, and that as a result it serves to interrupt rather than promote lesbian connection and interaction. My focus is not a new standard of behavior, but rather concerns what it means to be a moral agent under oppression.

Among lesbians, after the initial burst of this wave of the women's liberation movement, many of us began to focus on the kind of society we hoped for among women. We talked of learning to be more "open," and by that we meant vulnerable. And as we found our interactions to be less than utopian, we began to talk about the need for a feminist ethics. Those discussions often began with declarations of how (some other) lesbians were selfish, together with assertions of the importance of self-sacrifice. In other words, while fighting the fathers' politics, we began reaching for their ethical concepts to interpret and judge our interactions. In what follows I discuss the appeal to the feminine and the concept of self-sacrifice as a feminine virtue, because I want to challenge these concepts and realize a different concept of female agency formed within a lesbian context.

THE FEMININE PRINCIPLE

We appeal to altruism, to self-sacrifice, and in general, to feminine virtuousness in a desperate attempt to find grace and goodness within a system marked by greed and fear. Although these virtues may herald for us the possibility of ethics—the possibility of some goodness in an otherwise nasty world—they are the virtues of subservience, as Mary Daly has pointed out.[4]

Under masculinist ethics, virtue is obedience and subservience,[5] and the virtuous are those who remain subordinate (accessible). The function of masculinist ethics has been to insulate those on top and facilitate their access to the resources of those under them. (Discussions of medical ethics are particularly illustrative.)

Despite this, and because of the effects of men's behavior, we can be tempted to regard the feminine as more valuable than the masculine. Appealing to women's "moral superiority," many suffragists defended votes for women. Currently, some women are noting values that pass between women and are developing theories about these values, including an ethics of dependence.

For example, Nel Noddings has developed an ethics based on feminine recep-tivity. Her analysis of caring includes engrossment and motivational displacement on the part of the "one-caring," and reciprocity, which amounts to merely acknowledging one-caring, on the part of the "cared-for." In effect, her analysis of caring is unidirectional because it includes no requirement of reciprocity beyond acknowledgment on the part of the cared-for, and because the ethical self can emerge only through caring for others.[6] If an ethics of caring is to be morally successful in replacing an ethics based on principles and duty, then it must, among other things, acknowledge a self as both related and separate, a self that is, as I argue elsewhere, neither autonomous nor other-defined, but rather one among many.[7]

Carol Gilligan has argued that, in ethical matters, women tend to focus on interpersonal relations while men's ethical considerations involve principles.[8] In the process she has attempted a vindication of what she perceives as women's morality.

Claudia Card has written a telling critique. Among other things, she argues that Gilligan does not take into account women's oppression and, consequently, the damage to women of that oppression. And, she argues, the fact that women have developed necessary survival skills under oppression does not mean these skills contribute ultimately to human good. For example, while Gilligan revalues women's concern for approval as actually a concern for maintaining relationships, Card reminds us that the approval women seek is usually male approval, which is granted for "obedience to conventions requiring affiliation with men, respect for their views, empathy for them, etc." Or again, while Gilligan revalues the so-called weak ego boundaries of women as a capacity for affiliation, Card reminds us that only certain affiliations are pursued. Lesbian relations, for example, are more often than not a source of terror for women.[9]

In addition it may be that women have a greater capacity for empathy; however, women tend to direct that empathy to men of their own race and class, not to women of other races and classes, or even women of their own race and class. (Early radical feminists called this male-identification.) Further, Claudia Card points out that intimacy has not cured the violence in women's lives; instead, it "has given the violent greater access to their victims." She goes on: "Without validation of success in separating, we may learn to see our only decent option as trying to improve the quality of bad relationships." She adds: "More likely to be mistaken for a caring virtue is a misplaced gratitude women have felt toward men for taking less than full advantage of their power to abuse or for singling them out for the privilege of service in return for 'protection.' " Card argues that misplaced gratitude is a form of moral damage women have suffered, along with lying, cunning, deceit, and manipulation.[10]

Actually, I go a step farther and argue that, while men have designed "the feminine" for their own purposes, women have refined these virtues in defense and resistance, developing them as a means of obtaining some control (individual and limited) in situations which *presume* female self-sacrifice.[11] Women have developed the "giving" expected of them into survival skills, strategies for gaining some control in situations where their energy and attention are focused on others. That is, the power of control can be exercised from the subordinate position, and under heterosexualism women have refined and developed the feminine virtues for just that purpose. Under heterosexualism, female agency involves manipulation and cunning—for example, a woman getting what she needs for herself and her children by manipulating a man in such a way that he thinks it was all his idea. This is the essence of female agency under heterosexualism.

Manipulation, cunning, and deceit are not peculiar to women. Men are also extremely manipulative and deceitful, and can exhibit considerable cunning, for example, in keeping their dominance over their peers or subordinates from appearing overt, or in enlisting women to support them. The difference, finally, between men and women under heterosexualism may lie in who maintains dominance—though not, in every instance, in who maintains control.

Dominance is maintained by violence or the threat of violence, which, in the long run, means by destruction or the threat of destruction. If nothing else works, men will disrupt or destroy what is going on. Thus, to be different from men, women stress nonviolence. Under heterosexualism, manipulation and control are not challenged; what is challenged is only the threat of disruption or destruction. Women want men to "play fair" in the game of manipulation and control by not resorting to the one-upmanship of destruction.

Many claim that there is a feminine principle that must exert itself to counterbalance masculinism pervading world cultures, but what they seem to ignore is that the feminine has its origin in masculinist ideology and does not represent a break from it. Further, the counterbalance works both ways. Because of the nondiscriminatory nature of feminine receptivity, that is, a lack of evaluating or judging what the feminine responds to, the feminine requires the masculine to protect it from foreign invasion.

Within lesbian community, many lesbians embrace a feminine principle and suggest that self-sacrifice, altruism, mothering as unconditional loving, and vulnerability are desirable ethical norms in our relationships. I want to challenge this. In this essay I address the concept of self-sacrifice.

''SELFISHNESS'' AND ''SELF-SACRIFICE''

Consider, first, the use of the label "selfish." Those who are judged to be selfish are often those who do not respond to demands from others: the question of selfishness is a question of whether a person thinks only of herself. This consideration often develops into a complaint that the person deemed selfish does not act in ways that contribute to a social structure such as the nation, the family, the synagogue or church, the corporation, the sewing circle, or the collective. Significantly, when a person goes along with the group, even if she is only thinking of herself—being "selfish"—she may well be considered ethical for doing the "right" thing. On the other hand, someone who is perceived as selflessly opposing the group often is judged immoral and unethical. Thus someone can be "selfish" yet "good"—as well as "unselfish" yet "bad." It seems that selfishness is not of prime concern; rather, the label is used as an excuse to manipulate our participation toward someone else's end.

Second, masculinist ideology suggests that the true female nature affirms itself through self-sacrifice. Mary Daly defines "self-sacrifice" as the handing over of our identity and energy to individuals or institutions.[12] This ethical value encourages a woman to give up pursuit of her needs and interests in order to dedicate her efforts to pursuing others' needs and interests, usually those of her husband and children.

Self-sacrifice appears to be a sacrifice of self-interest. Yet women face limited options: men limit women's options through conceptual, physical, and economic coercion. As a result, when a woman engages in self-denial, acquiesces to male authority, and apparently sacrifices her own interests to those of a man in conformity with the dictates of the feminine stereotype, she may actually be acting from self-interest, doing what she deems necessary to her own survival.[13]

One consequence is that, except perhaps in extreme cases of female sexual slavery, when a woman is in a situation in which she is expected to shift her identity to that of a man or a child, the stage is set for her to work to control the arena wherein her identity is located. She has not sacrificed her self: by altruistically adopting another's interests, she has transferred that self, or rather it has been arrogated by the man.[14] She may have given up pursuit of her own unique interests and needs in favor of those of her husband (and to a lesser extent those of her children), but she will pursue their interests and needs as her own.

This in turn gives rise to a double bind of heterosexualism: she is expected to attend to everyone else's projects, but she has no final say in how they are realized. She thus becomes the nagging wife or the fairy-tale stepmother. For example, mothers may "live vicariously" through their children and some wives may be "domineering." Those mothers who pursue their children's needs and interests too enthusiastically are criticized for not being passive enough. The stereotype of the Jewish mother attests to the trap self-sacrifice sets up for women.

Third, the concepts of "self-sacrifice," "altruism," "selfishness," and "self-interest" may appear to be factual descriptions, but the implications we can draw from sentences containing these words depend significantly on how we use them. Someone may "self-sacrifice" because it makes her feel good, so she is actually acting from "self-interest." "Self-sacrifice" may even be "selfish" if someone refuses to take her own risks or becomes a burden if she doesn't take care of herself as a result. We can play around with these concepts and come up with all sorts of interesting results; through all this, acting in consideration of our own needs and limits does not exist as a moral consideration.

Fourth, the selfish/selfless (or egoism/altruism) dichotomy does not accurately categorize our interactions. Often we do not consider our interests and the interests of others as being in conflict.[15] Concern for ourselves does not imply disregarding the needs of others.[16] In addition, doing good for others need not involve disregarding ourselves.

Fifth, in challenging the concept of "self-sacrifice," I do not mean to suggest that the sort of "selfish" behavior which self-sacrifice is supposed to counter does not exist among lesbians. For example, a lesbian may consistently act as if her feelings are the only ones, that she is warranted in interrupting anything else going on to demand attention (the strategies for this are many and varied); however, even though the problem is real, the solution does not lie in advocating self-sacrifice. When a lesbian is acting this way, often it is because she does not have a firm sense of herself in relation to others and is threatened; advocating self-sacrifice will only compound the problem.

Egocentrism is the perception that the world revolves around oneself. It is important to have a healthy sense of oneself, centered and in relation to others. But egocentrism is our judgment that those around us have no other relationships, needs, commitments, or identity than what they have with us. Egocentrism is perceiving and judging others only in relation to ourselves. Hence it is a confusion of our needs, reactions, and choices with those of others. Egocentrism is a form of "selfishness," for it entails a lack of consideration for others—it involves a lack of awareness that others have needs distinct from our own.

In the community we tend to promote self-sacrifice as a virtue and a proper antidote for behavior resulting from egocentrism. But self-sacrifice cannot solve the problem because egocentrism involves a confusion of needs similar in form to the confusion that occurs with self-sacrifice: my perception of my needs and concerns becomes so entwined with my perception of others that anything relating to the other must relate to me and vice versa.

The difference is that in the case of self-sacrifice we cease to have a distinct sense of ourselves. In the case of egocentrism we cease to have a distinct sense of the other. Thus, advocating self-sacrifice as a corrective measure to selfishness really feeds an underlying problem of ego boundary: the solution actually nurtures the problem.

Sixth, another's "self-sacrifice" is not particularly helpful when we are pursuing our goals. Some of us joke about wanting a wife. But what helps me, for example, do my work is not someone giving up her goals to pursue mine and attempt to affect them. What helps is someone giving me encouragement, criticism—an exchange of ideas that rub against mine, someone who sparks and is sparked by an exchange.

Someone might argue that self-sacrifice is important in certain political situations. Yet lesbian burnout results from self-sacrifice in political projects, especially when the project does not develop in the direction or as quickly as the lesbian imagined—burnout that in turn results in virtual or even complete withdrawal from lesbian community. If a lesbian devotes herself to a project in such a way that her identity merges with it while her life goes on hold, and she does not gauge her own needs and limits, she may become unable to pull back at times and so become devastated if things don't go exactly and immediately as she believes they ought to. She may work frantically, as if responsible for the whole situation . . . until something snaps and she ceases to care, ceases to be able to respond. Self-sacrifice is not a means of engaging.

When we engage in political work, or projects and relationships, we need not regard this as taking us away from our everyday concerns, as being in conflict with our personal goals, and hence as a sacrifice. Nor is it useful to believe we must sacrifice in order to feel we are truly struggling. Rather, we can regard our work as a matter of pursuing our needs and interests, as part of our means of living in heteropatriarchy, as our means of creating meaning in our living. In this way we make choices, take risks, make mistakes, revalue our commitment as things progress, but we do not so easily lose our self in self-sacrifice and burnout.

This brings me to my main point. We tend to regard choosing to do something as a sacrifice. I want to suggest, instead, that we regard choosing to do something as a creation. From heterosexualism we tend to believe that any time we help another, we are sacrificing something. Thus we might regard helping a friend fix a carburetor, spending an evening listening to her when she's upset rather than going to a party, or helping her move as a matter of self-sacrifice. But these acts do not necessarily involve self-sacrifice. Rather, they involve a choice between two or more things to do. Often we have choices and we will have reasons for any choice we make. But that we have to make choices is not itself a matter of sacrifice.

There is another way of approaching this: we can regard our choosing to interact as part of how we engage in living. Such choices are a matter of focus, not sacrifice. That I attend certain things and not others, that I focus here and not there, is part of how I create value. Far from sacrificing myself, or part of myself, I am creating; I am weaving lesbian value.

Thus as I engage in lesbian living, I make choices—to start this relationship, to work on this project, to withdraw now, to dream now. I make daily choices; at one time I may choose to help another, at another time not. But in choosing to help another, I am not thereby sacrificing myself. Instead, this is part of what I involve myself in. When we regard interacting with others as a sacrifice and not as an engagement, it is time to reassess the relationship.

An idea is floating about to the effect that if we cannot do everything, if we have to choose some and let other things go, then we are sacrificing something. Given traditional Anglo-European philosophy and U.S. imperialist ideology, U.S. lesbians in particular tend to think the whole world exists for us, that everything is potentially ours (or should be), so that when we have to choose between two or more options, we feel we are sacrificing something or that we have lost something. But everything is not ours; everything is not even potentially ours. In fact, nothing out there that exists is ours. Thus in acting, engaging, making choices—in choosing one thing rather than another—we are not losing anything. In acting, engaging, making choices, we are creating something. We create a relationship, we create value. As we focus on lesbian community and bring our backgrounds, interests, abilities, and desires to it, we create lesbian meaning.

What exists here as lesbian community is not some predetermined phenomenon that we opted for but rather a result of what we've created. The same is true of all our relationships. The choice to engage here rather than there is not a sacrifice of what's "out there"; to engage is to create something that did not exist before. I want to suggest that revaluing choice is central to Lesbian Ethics.

For example, understanding choice as creation, not sacrifice, helps us better understand choices we make that are typically considered "altruistic." Often we are drawn to helping others. That's one reason so many are drawn to healing, to teaching, to volunteering to work at shelters, to practicing therapy, to working at community centers or in political campaigns, to going to Nicaragua—to all kinds of political work. In doing such work, we feel we are creating something, that we are participating in something, that we engage and make a difference.

If we decide to regard choice as a creation, not a sacrifice, situations requiring difficult decisions will still arise for us. Even so, we can regard our ability to make choices as a source of power, an enabling power, rather than a loss or sacrifice or compromise. Thus by revaluing choice we begin to revalue female agency: female agency begins to be not essentially a matter of sacrifice, but a process of engagement and creation.

CONCLUSION

I am not simply saying that at times we don't behave as well as we might. I am saying that the *structure* of the feminine virtues will thwart even our best efforts because these virtues don't function to promote female agency that stems from self-understanding and that is both related and separate. And far from facilitating our ethical interactions, the feminine virtues actually interrupt attempts among lesbians to connect and interact ethically by promoting control and distance and by erecting barriers. If we are to achieve a moral revolution, rather than possible moral reform or perhaps remaining stuck in the status quo, it is important to understand the feminine as born of the masculine.

If we regard choice as creation not sacrifice, we can regard our ability to make choices as a source of enabling power rather than as a source of sacrifice or compromise. As a result we can revalue female agency, developing it independently of the manipulation and control from the position of subordination of heterosexualism. Female agency becomes not essentially a matter of sacrifice, but rather a process of engagement and creation.

NOTES

1. This paper is excerpted from my book *Lesbian Ethics: Toward New Value* (1988, Institute of Lesbian Studies, P.O. Box 60242, Palo Alto, CA 94306). A longer version of

this paper is in Jeffner Allen, ed., *Lesbian Philosophies and Cultures* (Albany: SUNY Press, 1990). The material in this introduction includes bits and pieces from my introduction and is designed merely to orient the reader.

2. Some will wonder whether others besides lesbians fit into what I am calling Lesbian Ethics. My answer is that, of course, others can fit into what I am saying. Heterosexual women can fit into this schema, for example. However, heterosexual women fit exactly the way lesbians fit into heterosexual society. Lesbians fit there, but not as lesbians. Heterosexual women can fit here, though not as heterosexual women—that is, not as members of the category "woman."

3. I use "foundation" in the Wittgensteinian sense of an axis held in place by what surrounds it.

4. Note Mary Daly, *Beyond God the Father: Toward a Philosophy of Women's Liberation* (Boston: Beacon Press, 1973) and *Gyn/Ecology: The Metaethics of Radical Feminism* (Boston: Beacon Press, 1978).

5. Claudia Card, conversation.

6. Nel Noddings, *Caring: A Feminine Approach to Ethics & Moral Education* (Berkeley: University of California Press, 1984). My remarks are from "Some Remarks about Caring," a paper presented to a joint session of the Radical Philosophy Association and the Society for Women in Philosophy at the Central Division APA meetings in Cincinnati, April 1988.

7. Hoagland, *Lesbian Ethics*, chapters 3, 5.

8. Carol Gilligan, *In a Different Voice: Psychological Theory and Women's Development* (Cambridge, Mass.: Harvard University Press, 1982).

9. Claudia Card, *Virtues and Moral Luck*, Series 1, Institute for Legal Studies, Working Papers, University of Wisconsin-Madison, Law School, November 1985, 14–15.

10. Ibid., 16, 17, 23.

11. " 'Femininity,' Resistance, and Sabotage," in Mary Vetterling-Braggin, ed., *"Femininity," "Masculinity," and "Androgyny": A Modern Philosophical Discussion* (Totowa, N.J.: Littlefield, Adams, 1982), 85–98.

12. Mary Daly, *Gyn/Ecology*, 374–75.

13. Marilyn Frye, "In and Out of Harm's Way: Arrogance and Love," in *The Politics of Reality: Essays in Feminist Theory* (Trumansburg, N.Y.: Crossing Press, 1983).

14. Ibid., 66–72.

15. For further discussion, note Judith Tourmey, "Exploitation, Oppression, and Self-Sacrifice," in Carol C. Gould and Marx W. Wartofsky, eds., *Women and Philosophy* (New York: G. P. Putnam's Sons, 1976), 206–221; and Lawrence Blum, Marcia Homiak, Judy Housman, and Naomi Scheman, "Altruism and Women's Oppression," in Gould and Wartofsky, 222–247.

16. For further discussion, note James Rachels, "Morality and Self-Interest," in James Rachels and Frank A. Tillman, eds., *Philosophical Issues: A Contemporary Introduction* (New York: Harper & Row, 1972), 120–121.

Moral Understandings: Alternative "Epistemology" for a Feminist Ethics

MARGARET URBAN WALKER ▮▮▮▮▮▮▮▮▮▮

When Annette Baier asked a few years ago what women wanted in a moral theory, the answer she arrived at was that moral *theory* was just what women *didn't* want, if a moral theory is a "fairly systematic account of a fairly large area of morality, with a keystone supporting all the rest."[1] Yet the latter is what a still dominant tradition of moral philosophy—stretching from Socrates through Sidgwick to Rawls —*does* want: a fairly compact system of very general but directly action-guiding principles or procedures. Current philosophical practice still largely views ethics as the search for moral knowledge, and moral knowledge as comprising universal moral formulae and the theoretical justification of these.

If one asks the somewhat different question of what a *feminist ethics* is, or should look like, one might have in mind some different things. One is that feminist ethics clarifies the moral legitimacy and necessity of the kinds of social, political, and personal changes that feminism demands in order to end male domination, or perhaps to end domination generally.[2] Another conception of feminist ethics is that of one in which the moral perceptions, self-images, and senses of moral value and responsibility of women have been represented or restored. Philosophical ethics, as a cultural product, has until recently been almost entirely a product of some men's thinking. There are the usual reasons to suspect that those men will not have represented, or will not have represented truly, modes of life and forms of responsibility which aren't theirs, or which they could recognize fully only at the cost of acknowledging their interlocking gender, race, and class privileges. Although female voices alone may not be sufficient correctives to this, they promise to be important ones. Here the tasks of restoration, reconstruction, and new construction are not sharply divided; all involve suspension and reexamination of unquestioned assumptions and standard forms.

The second reconstructive project has made a certain family of themes—personal relations, nurturance and caring, maternal experience, emotional responsiveness, attunement to particular persons and contexts, sensitivity to open-ended responsibilities—a focus for feminist ethics.[3] At the same time these themes have become the object of sharp criticism by *other* feminists who ask whether the values and paradigms valorized in the reconstructive work are not mistaken and politically

retrograde; whether maternal paradigms, nurturant responsiveness, and a bent toward responsibility for others' needs aren't our oppressive history, not our liberating
future; whether "women's morality" isn't a familiar ghetto rather than a liberated
space.[4] Some feminists question whether the second, reconstructive project can
meet and nourish the first, politically normative one.[5]

Although many strands of this conversation beg consideration, my purpose is to
commend one strand of the reconstructive project for consideration as a part, but
only part, of an adequate and flexible feminist ethic. I find in the reconstructive
work a profound and original rebellion against the regnant paradigm of moral
knowledge mentioned in my opening paragraph. It might be called an *alternative
moral epistemology*, a very different way of identifying and appreciating the forms
of intelligence which define responsible moral consideration. This view does not
imagine our moral understandings congealed into a compact theoretical instrument
of impersonal decision for each person, but as deployed in shared processes of
discovery, expression, interpretation, and adjustment between persons. Facets of
this alternative view which appear repeatedly in reconstructive discussions are:
attention to the particular; a way of constructing morally relevant understandings
which is "contextual and narrative";[6] a picture of deliberation as a site of expression
and communication.

Here are my limited aims. First, I model this alternative epistemology of moral
understandings by describing its three elements and their affinities. Second, I
identify how its features challenge the still-hardy, mainstream universalist tradition
on moral knowledge. Finally, too briefly, I indicate some ways this particular result
of the reconstructive approach to feminist ethics answers to some concerns of the
first, politically normative approach. Refusing the canonical "theory" option does
not mean going without guidance in judgments and practices of countering domination. Neither does the alternative moral epistemology by itself require commitments to the specific moral values and paradigms lately in dispute among feminists.

I. ELEMENTS OF AN ALTERNATIVE
MORAL EPISTEMOLOGY

A substantial number of contemporary women writers on morality have sounded
the theme of attention to "particular others in actual contexts."[7] Iris Murdoch
(1970) sets an oft-cited precedent for this theme in her defense of *attention* ("loving
regard," "patient and just discernment") as the "characteristic and proper mark of
the active moral agent."[8]

In pointed opposition to the emphasis in most moral philosophy on conscientious
adherence to principle, Murdoch insists instead on the "endless task" of "good
vision: unsentimental, detached, unselfish, objective attention," which she calls
love.[9] More recent women writers who see acute and unimpeded perception of
particular human beings as the condition of adequate moral response concur in

Murdoch's epistemological point—her emphasis on a certain kind of understanding as central to morality.[10]

Ruddick finds in the virtues of maternal practices dispositions to be cultivated more widely: acceptance of another's separate consciousness making its own sense of the world; recognition of the common humanity of the other's familiar longings and impulses; surrendering expectations of repeatability in order to follow the distinct trajectory of a particular life.[11] Whitbeck sees a similar sensibility enabling practices (such as teaching the young, nursing the sick, tending the body) for "the (mutual) realization of people" which are typically considered "women's work."[12] Gilligan's reconstructed "care ethic" involves "the ability to perceive people in their own terms and to respond to their needs."[13] Benhabib explores the "epistemic incoherence" of strategies of reversibility and universalization once the concreteness of other individuals has been covered over by the "generalized" conception of others in terms of an abstract *status*.[14]

Attention to particular persons as *a*, if not *the*, morally crucial epistemic mode requires distinctive sorts of understanding, described usefully by Gilligan as "contextual and narrative" rather than "formal and abstract." The latter "abstracts the moral problem from the interpersonal situation," and the former invokes a "narrative of relationships that extends over time."[15] Two elements are at work here: context and concreteness of individuals with specific "history, identity, and affective-emotional constitution," and the special context that is a relationship, with *its* history, identity, and affective definition.[16]

The two are linked by the notion of a narrative, of the location of human beings' feelings, psychological states, needs, and understandings as nodes of a story (or of the intersection of stories) that has already begun, and will continue beyond a given juncture of moral urgency. Conceptually, this means that we don't and can't identify people's emotions, intentions and other mental states with momentary (and especially not momentary inner, private) phenomena. Instead, we identify these features of people by attending to how their beliefs, feelings, modes of expression, circumstances and more, arranged in characteristic ways and often spread out in time, configure into a recognizable kind of story. Practically, this means that individual embroideries and idiosyncrasies, as well as the learned codes of expression and response built up in particular relationships, and built up culturally around kinds of relationships, require of us acute attention to the minute and specific, to history and incident, in grasping cases in a morally adequate way. If the others I need to understand really are actual others in a particular case at hand, and not repeatable instances or replaceable occupants of a general status, they will require of me an understanding of their/our story and its concrete detail. Without this I really cannot know *how it is* with others toward whom I will act, or what the meaning and consequence of any acts will be.

Whitbeck argues for a view of persons as "fundamentally a history of relationships to other people," of actions as responses to the "whole configuration of relations" and of moral responsibilities as the essentially responsive, discretionary, and open-ended kind that relationships generate.[17] Sharon Bishop examines moral response as the attempt to mediate multiple, sometimes conflicting, moral claims that arise out of our many continuing connections with other people and our needs to maintain them with integrity and sensitivity.[18] The intertwining of selves and stories in narrative constructions which locate what is at stake, what is needed, and what is possible is at the heart of moral thinking for many women and feminist writers. The understanding of such stories requires many forms of intelligence; all are at work in the competent moral agent, on this view.[19]

One form of intelligence that very often, if not typically, offers crucial resources for the resolution of moral problems is the *ability to communicate* among persons involved or affected. Although this avenue to understanding is not always open, it often enough is, and its efficacy is so obvious that it is astonishing how little attention is paid it in most nonfeminist moral philosophy. Even in that strain of theory that postulates or simulates an original agreement or compact, the role of communication in, as it were, the moral event is routinely ignored, and the moral agent on the spot is depicted in lonely cogitations. Given the particularistic paradigm of understanding and the situated conception of responsibility already discussed, it is not surprising that the resource of communication is often stressed in women's writing on morality. Gilligan stresses the commitment in the "care" ethic she describes to "activating the network [of relationships] by communication"; Bishop's reconstrual of moral response as "offering compensation and mediating settlements" pictures us as engaging those affected by our moral choices in a common search for constructive ways of answering unsatisfiable or competing claims.[20] Benhabib even more directly challenges the "monological model of moral reasoning" with a proposal for a "communicative ethic of need interpretation," in which actual dialogue replaces hypothetical methods and fixed, prior constraints on "admissible" concerns.[21]

II. FROM MORAL KNOWLEDGE TO MORAL UNDERSTANDINGS

The three elements of attention, contextual and narrative appreciation, and communication in the event of moral deliberation might be seen as an alternative epistemology of moral understanding, or the basis of one. This view, gleaned from the works of a variety of female and feminist writers, provides an alternative to a now standard and canonical (which is to say, professionally institutionalized) view of the form and point of ethics (or its philosophical elaboration).[22] This view is both old and continuous enough to be called a tradition in the strongest sense, and we might call it the *universalist/impersonalist tradition*. In the words of one of its most explicit proponents, nineteenth-century utilitarian philosopher Henry Sidgwick, its goal is systematization of moral understanding, and its ideal of system is that of "precise general knowledge of what ought to be," encoded in "directive rules of conduct" which are "clear and decisive" and "in universal form."[23] The rationale for pursuing a "scientifically complete and systematically reflective form" in morals is that it "corrects" and "supplements" our scattered intuitions, and resolves "uncertainties and discrepancies" in moral judgement.[24] By useful abstraction it steers us away from, in Sidgwick's words, "obvious sources of error" which "disturb the clearness" of moral discernment.[25] For Sidgwick, such distractions include complexity of circumstances, personal interests, and habitual sympathies. Thus, according to Sidgwick, only precise and truly universal principles can provide for "perfection of practice no less than for theoretical completeness."[26]

This capsule description of standard intent and methodology aims to bring into relief its very general picture of morality as individuals standing before the bar of impersonal truth. Moral responsibility is envisioned as responsiveness to the impersonal truths in which morality resides; each individual stands justified if he or she can invoke the authority of this impersonal truth; the moral community of individuals is secured by the conformity (and uniformity) guaranteed by obedience to this higher authority.[27] From an epistemological angle, one might gloss this view as: adequacy of moral understanding increases as this understanding approaches systematic generality.

The alternative moral epistemology already outlined holds, to the contrary, that: adequacy of moral understanding decreases as its form approaches generality through abstraction. A view consistent with this will not be one of individuals standing singly before the impersonal dicta of Morality, but one of human beings connected in various ways and at various depths responding *to each other* by engaging together in a search for shareable interpretations of their responsibilities, and/or bearable resolutions to their moral binds. These interpretations and resolutions will be constrained not only by how well they protect goods we can share, but also by how well they preserve the very human connections that make the shared process necessary and possible. The long oscillation in Western moral thought between the impersonal and the personal viewpoints is answered by proposing that we consider, fully and in earnest, the *interpersonal* view.

The result of this alternative epistemology is not, then, an "opposite number" or shadow image of impersonalist approaches; it is instead a point of departure for a *variety* of different problematics, investigations, focal concerns, and genres of writing and teaching about ethics, many of which we have not, I suppose, yet clearly imagined. Some philosophical endeavors are obviously relevant: greater attention to the pragmatics of communication (of what people mean and do when they address each other, and not just what their words mean); exploration of how exemplary, particular cases are made points of reference for shareable judgments, how they are explicated and how analogies are drawn with them; understanding how various factors (semantic, institutional, political) shape our ability to arrive at shared interpretations; questioning barriers between philosophical, literary, critical, and empirical investigations of moral life. These endeavors will, however, be carried out in a cheerfully piecemeal fashion that neither expects nor requires their results to eventuate in a comprehensive systematization.

The analogue of this on the practical level is the expectation of constant "moral remainders," to adopt a phrase in recent philosophical use. "Moral remainders" refers to some genuine moral demands that, because their fulfillment conflicted with other genuine moral demands, are "left over" in episodes of moral choice, and yet are not just nullified.[28] Whether this sort of thing is even possible is an issue in contemporary moral philosophy.[29] But if moral life is seen as a tissue of moral understandings that configure, respond to, and reconfigure relations as they go, we should anticipate residues and carry-overs as the rule rather than the exception: one's choice will often be a selection of one among various imperfect responses, a response to some among various claims that can't all be fulfilled. So there will just as often be unfinished and ongoing business, compensations and reparations, postponements and returns. Moral problems on this view are nodal points in progressive histories of mutual adjustment and understanding, not "cases" to be closed by a final verdict of a highest court.

III. FROM EPISTEMOLOGY TO PRACTICE

Although I've cast the discussion here in terms of moral "epistemology," my point has been that there is a way of looking at the understanding critical to and distinctive of full moral capacity on which this understanding is *not* really an *episteme*, not a nomologically ordered theory. On the alternative view, moral understanding is a collection of perceptive, imaginative, appreciative, and expressive skills and capacities which put and keep us in unimpeded contact with the realities of ourselves and specific others.[30]

It's also true that a picture of moral understanding is not a whole moral view. Indeed, the alternative moral "epistemology" sketched here leaves open to consideration many questions about which sorts of values enable moral agents to express themselves and hear others, to interpret wisely, and to nourish each other's capacities for supple attentiveness. It also leaves open what other values not directly related to these expressive and receptive capacities are those a feminist ethics ought to endorse. It does not promote one kind of relationship as paradigmatic of moral encounter, and invites us to explore the resources and impediments to expression, reception, and communication in relationships of many kinds. Yet the priority it gives to voicing and hearing, to being answerable in and for specific encounters and relationships promises, I believe, potent critical resources.

First, an ethic based on this alternative picture of moral understanding is set to challenge fundamentally and consistently the way the universalist tradition has institutionalized *indirect* ways of relating as moral *paradigms*. By "indirect" here I mean ways of appreciating persons and situations mediated through what are typically some few, entrenched parameters of status, right, principle, or duty. The alternative picture discussed here confronts this "policed sociability"[31] of universalism with an alternative ideal of *moral objectivity*: that of unimpeded, undistorted, and flexible appreciation of unrepeatable individuals in what are often distinctive situations and relationships. Morally relevant categories on this view include the full, nuanced range of expressive resources for articulating and constructing interpersonal life. By contrast, the ways of describing and expressing to which universalist morality permits moral relevance are typically limited to those which are "repeatable," "universalizable," "impartial," or "impersonal"—that is, those that embody the forms of detachment that are taken by universalism as constitutive of "the moral point of view."

From the alternative framework, we can see universalist morality as "curbing our imaginations" by enforcing communicative and reflective strategies that are interpersonally *evasive*.[32] Universalism, for example, tends to regiment moral thinking so that negligent or willful inattention to need and expectation in the course of daily life is readily seen as "mere insensitivity," a nonmoral failing, when it is not in dereliction of explicit "duties." Worse, it legitimates *uniformly* assuming the quasi-administrative or juridical posture of "the" (i.e., universal) moral point of view. Yet in many cases, assuming that viewpoint may foreclose the more revealing if sometimes painful path of expression, acknowledgement, and collaboration that could otherwise lead to genuinely responsive solutions. Feminists have special and acute needs to fend off this systematic depersonalizing of the moral and demoralizing of the personal. For on a practical level, what feminists aspire to depends as much on restructuring our senses of moral responsibility in intimate partnerships, sexual relations, communities of personal loyalty, and day-to-day work relations as it clearly does on replacing institutional, legal, and political arrangements.

Second, the alternative picture invites us not to be too tempted by the "separate spheres" move of endorsing particularism for personal or intimate relations, universalism for the large-scale or genuinely administrative context, or for dealings with unknown or little-known persons. Although principled, generalized treatments may really be the best we can resort to in many cases of the latter sort, it is well to preserve a lively sense of the *moral incompleteness* or inadequacy of these resorts. This is partly to defend ourselves against dispositions to keep strangers strange and outsiders outside; it is also to prevent our becoming comfortable with essentially distancing, depersonalizing, or paternalistic attitudes that may not really *be* the only resorts if roles and institutions can be shaped to embody expressive and communicative possibilities. On the alternative view of moral-practical intelligence discussed, it is crucial to examine how structural features of institutionalized relations combine with typical situations to enable or deform the abilities of all concerned to hear and to be heard.[33]

Finally, this kind of moral epistemology reminds us that styles of moral thinking are ways of answering to *other people* in terms of some responsibilities that are commonly recognized or recognizable in some community. Philosophical representations of these styles will both reflect and reinforce the relations of authority, power, and responsibility they encode. For moral philosophy to be sincerely reflective, it must attend focally to questions often considered "philosophically" inappropriate: questions about the *rhetoric* and *politics of ethics*. These are questions about the discursive and expressive formats that have been declared appropriate to the task of representing moral life, and about who has the standing (and the access to institutionalized forums) to make, and to challenge, the "rules" (including substantive assumptions) of the genre. When we construct and consider representations of our moral situations, we need to ask: what actual community of moral responsibility does this representation of moral thinking purport to represent? Who does it actually represent? What communicative strategies does it support? Who will be in a position (concretely, socially) to deploy these strategies? Who is in a position to transmit and enforce the rules that constrain them? In what forms of activity or endeavor will they have (or fail to have) an application, and who is served by these activities?[34]

A moral philosophy is a particular rhetoric, sustained and deployed by certain groups of people in certain places; its apparent form may belie its real application and meaning. For example, philosophers have long insisted on the formal universality of norms, concepts, or procedures as the key moral bulwark against bias and injustice. Yet the rhetoric of universality has been entirely compatible, as feminist philosophers have repeatedly shown, with the most complete (and often intentional) exclusion of women as moral agents from such loftily universal constructs as the social contract, pure practical rationality, or the good life for man, and with bypassing altogether in application whole areas of life that are the province of women (voluntarily or not), such as the rearing of children.[35]

Further, not only the substance and presuppositions but also the standard discursive forms of moral philosophy—its canonical styles of presentation, methods of argument, characteristic problems—require pragmatic evaluation. These forms include stark absence of the second person and the plural in projections of philosophical deliberation; virtual exclusion of collaborative and communicative modes of formulating and negotiating moral problems; regimentation of moral "reasoning" into formats of deductive argument; reliance on schematic examples in which the few "morally relevant" factors have already been selected, and in which social–political context is effaced; and omission of continuing narratives that explore the interpersonal sequels to moral "solutions." These are rhetorical conventions that curb the moral imaginations of academic philosophers drastically. Alarmingly, we visit them on our students as we "refine" their moral thinking, obscuring morally significant features of everyday life, personal relations, and the social conditions that structure them.

There are alternatives to the abstract, authoritarian, impersonal, universalist view of moral consciousness. The picture of direct mutual response and responsibility is not a whole ethics, but it is one way of rotating the axis of our investigation around the fixed point of our real need.[36]

Notes

An earlier version of this essay was published in *Hypatia* 4 (1989).

1. Annette Baier, "What Do Women Want in a Moral Theory?" *Nous* 19 (1985), 55.

2. This view of feminist ethics does not rule out in principle that some currently prominent view in philosophical ethics, properly applied, can be a feminist ethics. Although this possibility seems less live currently, early feminist discussions of issues like abortion, rape, and pornography often invoked standard notions of rights, respect, or the promotion of happiness. And it is still a fact that in our given political culture, appeals to moral standards that cohere with liberal political ideas are potent and indispensable tools in pursuing feminist social and legal objectives.

3. Pioneering work in this area includes Baier, 53–63; Baier, "Trust and Anti-Trust," *Ethics* 96 (1986), 231–260; Baier, "The Need for More than Justice," in Marsha Hanen and Kai Nielsen, eds., *Science, Morality and Feminist Theory* (Calgary, Alberta: University of Calgary Press, 1987); Carol Gilligan, *In a Different Voice* (Cambridge: Harvard University Press, 1982); Nel Noddings, *Caring: A Feminine Approach to Ethics and Moral Education* (Berkeley: University of California Press, 1984); Adrienne Rich, *Of Woman Born* (New York: W. W. Norton, 1976); Adrienne Rich, *On Lies, Secrets, and Silence* (New York: W. W. Norton, 1979); Sara Ruddick, "Maternal Thinking," in Joyce Trebilcot, ed., *Mothering* (Totowa, N.J.: Rowman and Allanheld, 1984); Carol Whitbeck, "A Different Reality: Feminist Ontology," in Carol C. Gould, ed., *Beyond Domination* (Totowa, N.J.: Rowman and Allanheld, 1983): 64–88; and others.

4. See Jean Grimshaw, *Philosophy and Feminist Thinking* (Minneapolis: University of Minnesota Press, 1986); Claudia Card, "Virtues and Moral Luck," Working Series 1.4, Institute for Legal Studies, University of Wisconsin-Madison, Law School, 1985; Jeffner Allen, *Lesbian Philosophy: Explorations* (Palo Alto, Calif.: Institute for Lesbian Studies, 1986); Lorraine Code, "Second Persons," in Hanen and Nielsen, eds., *Science, Morality and Feminist Theory*; and Barbara Houston, "Rescuing Womanly Virtues: Some Dangers of Moral Reclamation," in Hanen and Nielsen, for example. Grimshaw is specially critical of claims that women's moral *thinking* is characteristically different; Code criticizes "maternalism"; Houston discusses objections by Card, Allen, and others. For critical reactions to Gilligan's work in particular, see Debra Nails, Mary Ann O'Loughlin, and James C. Walker, *Social Research* 50.3 (Autumn 1983); Linda K. Kerber et al., "On *In a Different Voice*: An Interdisciplinary Forum," *Signs* 11.2 (1986), 304–333; and Meredith Michaels, "Morality Without Distinction," *The Philosophical Forum* 17 (1989), 175–187.

5. I don't mean to make this dialogue sound too bipolar. Virginia Held ("Feminism and Moral Theory," in Eva Feder Kittay and Diana T. Meyers, eds., *Women and Moral Theory* [Totowa, N.J.: Rowman and Littlefield, 1987], 111–128) is cautious on the issue of jettisoning principles to particularism. Marilyn Friedman ("Beyond Caring: The De-moralization of Gender," in Hanen and Nielsen, eds., *Science, Morality and Feminist Theory*, 87–110) combines a plea for the integration of justice and caring values with the view that the character of particularized moral commitments does not combine with rule-based respect. Both Held and Friedman tentatively suggest the application of different moral approaches to different "spheres" of life or different kinds of relationships. But see my section III on the "separate spheres" idea.

6. Gilligan, *In a Different Voice*, 19.

7. Held, "Feminism and Moral Theory," 118.

8. Iris Murdoch, *The Sovereignty of Good* (London: Routledge & Kegan Paul, 1985), 40, 38, 34.

9. Ibid., 28, 65–66. Murdoch herself credits her conception of a "just and loving gaze directed upon an individual reality" (Murdoch, 34) to Simone Weil, whose views are complicated enough (and ambivalent enough, from the viewpoint I'm discussing here) to require quite separate consideration.

10. Many may not share the Platonism, Freudian Psychology, theory of art, or other views to which Murdoch joins her views on love. One subtle critique of the deep social conservatism of Murdoch's views is provided by Sabina Lovibond, *Realism and Imagination in Ethics* (Minneapolis: University of Minnesota Press, 1983), 189–200.

11. Ruddick, "Maternal Thinking," 218–220.

12. Whitbeck, "A Different Reality," 65.

13. Carol Gilligan, "The Conquistador and the Dark Continent: Reflections on the Psychology of Love," Daedalus 113 (1984), 77.

14. Seyla Benhabib, "The Generalized and the Concrete Other," in Kittay and Meyers, eds., Women and Moral Theory, 164. See also Held; Noddings, chapters 1, 4. See also Martha Nussbaum, "Flawed Crystals: James's The Golden Bowl and Literature as Moral Philosophy," New Literary History 15 (1983), 25–50, on reviving the Aristotelian notion of perception as "appropriate acknowledgement" of the particular person in the face of the blinding urge to preserve preconceived, harmonious orderings of abstracted value.

15. Gilligan, In a Different Voice, 32, 28.

16. Benhabib, "The Generalized and the Concrete Other," 163.

17. Whitbeck, "A Different Reality," 76.

18. Sharon Bishop, "Connections and Guilt," Hypatia 2 (1987), 7–23.

19. See Cora Diamond ("Having a Rough Story about What Moral Philosophy Is," New Literary History 15 [1983], 155–169) on the importance of grasping the moral "texture" of individuals (an idea she attributes to Iris Murdoch).

20. Gilligan, In a Different Voice, 30; Bishop, "Connections and Guilt," 12.

21. Benhabib, "The Generalized and the Concrete Other," 167, 169.

22. The difference between representing morality and "rationally reconstructing" it philosophically is not always clear, and this is itself a source of deep problems, substantively and methodologically. Kathryn Addelson ("Moral Passages," in Kittay and Meyers, eds., Women and Moral Theory), for example, deeply challenges the appropriateness and moral legitimacy of an academic practice of philosophical ethics (if I understand her correctly). I take this challenge quite seriously, even as I right now continue to do a version of academic philosophical ethics.

23. Henry Sidgwick, The Methods of Ethics (Indianapolis: Hackett Publishing, 1981 [1907]), 1, 2, 199, 228. Sidgwick's work richly repays study if one wants to see in explicit and self-conscious form the "rules" of the genre of today's philosophical ethics. But one could find the same rules formulated (or implicitly honored) in any number of mainstream twentieth-century authors.

24. Ibid., 425.

25. Ibid., 214.

26. Ibid., 262.

27. Since writing this I have discovered a parallel characterization in Anthony Skillen's description of modern, bourgeois moral consciousness as a blend of "abstract authoritarianism" and "generalized disciplinarianism." Anthony Skillen, Ruling Illusions (Atlantic Highlands, N.J.: Humanities Press, 1978), 153.

28. A standard example would be that in which two promises, each sincerely and responsibly made, turn out to be contingently incapable of both being kept. In such cases, whichever commitment I fulfill, another will have been neglected. Bishop (13ff) discusses the importance of taking the longer view of such cases.

29. A number of widely known essays that debate the issues about dilemmas and moral remainders are collected in Christopher Gowans, Moral Dilemmas, (New York: Oxford University Press, 1987).

30. A moral epistemology of the sort described finds common or overlapping cause with a number of other contemporary deviations from dominant views. For critics of impartiality on behalf of the personal life, see Bernard Williams, Moral Luck (Cambridge: Cambridge University Press, 1981); Lawrence Blum, Friendship, Altruism and Morality (London: Routledge and Kegan Paul, 1980); and Michael Stocker, "The Schizophrenia of Modern Ethical Theories," Journal of Philosophy 73 (1976), 453–466. On interrogating moral views for their concrete social and historical conditions, see Alasdair MacIntyre, After Virtue (Notre Dame, Ind.: University of Notre Dame Press, 1981). For insistence on the primacy of judgments in particular cases, see the new Aristotelians, Martha Nussbaum, The Fragility of Goodness (New York: W. W. Norton, 1986), and David Wiggins, "Deliberation and Practical

Reasoning," in Joseph Raz, ed., *Practical Reasoning* (Oxford: Oxford University Press, 1978). For other versions of "responsibility ethics," which situate moral claims in relational struc- tures of power and dependency, see Robert Goodin, *Protecting the Vulnerable* (Chicago: University of Chicago Press, 1985), and Hans Jonas, *The Imperative of Responsibility* (Chicago: University of Chicago Press, 1984). On morality as a tissue of acknowledgments and refusals, see Stanley Cavell, *The Claim of Reason* (Oxford: Oxford University Press, 1979), parts 3, 4. And on morality as constituted by social practices and as expressive of relations of authority in, respectively, a Marxist and a Wittgensteinian-Hegelian vein, see Skillen, *Ruling Illusion*, and Lovibond, *Realism and Imagination*. All these may be, used selectively, resources for a different kind of ethics. Yet feminists might remain wary of unwanted residues and omissions in some of these views.

31. Skillen, *Ruling Illusions*, 170.

32. Lovibond, *Realism and Imagination*, 199.

33. Some characteristically modern forms of moral universalism may project a sort of "moral colonialism" (the "subjects" of my moral decisions disappear behind uniform "policies" I must impartially "apply") because they were forged historically with an eye to actual colonization—industrial or imperial. See Skillen, *Ruling Illusions*, chapter 4, on both Kantian and utilitarian disciplinarianism and Bernard Williams, *Ethics and the Limits of Philosophy* (Cambridge, Mass.: Harvard University Press, 1985), chapter 6 on Sidgwickian "government house utilitarianism."

34. On the political aspects of construction and deployment of modes of rationality and styles of thought with respect to gender, see essays in Kittay and Meyers, eds., *Women and Moral Theory* by Sara Ruddick, "Remarks on the Sexual Politics of Reason," 237–260; Kathryn Addelson, "Moral Passages," 87–110; Sandra Harding, "The Curious Coincidence of Feminine and African Moralities," 296–315. See also Cheshire Calhoun, "Justice, Care, Gender Bias," *Journal of Philosophy* 85 (1988), 451–463, for a discussion of the way philosophers' neglect of certain topics reinforces moral ideologies.

35. Baier, "Trust and Anti-Trust" and "The Need for More than Justice," is particularly humane and lucid on this topic.

36. Special thanks to Sandra Bartky for very good suggestions on an early draft of this essay, and to Helen Bequaert-Holmes and Laura Purdy, editors of the *Hypatia* Special Issue on Medical Ethics (vol. 4, no. 2, 1989) in which this essay originally appeared, for many helpful suggestions.

A Global Perspective on Feminist Ethics and Diversity

CHARLOTTE BUNCH

I want to begin with a story I once heard about Gandhi being interviewed by the British press during the Indian Independence struggle. When asked "What do you think of Western civilization?" he is said to have paused and replied: "What a wonderful idea!"

This story illustrates the importance of the question of perspective, of how our view of reality is shaped by our experiences and by where we stand in relation to the issues being discussed. One fundamental objective of feminism has been exposing the limitations of male-biased perspectives where women's views have been left out. But women sometimes critique male distortions without seeing race, class, age, heterosexual, ablebodied and cultural biases as well. Here I focus primarily on ethnocentric bias not because it is more important than other distortions, but because addressing it seems urgent for the development of feminism at this time.

The question of perspective is central to one of the basic tenets of feminism: "the personal is political." As the Indian feminist Gita Sen has noted, "Seen through a woman's eyes the personal is always political. It is perhaps as profound a sign as any of the fragmentation of identity that is a hallmark of our times that we have had to say so. And to justify our saying so."[1] The concept of the personal as political reflects a vital insight of feminism, but the personal is not all we need for our politics. We must also learn from the experiences of others since each of our perspectives is necessarily limited and culture-bound. While feminism begins with our own lives, we need to see how our personal experiences have been shaped and perspectives distorted by society, by the limitations and biases of our families, our race, our class, our culture, and our professions.

Another problem with understanding the implications of the personal as political is reflected in confusion between ethical principles/values and whether one's behavior is politically correct in a narrow individualistic sense—whether that's about how you cut your hair or where you go shopping. It is important to think about the political aspects of personal behavior, but the emphasis on such correctness has often led women to become obsessed with individual guilt, rather than to develop a political perspective on what can be done about these things. Trying to be politically correct often has a moralistic tone that implies if you do all the "right" things, then you can wash your hands of responsibility for being part of an oppressive culture. But there is no way to deny that responsibility, no matter how correct one's personal behavior. There is, however, the possibility of being ethical or taking responsibility for doing whatever one can about society. Ethics is, then, a critical part of politics not to be confused with moralism; ethics should inform political decisions which then embody and make concrete ethical commitments.

Today it is critical that we learn to think about such feminist questions globally. This is not a luxury or something one does as a hobby, but must be incorporated into our everyday lives. There is a tendency in the U.S. to view international as totally other than local, but that is a separation we cannot afford. Developing a global perspective is not learning a body of facts, it is a matter of one's approach. No one person can give you a global perspective, including me. But I can share reflections on my own journey as a WASP USAmerican seeking to understand the world from the perspectives of "other" experiences.

My global journey began in the 1960s in the Civil Rights movement in North Carolina, which first taught me that I could more profoundly understand myself by learning about the world as viewed by black people in the South. The reconstruction of my view of the world begun then led to the process of reconceptualizing myself. Since then I have tried to put myself in situations where I would see, experience, and learn from difference. I have sought to understand other ways of seeing reality through my choice of reading, conversations, public events, actions to take, and so on. Even whom you listen to and are around informally shapes how you perceive the world. For example, I watched the 1988 Democratic and Republican conventions with Latin Americans. It was embarrassing to look through their eyes at rhetoric like "Keeping America Number One" or "they can't do that to an American," implying that we have rights that other citizens in the world don't deserve. There are many opportunities in the U.S. to hear various views of this country from the outside since there are many foreign students, scholars, visitors, refugees, and immigrants here.

Speaking of U.S. elections, a feminist ethics from a global perspective reminds us that when we vote, we don't vote just for ourselves. We vote in solidarity and on behalf of all those in the world who can't vote in U.S. elections but whose lives will be affected by them. Thus a global perspective is more than just going to another country. It means looking at whatever one does here—in an election or direct action or a classroom—and seeking to understand the global implications of that situation. A global perspective requires seeing beyond the domestic versus international split and moving beyond nation-state boundaries as the defining parameters of our lives.

Global also means *integral*, taken from its Spanish definition as holistic, not just seeing the parts of a question as separate but seeing how things are connected. It means looking for the relationship between various factors usually thought of in isolation—political, economic, cultural, and spiritual—or how what happens in one part of the world is connected to another. For example, we see the interconnectedness of women's economic and sexual subordination or of how violence against women is related to the violence of militarism. Thus we see that all forms of violence reinforce each other, from racism and homophobia to sexual assault and warfare—all are based in the dynamic of domination of one group by another backed up by physical and economic force.

A global perspective on feminist ethics requires a global vision of feminism—a feminism that is inclusive and seeks to reflect a wide diversity of women's experiences and views. It is possible to work toward this today because the 1980s brought an enormous growth in women's movements around the world, making feminism more reflective of women's diversity. One group that has articulated the significance of these movements is DAWN—Development Alternatives with Women in a New Era. This group of Third World women activists and researchers prepared a book for the 1985 End of the Decade Women's World Conference in Nairobi, declaring:

> There is and must be a diversity of feminisms, responsive to the different needs and concerns of different women, and defined by them for themselves. This diversity builds on a common opposition to gender oppression and hierarchy which, however, is only the first step in articulating and acting upon a political agenda.
>
> For many women of the world, problems of nationality, class and race are inextricably linked to their specific oppression as women. Their definition of feminism to include the struggle against all forms of oppression is legitimate and necessary. In many instances gender equality must be accompanied by changes on those other fronts as well. But, at the same time, the struggle against gender subordination cannot be compromised in the struggle against other forms of oppression, or be relegated to a future when they may be wiped out. . . . This is why we need to affirm that feminism strives for the broadest, deepest development of society and human beings, free of all systems of domination.[2]

This process of diversification and particularization of feminism has surfaced in groups not often heard about before. One example is the Network of Women Living under Muslim Laws, with women from North Africa, the Middle East, South Asia and Europe working to see what forms of feminism are meaningful to women's evolving struggles in their varying cultures. The network has exchanges among women from different Muslim communities coming together for meetings or going to work with groups in other countries for a short period. Through the efforts of such women, a body of work about what it means to be feminist in a Muslim context is emerging.

Another example is a lesbian feminist network in Latin America, which has evolved in the past decade, with groups in Brazil, Chile, Peru, Mexico, Costa Rica, and the Dominican Republic among others. Their first regional conference in Mexico in 1987 brought together over 250 Latina lesbians, many of whom are building an ongoing network of women challenging the particular forms that heterosexism takes in their region. The Muslim women and the lesbians in Latin America are some of the many women's voices speaking out today that the media ignore when they keeps trying to declare feminism in decline. Yet, such global activism has been the cutting edge of feminism in the last decade.

Much emphasis in this decade has been on diversity, but there has also been recognition of commonality. The DAWN statement, for example, talks about common opposition to gender subordination and to domination in all its forms. The global feminist vision of justice seeks to end gender subordination along with other forms of domination to which it is connected. On the individual level, a common goal has been the empowerment of every woman to gain more control over her life.

This global approach to feminist ethics requires seeing feminism as a standpoint or a political perspective on the world. It is a way of understanding ourselves and the world around us, of interpreting our reality and guiding our actions. It begins with any woman's experiences that have been denied, and moves from there to a broader view of diverse women's experiences. It also reinterprets men's experiences and definitions of reality from the point of view of women. For, though a feminist standpoint starts with women's lives at the center, it is not synonymous with being female or just about a single set of issues; rather, it is about reinterpreting any issue from this approach, which anyone can choose to develop.

THE ISSUE OF DIFFERENCE

In looking at feminist writings on ethics, I felt there was not enough attention paid to the question of diversity and difference among women. The issue of differences among people is probably the key question for feminism today. The way our societies deal with differences of race, class, culture, nation, sex, sexual preference, and so on, and those between people and the rest of nature, is part of the cycle of patriarchal domination and destruction that is bringing the planet to the point of self-destruction. This question of differences in all its manifestations is quite simply a question of survival. It is an issue not only of differences within feminist groups, which is often how it gets discussed, but also of how we challenge the basic ways we've been socialized to view the question of difference. It's not only that we need to learn more about different people, but also that we have to learn how to view diversity differently. We need new ways of thinking about the issue of difference.

For example, much of the debate about feminism has focused on the nature versus nurture question of whether differences of sex are innate or socially constructed. My assumption is that they are not biological, or at least that we cannot know much about what's innate for some time because our gender concepts are deeply ingrained. But what interests me more is why we are so focused on that question.

I see the crucial question as: Why does difference have to mean inequality? The basic issue is not whether gender differences are biological—even if we should discover they are, why does that have to lead to inequality? Our fears in looking at the issue of biological differences are rooted in patriarchal culture, where we know only difference as inequality. We know little about societies where diversity is respected as truly complementary and equal. There's often been rhetoric about women and men being complementary, but we know that's usually a cover-up for female oppression. The question therefore is whether it is possible to separate issues of diversity from domination. Is it possible to think and live in a way that relates to difference from another set of assumptions? If we could separate difference from domination, we could move toward a genuine discussion of the biology, nature/nurture question in which we wouldn't have to fear the results, because they would no longer be so loaded.

Talk about diversity can fall into sloppy pluralism in which everything is diverse and nothing matters. But if we do not equate difference with inequality and domination, it is possible to have genuine debate about differences without carrying power-over baggage. We could argue with respect over what is most effective and liberating, rather than fall into our culture's obsession with who is number one/correct and therefore has the right to dominate others.

For example, we wouldn't be talking after a presidential debate about who won, but of how much the debate showed us about the candidate's character or of the directions he might take the nation. What does winning a debate have to do with being a good president? It doesn't tell us who expressed the values and concerns we have. The emphasis should be on whose vision and plans we see as the most humane, motivating, or viable rather than on who won the contest. This example reveals how the dynamic of domination distorts public life.

There could be no more fundamental, ethical revolution in how we see ourselves than altering this dynamic, this model by which all differences are viewed as a matter of fear and domination. Violence throughout the world is fueled by this dynamic, which leads people to concentrate on who is going to be on top, who is going to dominate and who will lose, rather than on how we might all survive better together.

POSITIVE APPROACHES TO DIVERSITY

I would like to suggest positive ways of thinking about diversity because there is a tendency to see it as a problem to be solved. This reminds me of the way people once talked about "the woman question," or "the negro problem," mistakenly implying that the problem was women or blacks, rather than understanding that the problem was racism and sexism. So too with the issue of diversity, there is nothing inherently problematic or wrong about the existence of differences between people. On the contrary, differences can be a source of richness, insight, and variety. But many fear and avoid differences because of this negative assumption that one side has to be right or better or dominate the other.

This difficulty with difference occurs not only around identity issues such as sex or race but also in relation to political differences. For example, in feminist debates over whether sex, race, or class was the most important factor of oppression, there was often little space to discuss the really vital issue of how the three interact in affecting women's lives. Or in arguments over feminist ethics, it's not a question of whether justice or caring is more important, but of whether we can create a more equal relationship between these principles.

Feminist ethics that builds on interrelatedness and balances differing values requires that we live with complexity and see diversity positively. The problem is not diversity but how we approach differences and the power, privilege, and prejudice that our culture has structured around it. Audre Lorde has illuminated this question:

> As a 49-year-old Black lesbian feminist socialist mother of two, including one boy, and a member of an interracial couple, I usually find myself part of some group defined as other, deviant, inferior or just plain wrong. . . . Certainly there are very real differences between us, differences of race, of age, of sex and sexual preference. But it is not those differences between us that are separating us. It is rather our refusal to recognize those differences and to examine the distortions which result from our misnaming them and their effects upon human behavior and expectation.[3]

In stating that it is not the differences, but the way in which we relate to them that is the problem, Lorde points us toward examining how people deny diversity or pretend it doesn't have a social or political impact on all of us. Only through acknowledging diversity and dealing with the problems that society has created around it can we begin to have unity through respecting and valuing diversity. In order for diversity to function fully as a creative source of richness and possibility, it must be de-coupled from economic, political, and social power and privileges. Differences will divide us as long as they are the basis upon which any group is denied power and resources. This de-coupling is the critical political task; the personal work is to change how each of us thinks about and functions with regard to these issues. The two tasks go hand in hand.

When diversity is understood as richness of possibility, it is possible to move beyond tolerance toward a genuine engagement around difference. Don't get me wrong—I'm for tolerance over intolerance any day. But feminist appreciation of diversity must move beyond tolerance to valuing diversity not by condescendingly allowing others to live but by learning from them. This helps us see the changes necessary in the world more clearly and broadens our perspective on ourselves. This approach to diversity is not always easy or comfortable to carry out, but it is both politically necessary and personally rewarding to try it.

In the effort to learn from and value diversity, we must put it at the center of our inquiries. Too often in women's studies and movements, diversity is something that gets added on at the end. For example, a class studies "women" and then looks at "other" groups of women—lesbians, older women, Latinas, and so on—which implies that the first study of white, middle-class, heterosexual U.S. women of a certain age is the norm and all the rest (the majority of the female population) in added on to that essence of womanhood.

We must not assume that there is any one female core experience and, instead, view the diversity of women as the center from which we then explore commonness. To look at a question in this way, one might start with a nondominant group's experience rather than from the dominant position. As Bell Hooks has pointed out in *Feminist Theory: From Margin to Center*, in viewing that which is defined as marginal one comes to understand the norm more profoundly and to understand the impact of the norm and its distortion of reality.[4] For example, in discussing motherhood, begin with lesbian mothers or teenage mothers. Starting with those who don't fit the norm and seeing the institution from that perspective will alter how one views the issue.

GLOBAL FEMINIST ETHICS

Following this approach to diversity, it is useful to look at feminist ethics as discussed in other countries. Gita Sen, in "Ethics in Third World Development: A Feminist Perspective," declares that the ethics of development in our time has to do with the simple survival of human beings and of humanness. Thus she speaks of ethics not as a secondary or academic matter, but as the heart of human survival. She suggests that by looking at women's survival efforts in the Third World, we see not only women's ethics coming out of that struggle but also the basis for developing values for the culture.[5]

Sen's is not an abstract inquiry; she states that she is trying to convince government and development planners to listen to poor, Third World women as the source of ideas that could provide solutions to the problems of development in their countries. She challenges them to see that the way in which poor women have managed to survive in spite of incredible odds is by coming up with creative strategies that can also be useful to government planning. She does not claim that every survival strategy is therefore a feminist ethic or that every poor woman is more moral. Rather she says that these women's experiences have produced new ways of looking at and solving their countries' problems.

I sought to apply this approach by looking at insights and strategies that have emerged from the survival struggles of various disenfranchised groups. For example, the black civil-rights movement created a context for looking at the world from the perspective of the oppressed that opened the way for many changes in U.S. culture. It offered a view of how racial domination distorted society and its concept of humanness that not only affected blacks but changed the way many of us saw the world in other areas as well. The way we saw U.S. involvement in Vietnam changed. The way we saw ourselves as women changed.

Within the U.S. feminist movement a similar development took place when lesbians reinterpreted women's reality from the perspective of the marginalized. Lesbians provided insights about what it means to be woman identified and how male identification restrained women's search for identity and options. Being outside the dominant institution of heterosexuality, lesbians could see not just our experience of it but also how its compulsory structure affected women generally. Thus we could suggest that if every woman did not mind being called a lesbian and refused to run away from the issue, it would lose its power to control us and there would be a powerful upsurge in women's self-image and freedom. Whether one is lesbian or straight, if that fear restrains women's activities, homophobia affects us. Some women have acted on these insights from the margins while others haven't, but the ideas are now there for all to draw on.

Women of color and Third World women have been doing something similar for feminism in the eighties. They have been producing insights in many areas that women in the dominant culture often don't see, but that all of us can learn from. I'm not focusing on such women as the most oppressed or as victims—even though we must never forget that many have been brutally victimized. I'm talking about Third World women as actors who are struggling to change their lives and who have found keys to survival for themselves and in so doing are producing ideas useful to all concerned with change. This is not about some mythological, super-oppressed superwomen who are going to rise up and save the world, but about how insights and social alternatives are born from the struggles of everyday life.

Let me illustrate. During the recent dictatorship in Argentina, the women of the Plaza de Mayo—mostly mothers and grandmothers of people who disappeared during the crackdown on dissidents—began a silent vigil every week in the Plaza holding placards with photos and names of their missing loved ones. In the midst of a ruthless dictatorship, when most were denying that anything was wrong, this simple act was a courageous ethical stand taken out of the pain in these women's lives. They refused to be silent and stood up to power, bearing witness to a reality that was being denied.

That action had an impact throughout the world as an example of a nonviolent way to stand up to militarism. The women did not single-handedly bring down the dictatorship, but they played an important role in bringing people to see the ethical necessity of facing up to what was happening. They opened up space in a closed society and provided the impetus for expanding the concept of human rights in such situations. Before that, disappearances weren't recognized as a form of human-rights abuse, just as violence against women is not understood as a human-rights abuse today, since there is no clear understanding of government responsibility for individual violations of human rights. The work of the women of the Plaza de Mayo will also help in the effort to broaden the understanding of human rights of women generally.

Another example is the movement of women in Peru and other Andean countries around "comedores populares"—community dining rooms where poor women band together to feed their families communally. They not only meet the survival needs of their families better, but also through taking action together, an empowering process occurs. Working together in the communal kitchens, the women talk about their lives and become politically active around issues ranging from food prices to domestic violence. One group passed out whistles to women in the neighborhood so that if anyone was being beaten, she could blow a whistle, or if one heard another being beaten, she blew her whistle until many women in the community were blowing their whistles to shame the man and stop the violence.

I could talk about many more examples of women taking action to break the silent acceptance of domination and bring change in their situations. In Kenya women of the Greenbelt movement have planted trees where the desertification process threatens to destroy more land and leave many families with no work or food. In India the Chipko movement was led by tribal women who literally hugged trees that were to be chopped down for "development" to prevent their destruction, which would have led to the destruction of their communities. In these actions, women are demanding an ethical accounting for the human costs of development, forcing governments and planners to consider people's needs.

Women are also bringing change in basic concepts that define how we see issues. In Chile feminists initiated a slogan that has caught on throughout Latin America: "democracia en el pais y en la casa" (democracy in the country and in the home). This concept shows the link between democracy as a public issue, which is important to people in the region, and democracy as a concept of the right to self-determination in the home. In this country we call that linkage "the personal is political" and talk about connections between the public and the private sphere. By connecting feminism to the concept of democracy, the Chileans have created a more powerful way to talk about women's rights in the language of ideals that are important to the region.

Feminists are also examining human-rights discourse and struggling with the question of whether feminist ethics is based too much on individualism. Human rights is a useful concept for defending women's rights, but women are also seeking a different relationship between individual and community rights. Here, too, we may benefit from insights from other cultures. A woman from West Africa explained that gaining the right to abortion in her country must be based on getting the community to understand that a woman's control over her body is in the interest of the community. She felt she couldn't argue that women have this as an individual right because her culture doesn't conceive of individual rights as taking precedence over the community. Our challenge as feminists is not to give up such individual human rights, but to find ways to move away from the idea that these are isolated and separate from the needs of the community. How do we bring more integration of community and individual needs/rights? This is one of the areas where feminists hope to move beyond old dichotomies and dualisms that separate issues of concern. Is there not some way to reconceptualize these things that doesn't put them in opposition?

Many feminist discussions about ethics seek to bring what our society poses as opposites, such as a nurturing ethic versus a justice ethic, into a new relationship. Ways to get beyond our cultural binds may well come from seeing the issues as they are viewed by women in other countries. The next step in the discourse about feminist ethics should be to look at how questions are being addressed in other places and see what we can both learn from others as well as offer from our work. A global feminist ethic of respect for diversity is required if we are to learn from each other. This means building an exchange based on respect that grows out of acknowledging the richness of our differences while also struggling against the ways in which these divide us through an imbalance of power and privilege. Such an exchange does not deny any of our realities but it pushes us to learn to understand them more broadly by seeing other aspects of the world as well. An ethic of responsibility for our actions and solidarity and reciprocity in our interactions with each other can lay the groundwork for this exchange to become a truly global, feminist movement.

Notes

1. Gita Sen, "Ethics in Third World Development: A Feminist Perspective." The Rama Mehta Lecture, Radcliffe College, Harvard University, April 28, 1988, manuscript p. 4.

2. Gita Sen and Caren Grown (for DAWN), *Development, Crises and Alternative Visions: Third World Feminist Perspectives* (N.Y.: Monthly Review Press, 1987), 18–19.

3. Audre Lorde, "Age, Race, Class and Sex: Women Redefining Difference," *Sister Outsider* (Trumansburg, N.Y.: The Crossing Press, 1984), 114–115.

4. Bell Hooks, *Feminist Theory: From Margin to Center* (Boston: South End Press, 1984).

5. Sen, "Ethics," 14. Another useful look at feminist ethics from other cultures is *Speaking of Faith: Global Perspectives on Women, Religion, and Social Change*, Diana L. Eck and Devaki Jain, eds. (New Delhi: Kali for Women Press, 1986).

A BIBLIOGRAPHY IN FEMINIST ETHICS

Ackelsberg, Martha. " 'Sisters' or 'Comrades'? The Politics of Friends and Families." In *Families, Politics, and Public Policy*, ed. Irene Diamond, pp. 339–356. New York: Longman, 1983.

Acker, S. "Feminist Theory and the Study of Gender and Education." *International Review of Education* 33.4 (1987): 419–435.

Adams, Margaret. "The Compassion Trap." In *Woman in Western Thought*, ed. Martha Lee Osborne, pp. 235–248. New York: Random House, 1979.

Addelson, Kathryn Pyne. "Moral Passages." In *Women and Moral Theory*, ed. Eva Feder Kittay and Diana T. Meyers, pp. 87–110. Totowa, N.J.: Rowman and Littlefield, 1987.

———. "Nietzsche and Moral Change." In *Woman in Western Thought*, ed. Martha Lee Osborne, pp. 235–248. New York: Random House, 1979.

Adler, Jonathan E. "Moral Development and the Personal Point of View." In *Women and Moral Theory*, ed. Eva Feder Kittay and Diana T. Meyers, pp. 205–234. Totowa, N.J.: Rowman and Littlefield, 1987.

Allen, Christine. "Sex Unity, Polarity, or Complementarity." *International Journal of Women's Studies* 6.4 (September/October 1983): 311–325.

Allen, Jeffner. *Lesbian Philosophy: Explorations*. Palo Alto, Calif.: Institute for Lesbian Studies, 1987.

———. "Through the Wild Region: An Essay in Phenomenological Feminism." *Review of Existential Psychology and Psychiatry* 18 (1982–1983): 241–256.

Andolsen, Barbara Hilkert. "Agape in Feminist Ethics." *Journal of Religious Ethics* 9 (Spring 1981): 69–82.

Andolsen, Barbara; Gudorf, Christine; and Pellauer, Mary D., eds. *Women's Consciousness, Women's Conscience: A Reader in Feminist Ethics*. Minneapolis, Minn.: Winston Press, 1985.

Andre, Judith. "Power, Oppression and Gender." *Social Theory and Practice* 11 (Spring 1985): 107–121.

Ayim, M., and Houston, B. "The Epistemology of Gender Identity: Implications for Social Policy." *Social Theory and Practice* 11 (Spring 1985): 25–59.

Baier, Annette C. "The Need for More Than Justice." In *Science, Morality and Feminist Theory*, ed. Marsha Hanen and Kai Nielsen. Calgary, Alberta: University of Calgary Press, 1987.

———. "Trust and Anti-Trust." *Ethics* 96 (1989): 231–260.

———. "What Do Women Want in a Moral Theory?" *Nous* 19 (1985): 55–63.

Baker, Gale S. "Is Equality Enough?" *Hypatia* 2.1 (Winter 1987): 63–65.

Baker, John. "Philosophy and the Morality of Abortion." *Journal of Applied Philosophy* 2 (October 1985): 261–270.

Bartky, Sandra. "Narcissism, Femininity and Alienation." *Social Theory and Practice* 8 (Summer 1982): 127–144.

Belenky, Mary Field; Clinchy, Blythe McVicker; Goldberger, Nancy Rule; and Tarule, Jill Mattuck. *Women's Ways of Knowing: The Development of Self, Voice, and Mind*. New York: Basic Books, 1986.

Bell, Nora Kizer. "Women and AIDS: Too Little, Too Late?" *Hypatia* 4.3 (Fall 1989): 3–22.

Benhabib, Seyla. "The Generalized and the Concrete Other: The Kohlberg-Gilligan Controversy and Feminist Theory." *Praxis International* 5 (January 1986): 402–424.

————. "The Generalized and the Concrete Other: The Kohlberg-Gilligan Controversy and Moral Theory." In *Women and Moral Theory*, ed. Eva Feder Kittay and Diana T. Meyers, pp. 154–177. Totowa, N.J.: Rowman and Littlefield, 1987.

————. "Judgement and the Moral Foundations of Politics in Arendt's Thought." *Political Theory* 16 (February 1988): 29–51.

Benjamin, Jessica. "A Desire of One's Own: Psychoanalytic Feminism and Intersubjective Space." In *Feminist Studies/Critical Studies*, ed. Teresa de Lauretis, pp. 78–101. Bloomington: Indiana University Press, 1986.

Bishop, Sharon. "Connections and Guilt." *Hypatia* 2.1 (1987): 7–23.

Blum, Lawrence. "Gilligan and Kohlberg: Implications for Moral Theory." *Ethics* 98 (April 1988): 472–491.

Blum, Lawrence; Homiak, Marcia; Housman, Judy; and Scheman, Naomi. "Altruism and Women's Oppression." In *Women and Philosophy*, ed. Carol Gould and Marx W. Wartofsky, pp. 222–247. New York: G. P. Putnam and Sons, 1976.

Boralevi, Lea Campos. "Utilitarianism and Feminism." In *Women in Western Political Philosophy*, ed. Ellen Kennedy, pp. 159–178. New York: St. Martin's Press, 1987.

Brabeck, M. M. "Feminist Perspectives on Moral Education and Development (symposium)." *Journal of Moral Education* 16 (October 1987): 163–248.

Brock-Utne, B. "Gender and Cooperation in the Laboratory [A Feminist Analysis]." *Journal of Peace Research* 26 (February 1989): 47–56.

Bussey, Kay, and Maughan, Betty. "Gender Differences in Moral Reasoning." *Journal of Personality and Social Psychology* 42.4 (April 1982): 701–706.

Cady, Susan; Ronan, Marian; and Taussig, Hal. *Sophia: The Future of Feminist Spirituality.* San Francisco: Harper and Row, 1986.

Cahill, Lisa Sowle. "Commentary: Beneath the Surface of the Abortion Dispute." In *Abortion: Understanding Differences*, edited by Sidney Callahan, pp. 225–228. New York: Plenum Press, 1984.

Calhoun, Cheshire. "Justice, Care, Gender Bias." *Journal of Philosophy* 85 (1988): 451–463.

Callahan, Daniel. "Autonomy: A Moral Good, Not a Moral Obsession." *Hastings Center Report* 14.5 (October 1984): 40–42.

Callahan, Sidney. "The Role of Emotion in Ethical Decision-Making." *Hastings Center Report* 18.3 (June/July 1988): 9–14.

Cancian, Francesca M. "The Feminization of Love." *Signs* 11 (Summer 1986): 692–709.

Card, Claudia. "Lesbian Attitudes and the Second Sex." *Hypatia* 3 (1985): 209–214.

————. "Virtues and Moral Luck," Series I, Institute for Legal Studies, Working Papers, University of Wisconsin-Madison, Law School, November, 1985.

————. "Women's Voices and Ethical Ideals: Must We Mean What We Say?" *Ethics* 99.1 (October 1988): 125–135.

Cheney, Jim. "Eco-Feminism and Deep Ecology." *Environmental Ethics* 9.2 (Summer 1987): 115–145.

Clark, L. M. G., and Lange, L., eds. *The Sexism of Social and Political Theory.* Toronto: University of Toronto Press, 1979.

Code, Lorraine B. "Autonomy Reconsidered." *Atlantis* 13 (1988): 27–35.

————. *Epistemic Responsibility.* Hanover, N. H.: University Press of New England for Brown University, 1987.

————. "Is the Sex of the Knower Epistemologically Significant?" *Metaphilosophy* 12 (July–October 1981): 267–276.

————. "Responsibility and the Epistemic Community: Woman's Place." *Social Research* 50.3 (Autumn 1983): 537–555.

————. "Simple Equality is Not Enough." *Australasian Journal of Philosophy* Supplement 64 (June 1986): 48–65.

Cohen, Cheryl H. "The Feminist Sexuality Debate: Ethics and Politics." *Hypatia* 1.2 (Fall 1986): 71–86.

Cooey, Paula M.; Farmer, Sharon A.; and Ross, Mary Ellen, eds. *Embodied Love: Sensuality and Relationship as Feminist Values*. San Francisco: Harper and Row, 1987.

Daly, Mary. *Gyn/Ecology: The Metaethics of Radical Feminism*. Boston: Beacon Press, 1978.

———. *Pure Lust: Elemental Feminist Philosophy*. Boston: Beacon Press, 1984.

Davion, Victoria. "Do Good Feminists Compete?" *Hypatia* 2.2 (Summer 1987): 55–63.

deSoussa, Ronald B., and Morgan, Kathryn Pauly. "Philosophy, Sex, and Feminism." *Atlantis* 13 (Spring 1988): 1–10.

Dietz, Mary. "Citizenship with a Feminist Face: The Problem with Maternal Thinking." *Political Theory* 13 (February 1985): 19–37.

Diller, Ann, and Houston, Barbara. "Trusting Ourselves to Care." *Resources for Feminist Research* 16 (1987): 35–38.

Dillon, Robin S. "Self-Respect and Justice." Ph.D. dissertation, University of Pittsburgh, 1977.

Doe, J. "There to Comfort, Not to Judge." *Nursing 88* 18 (September 1988): 82–83.

Donenberg, Geri R., and Hoffman, Lois W. "Gender Differences in Moral Development." *Sex Roles* 18 (June 1988): 701–717.

Duran, Jane. "A Philosophical Perspective on Gender." *Philosophy in Context* 17 (1987): 52–60.

Eisenstein, Zillah. *The Radical Future of Liberal Feminism*. New York: Longman, 1981.

Elshtain, Jean B. "Critical Reflections on Realism, Just Wars, and Feminism." In *Nuclear Weapons and the Future of Humanity*, ed. Avner Cohen, pp. 255–272. Totowa, N.J.: Rowman and Allanheld, 1986.

———, ed. *The Family in Political Thought*. Amherst: University of Massachusettes Press, 1982.

———. "Feminism, Family, and Community." *Dissent* 29.4 (Fall 1982): 442–449.

———. "On Beautiful Souls, Just Warriors, and Feminist Consciousness." *Women's Studies International Forum* 5.3/4 (Winter 1982): 341–348.

———. *Public Man, Private Woman*. Oxford: Martin Robertson, 1981.

———. "Reflections on War and Political Discourse: Realism, Just War, and Feminism in a Nuclear Age." *Political Theory* 13 (February 1985): 39–57.

———. "Women as Mirror and Other: Toward a Theory of Women, War, and Feminism." *Humanities and Society* 5 (Winter/Spring 1982): 29–44.

Farganis, Sondra. *The Social Reconstruction of the Feminine Character*. Totowa, N.J.: Rowman and Littlefield, 1986.

Farrell-Smith, Janet. "Possessive Power." *Hypatia* 1.2 (Fall 1986): 103–120.

Ferguson, Kathy E. *The Feminist Case Against Bureaucracy*. Philadelphia: Temple University Press, 1984.

Fischer, Bernice. "Guilt and Shame in the Women's Movement: The Radical Ideal of Action and its Meaning for Feminist Intellectuals." *Feminist Studies* 10 (Summer 1984): 185–212.

Fischer, Claude. *To Dwell Among Friends*. Boston: Beacon Press, 1986.

Flanagan, Owen J., Jr. "Virtue, Sex, and Gender: Some Philosophical Reflections on the Moral Psychology Debate." *Ethics* 92.3 (April, 1982): 499–512.

Flanagan, Owen; and Jackson, Kathryn. "Justice, Care, and Gender: The Kohlberg-Gilligan Debate Revisited." *Ethics* 97.3 (April 1987): 622–637.

Flax, Jane. "Political Philosophy and the Patriarchal Unconscious: A Psychoanalytic Perspective on Epistemology and Metaphysics." In *Discovering Reality*, ed. Sandra Harding and Merrill B. Hintikka, pp. 245–281. Dordrecht: D. Reidel, 1983.

Ford, M. R.; and Lowery, C. R. "Gender Differences in Moral Reasoning: A Comparison of the Use of Justice and Care Orientations." *Journal of Personality and Social Psychology* 50.4 (April 1986): 777–783.

Fraser, Nancy. "Toward a Discourse Ethic of Solidarity." *Praxis International* 5.4 (January 1986): 425–429.

Friedman, Marilyn. "Beyond Caring: The De-Moralization of Gender." In *Science, Morality and Feminist Theory*, ed. Marsha Hanen and Kai Nielsen, pp. 87–110. Calgary, Alberta: University of Calgary Press, 1987.

———."Care and Context in Moral Reasoning." In *Women and Moral Theory*, edited by Eva Feder Kittay and Diana T. Meyers, pp. 190–204. Totowa, N.J.: Rowman and Littlefield, 1987.

Friedman, William J.; Robinson, Amy B.; and Friedman, Brit L. "Sex Differences in Moral Judgements? A Test of Gilligan's Theory." *Psychology of Women Quarterly* 11 (March 1987): 37–46.

Fry, Sara T. "The Role of Caring in a Theory of Nursing Ethics." *Hypatia* 4.2 (Summer 1989): 88–103.

Frye, Marilyn. *The Politics of Reality: Essays in Feminist Theory*. Trumansburg, N.Y.: The Crossing Press, 1983.

Garry, Ann. "Narcissism and Vanity." *Social Theory and Practice* 8 (Summer 1982): 145–154.

Genova, Judith, ed. *Power, Gender, Values*. Edmonton, Alberta: Alberta Academic, 1987.

Gilligan, Carol. "The Conquistador and the Dark Continent: Reflections on the Psychology of Love." *Daedalus* 113.2 (Summer 1984): 75–95.

———. *In a Different Voice: Psychological Theory and Women's Development*. Cambridge, Mass.: Harvard University Press, 1982.

———. "Moral Orientation and Moral Development." In *Women and Moral Theory*, ed. Eva Feder Kittay and Diana T. Meyers, pp. 19–36. Totowa, N.J.: Rowman and Littlefield: 1987.

———. "New Maps of Development: New Visions of Education." *Philosophy of Education: Proceedings* 38 (1982): 47–62.

———. "Woman's Place in Man's Life-Cycle." *Harvard Educational Review* 47.4 (1977): 481–517.

Gilligan, C., and Attanucci, J. "Two Moral Orientations: Gender Differences and Similarities." *Merrill-Palmer Quarterly* 34 (July 1988): 223–237. (bibliography)

———. "Two Moral Orientations: Gender Differences and Similarities." *Merrill-Palmer Quarterly* 34 (October 1988): 451–456. (discussion)

Goldberg, Roberta. "The Determination of Consciousness through Gender, Family, and Work Experience." *Social Science Journal* 21 (October 1984): 75–86.

Gould, Carol C., ed. *Beyond Domination: New Perspectives on Women and Philosophy*. Totowa, N.J.: Rowman and Allanheld, 1984.

Gould, Ketayun. "Old Wine in New Bottles: A Feminist Perspective on Gilligan's Theory." *Social Work* 33.5 (September/October 1988): 411–415.

Grant, Judith. "I Feel Therefore I Am: A Critique of Female Experience as the Basis for a Feminist Epistemology." *Women and Politics* 7.3 (Fall 1987): 99–114.

Grimshaw, Jean. *Feminist Philosophers*. Brighton: Wheatsheaf Books, 1986.

———. *Philosophy and Feminist Thinking*. Minneapolis: University of Minnesota Press, 1986.

Gudorf, Christine. "How Will I Recognize My Conscience When I Find It?" *Philosophy and Theology: Marquette University Quarterly* 1 (Fall 1986): 64–83.

Hampson, M. Daphne. "On Power and Gender." *Modern Theology* 4 (April 1988): 234–250.

Hanen, Marsha. "Justification, Coherence and Feminism." In *Ethics and Justification*, ed. Douglas Odegard, pp. 39–54. Toronto: Edmonton Academic, 1988.

Hanen, Marsha, and Nielsen, Kai. *Science, Morality and Feminist Theory*. Calgary,: University of Calgary Press, 1987.

Haney, Eleanor Humes. "What Is Feminist Ethics: A Proposal for Continuing Discussion." *Journal of Religious Ethics* 8 (Spring 1980): 115–124.

Harding, Sandra. "Beneath the Surface of the Abortion Dispute." In *Abortion: Understanding Differences*, ed. Sidney Callahan, pp. 203–224. New York: Plenum Press, 1984.

———. "The Curious Coincidence of Feminine and African Moralities." In *Women and*

Moral Theory, ed. Eva Feder Kittay and Diana T. Meyers, pp. 296–315. Totowa, N.J.: Rowman and Littlefield, 1987.

———. "Is Gender a Variable in Conceptions of Rationality: A Survey of Issues." *Dialectica* 36 (1982): 225–242.

Harding, S., and Hintikka, M. B., eds. *Discovering Reality: Feminist Perspectives on Epistemology, Metaphysics, Methodology and Philosophy of Science*. Boston: D. Reidel, 1983.

Hardwig, John. "Should Women Think in Terms of Rights?" *Ethics* 94.3 (April 1984): 441–455.

Harris, J. R. "Ethical Values and Decision Processes of Male and Female Business Students." *Journal of Education for Business* 64 (February 1989): 234–238.

Harrison, Beverley Wildung. "Our Right To Choose: The Morality of Procreative Choice." In *Women's Consciousness, Women's Conscience: A Reader in Feminist Ethics*, ed. Barbara Hilkert Andolsen et al., pp. 101–120. Minneapolis: Winston Press, 1985.

———. "The Power of Anger in the Work of Love: Christian Ethics for Women and Other Strangers." *Union Seminary Quarterly Review* 36 (1981): 41–47.

Hartouni, Valerie A. "Antigone's Dilemma: A Problem in Political Membership." *Hypatia* 1 (Spring 1986): 3–20.

Hartsock, Nancy C. M. *Money, Sex, and Power*. Boston: Northeastern University Press, 1983.

Heise, Helen. "Eyeshadow, Aesthetics and Morality." *Hypatia* 2 (1984): 365–373.

Held, Virginia. "Feminism and Moral Theory." In *Women and Moral Theory*, ed. Eva Feder Kittay and Diana T. Meyers, pp. 111–128. Totowa, N.J.: Rowman and Littlefield, 1987.

———. "Non-Contractual Society." *The Canadian Journal of Philosophy* Supplementary 13 (1987): 111–138.

———. *Rights and Goods*. New York: The Free Press, 1984.

Heller, Agnes. "The Emotional Division of Labor Between the Sexes." *Social Praxis: International and Interdisciplinary Journal of Thought* 7 (1980): 205–218.

Higgins, Ann. "A Feminist Perspective on Moral Education." *Journal of Moral Education* 16.3 (October 1987): 240–248.

Hoagland, Sarah Lucia. "Femininity, Resistance, and Sabotage." In *Femininity, Masculinity, and Androgyny*, ed. Mary Vetterling-Braggin, pp. 85–98. Totowa, N.J.: Littlefield Adams, 1982.

———. *Lesbian Ethics*. Palo Alto, Calif.: Institute of Lesbian Studies, 1988.

Hochschild, Arlie Russell. *The Managed Heart: Commercialization of Human Feeling*. Berkeley, Calif.: University of California Press, 1983.

———. "The Sociology of Feeling and Emotion: Selected Possibilities." In *Another Voice*, ed. Marcia Millman and Rosabeth Moss Kanter, pp. 280–307. New York: Anchor Books, 1975.

Holmes, Helen Bequaert. "A Call to Heal Medicine." *Hypatia* 4.2 (Summer 1989): 1–8.

———. "Can Clinical Research be both Ethical and Scientific?" *Hypatia* 4.2 (Summer 1989): 156–168.

———. "A Feminist Analysis of the Universal Declaration of Human Rights." In *Beyond Domination*, ed. Carol Gould, pp. 250–264. Totowa, N.J.: Rowman and Allanheld, 1984.

Hoskins, Betty B., and Holmes, Helen Bequaert. "When Not to Choose: A Case Study." *Journal of Medicine and Human Bioethics* 6 (Spring/Summer 1985): 28–37.

Jaggar, Alison M. *Feminist Politics and Human Nature*. Totowa, N.J.: Rowman and Allanheld, 1983.

Jaggar, Alison M., and McBride, William L. " 'Reproduction' as Male Ideology." *Hypatia* 2 (1985): 185–196.

Janeway, Elizabeth. "Improper Behavior: Imperative for Civilization." *Hypatia* 2 (Winter 1987): 165–177.

Katzenstein, Mary Fainsod, and Laitin, David D. "Politics, Feminism, and the Ethics of Care." In Women and Moral Theory, ed. Eva Feder Kittay and Diana T. Meyers, pp. 261–281. Totowa, N.J.: Rowman and Littlefield, 1987.

Keller, Catherine. From a Broken Web: Separation, Sexism and Self. Boston: Beacon Press, 1986.

Kerber, Linda, et al. "In a Different Voice: An Interdisciplinary Forum." Signs 11.2 (1986): 304–333.

Ketchum, Sara Ann. "Female Culture, Woman Culture and Conceptual Change: Toward a Philosophy of Women's Studies." Social Theory and Practice 6 (Summer 1980): 151–162.

———. "Selling Babies and Selling Bodies." Hypatia 4.3 (Fall 1989): 116–127.

Kidwell, Jeaneen M.; Stevens, Robert E.; and Bethke, Art L. "Differences in Ethical Perceptions Between Male and Female Managers: Myth or Reality?" Journal of Business Ethics 6 (August 1987): 489–493.

Kittay, Eva Feder, and Meyers, Diana T. "Moral Orientation and Moral Development." In Women and Moral Theory, ed. Eva Feder Kittay and Diana T. Meyers, pp. 19–33. Totowa, N.J.: Rowman and Littlefield, 1987.

———, eds. Women and Moral Theory. Totowa, N.J.: Rowman and Littlefield, 1987.

Koonz, Claudia. Mothers in the Fatherland: Women, the Family, and Nazi Politics. New York: St. Martin's Press, 1987.

Krieger, Linda J. "Through a Glass Darkly: Paradigms of Equality and the Search for a Woman's Jurisprudence." Hypatia 2.1 (Winter 1987): 45–61.

Lauritzen, Paul. "A Feminist Ethic and the New Romanticism—Mothering as a Model of Moral Relations." Hypatia 4.2 (Summer 1989): 29–44.

Leach, Mary S. "Towards Caring about the Feminine." Philosophy of Education: Proceedings 41 (1985): 359–363.

Lemoncheck, Linda. Dehumanizing Women: Treating Persons as Sex Objects. Totowa, N.J.: Rowman and Allanheld, 1985.

Lifton, P. D. "Individual Differences in Moral Development: The Relation of Sex, Gender, and Personality to Morality." Journal of Personality 53.1 (June 1985): 306–334.

Lloyd, Genevieve. The Man of Reason: 'Male' and 'Female' in Western Philosophy. Minneapolis: University of Minnesota Press, 1984.

———. "Reason, Gender and Morality in the History of Philosophy." Social Research 50 (August 1983): 490–513.

Longino, Helen E. "Science, Objectivity and Feminist Values." Feminist Studies 14 (Fall 1988): 166–177.

Lorber, Judith. "Choice, Gift, or Patriarchal Bargain? Women's Consent to in vitro Fertilization in Male Infertility." Hypatia 4.3 (Fall 1989): 23–36.

Love, Charles E. "Universalization, Projects, and the New Feminine Ethic." Philosophy of Education: Proceedings 42 (1986): 73–82.

Lovibond, Sabina. Realism and Imagination in Ethics. Minneapolis: University of Minnesota Press, 1983.

Lugones, Maria. "Playfulness, 'World' Traveling, and Loving Perception." Hypatia 2.2 (Summer 1987): 3–19.

MacKinnon, Catharine A. "Desire and Power: A Feminist Perspective." In Marxism and the Interpretation of Culture, ed. Cary Nelson, pp. 105–121. Urbana: University of Illinois Press, 1988.

MacLaren, Elizabeth. "Dignity." Journal of Medical Ethics 3 (1977): 40–41.

Maguire, Daniel C. "The Feminization of God and Ethics." Christianity and Crisis (March 15, 1982): 59–67.

———. The Moral Choice. Garden City, N.Y.: Doubleday, 1978.

Mahowald, M., ed. Philosophy of Woman. Indianapolis: Hackett, 1978. 2d ed., 1983.

Manning, Rita. "The Random Collective as a Moral Agent." *Social Theory and Practice* 11 (Spring 1985): 97–105.

Mariette, Don E., Jr. "Environmentalism, Feminism and the Future of the American Society." *The Humanist* 44.3 (May–June 1984): 15–18, 30.

Markus, Maria. "Women, Success, and Civil Society: Submission to, or Subversion of, the Achievement Principle." *Praxis International* 5 (January 1986): 430–442.

Marquis, Don. "An Ethical Problem Concerning Recent Therapeutic Research on Breast Cancer." *Hypatia* 4.2 (Summer 1989): 140–155.

McCormick, Thelma. "Feminism and the New Crisis in Methodology." In *The Impact of Feminism in Research Methodologies*, ed. Winnie Tomm. Waterloo, Ontario: Wilfrid Laurier University Press, 1989.

Messer-Davidow, Ellen. "Knowers, Knowing, Knowledge: Feminist Theory and Education." *Journal of Thought* 20 (Fall 1985): 8–24.

Meyers, Diana T. "Personal Autonomy and the Paradox of Feminine Socialization." *Journal of Philosophy* 84 (November 1987): 619–629.

———. "The Politics of Self-Respect: A Feminist Praxis." *Hypatia* 1 (Spring 1986): 83–100.

Michaels, Meredith. "Morality Without Distinction." *The Philosophical Forum* 17 (1986): 175–187.

Miller, Jean Baker. *Toward a New Psychology of Women*. Boston: Beacon Press, 1976.

Morgan, Kathryn Pauly. "Romantic Love, Altruism, and Self-Respect." *Hypatia* 1.1 (Spring 1986): 117–148.

———. "Women and Moral Madness." *Canadian Journal of Philosophy* 17.3 (September 1987).

Mullet, Sheila. "Consensual Discourse and the Ideal of Caring." *Atlantas* 13 (Spring 1988): 24–26.

Muuss, R. E. "Carol Gilligan's Theory of Sex Differences in the Development of Moral Reasoning During Adolescence." *Adolescence* 22 (Fall 1987): 229–243.

Nails, Debra. "Social Scientific Sexism: Gilligan's Mismeasure of Man." *Social Research* 50.3 (Autumn 1983): 643–664.

———, ed. "Women and Morality [symposium]." *Social Research* 50.3 (Autumn 1983): 487–695.

Narayan, Uma. "Working Together Across Difference: Some Considerations on Emotions and Political Practice." *Hypatia* 3.2 (Summer 1988): 31–47.

Nebraska Sociological Feminist Collective. *A Feminist Ethic for Social Science Research*. Lewiston, N.Y.: Edwin Mellen Press, 1988.

Nelson, Hilde Lindemann and James Lindemann. "Cutting Motherhood in Two: Some Suspicions Concerning Surrogacy." *Hypatia* 4.3 (Fall 1989): 85–94.

Nicholson, Linda. "Feminist Theory: The Private and the Public." In *Beyond Domination*, ed. Carol Gould, pp. 221–232. Totowa, N.J.: Rowman and Allanheld, 1984.

———. "Women, Morality, and History." *Social Research* 50.3 (Autumn 1983): 514–536.

———. "Women's Work: Views from the History of Philosophy." In *Femininity, Masculinity, and Androgyny*, ed. Mary Vetterling-Braggin, pp. 203–221. Totowa, N.J.: Littlefield Adams, 1982.

Noddings, Nel. *Caring: A Feminine Approach to Ethics and Moral Education*. Berkeley, Calif.: University of California Press, 1984.

———. "Creating Rivals and Making Enemies." *Journal of Thought* 22 (Fall 1987): 23–31.

———. "Do We Really Want to Produce Good People?" *Journal of Moral Education* 16 (October 1987): 177–188.

———. "In Search of the Feminine." *Philosophy of Education: Proceedings* 41 (1985): 349–358.

———. "Women and Power." *Philosophy of Education: Proceedings* 36 (1980): 98–102.

Nunner-Winkler, Gertrude. "Two Moralities: A Critical Discussion of an Ethic of Care and Responsibility Versus an Ethic of Rights and Justice." In *Morality, Moral Behavior and Moral Development*, ed. William Kurtines and Jacob Gewirtz. New York: John Wiley and Sons, 1984.

Nussbaum, Martha. " 'Finely Aware and Richly Responsible': Moral Attention and the Moral Task of Literature." *Journal of Philosophy* 82 (October 1985): 516–529.

Nye, Andrea. *Feminist Theory and Philosophy of Man.* London: Croom Helm, 1988.

———. "Preparing the Way for a Feminist Praxis." *Hypatia* 1 (Spring 1986): 101–116.

———. "Woman Clothed with the Sun: Julia Kristeva and the Escape from/to Language." *Signs* 12 (Summer 1987): 664–686.

O'Loughlin, Mary Ann. "Responsibility and Moral Maturity in the Control of Fertility—or, A Woman's Place Is in the Wrong." *Social Research* 50.3 (Autumn 1983): 556–576.

Okin, Susan Moller. "Women and the Making of the Sentimental Family." *Philosophy and Public Affairs* 11 (Winter 1982): 65–88.

———. *Women in Western Political Thought*. Princeton, N.J.: Princeton University Press, 1979.

Osborne, M. L., ed. *Woman in Western Thought*. New York: Random House, 1979.

Overall, Christine. *Ethics and Human Reproduction: A Feminist Analysis*. Boston: Allen and Unwin, 1987.

Parsons, Susan F. "Feminism and the Logic of Morality: A Consideration of Alternatives." *Radical Philosophy* 47 (Autumn 1987): 2–12.

———. "Feminism and Moral Reasoning." *Australasian Journal of Philosophy* Supplement 64 (June 1986): 75–90.

———. "The Intersection of Feminism and Theological Ethics: A Philosophical Approach." *Modern Theology* 4 (April 1988): 251–266.

Pateman, Carol. *The Problem of Political Obligation: A Critique of Liberal Theory*. Berkeley: University of California Press, 1979.

Patterson, Eleanora. "Suffering." In *Reweaving the Web of Life*, ed. Pam McAllister, pp. 165–174. Philadelphia: New Society Publishers, 1982.

Pellauer, Mary D. "Moral Callousness and Moral Sensitivity: Violence Against Women." In *Women's Consciousness, Women's Conscience*, ed. Barbara Hilkert Andolsen, Christine E. Gudorf, and Mary Pellauer, pp. 33–50. San Francisco: Harper and Row, 1987.

Poff, Deborah C., and Michalos, Alex C. "Feminism and the Quality of Life." *Social Indicators Research* 20 (October 1988): 445–472.

Powell, G. N.; Posner, Barry; and Schmidt, Warren. "Sex Effects on Managerial Value Systems." *Human Relations* 37.11 (November 1984): 909–921.

Pratt, Michael W.; Golding, Gail; and Hunter, William J. "Does Morality Have a Gender? Sex, Sex Role and Moral Judgment Relationships Across the Adult Lifespan." *Merrill-Palmer Quarterly* 30 (October 1984): 321–340.

Purdy, Laura M. "Feminist Healing Ethics." *Hypatia* 4.2 (Summer 1989): 9–14.

Rabine, Leslie Wahl. "A Feminist Politics of Non-Identity." *Feminist Studies* 14 (Spring 1988): 11–31.

Ravven, Heidi M. "Has Hegel Anything to Say to Feminists?" *The Owl of Minerva* 19 (Spring 1988): 149–168.

Raymond, Janice. "Female Friendship and Feminist Ethics." In *Women's Consciousness, Women's Conscience*, ed. Barbara Hilkert Andolsen et al., pp. 161–174. Minneapolis: Winston Press, 1985.

———. *A Passion for Friends*. Boston: Beacon Press, 1986.

Reimer, Michelle S. "Gender Differences in Moral Judgments: The State of the Art." *Smith College Studies in Social Work* 54 (November 1983): 1–12.

Rhodes, Margaret L. "Gilligan's Theory of Moral Development as Applied to Social Work." *Social Work* 30.2 (March/April 1985): 101–105.

Rich, Adrienne. *On Lies, Secrets, and Silence*. New York: W. W. Norton and Company, 1979.

Robb, Carol S. "A Framework for Feminist Ethics." *Journal of Religious Ethics* 9 (Spring 1981): 48–68.

Rose, Hilary. "Dreaming the Future." *Hypatia* 3 (Spring 1988): 119–137.

Rothbart, Mary K.; Hanley, Dean; and Albert, Marc. "Gender Differences in Moral Reasoning." *Sex Roles* 15 (December 1986): 645–653.

Rothschild, Joan, ed. *Machina Ex Dea: Feminist Perspectives on Technology.* New York: Pergamon Press, 1983.

Rowland, Robyn. "Making Women Visible in the Embryo Experimentation Debate." *Bioethics* 1 (April 1987): 179–188.

Ruddick, Sara. "Maternal Thinking." *Feminist Studies* 1 (Summer 1980): 342–367.

———. "Maternal Thinking." In *Women and Values*, edited by Marilyn Pearsall, pp. 340–351. Belmont, Calif.: Wadsworth, 1986.

———. "Pacifying the Forces: Drafting Women in the Interests of Peace." *Signs* 8.3 (Spring 1983): 471–489.

———. "Preservative Love and Military Destruction: Some Reflections on Mothering and Peace." In *Mothering: Essays in Feminist Theory*, ed. J. Trebilcot, pp. 231–262. Totowa, N.J.: Rowman and Allanheld, 1983.

———. "Remarks on the Sexual Politics of Reason." In *Women and Moral Theory*, ed. Eva Feder Kittay and Diana T. Meyers, pp. 237–260. Totowa, N.J.: Rowman and Littlefield, 1987.

Ruether, Rosemary Radford. "Feminism and Peace." In *Women's Consciousness, Women's Conscience*, ed. Barbara Hilkert Andolsen et al. pp. 63–74. Minneapolis: Winston Press, 1985.

———. *New Woman, New Earth: Sexist Ideologies and Human Liberation.* New York: Seabury, 1983.

Sayers, Janet. "Feminism and Mothering: A Kleinian Perspective." *Women's Studies International Forum* 7.4 (1984): 237–241.

Scheman, Naomi. "Individualism and the Objects of Psychology." In *Discovering Reality: Feminist Perspectives on Epistemology, Metaphysics, Methodology and Philosophy of Science*, ed. S. Harding and M. B. Hintikka, pp. 225–244. Boston: D. Reidel, 1983.

Scott, Joan W. "Deconstructing Equality-versus-Difference: Or, the Uses of Post-structuralist Theory for Feminism." *Feminist Studies* 14 (Spring 1988): 33–50.

Segers, Mary C. "The Catholic Bishops' Pastoral Letter on War and Peace." *Feminist Studies* 11 (Fall 1985): 619–647.

Shapiro, J. P., and Smith-Rosenburg, C. "The 'Other Voices' in Contemporary Ethical Dilemmas: The Value of the New Scholarship on Women in the Teaching of Ethics." *Women's Studies International Forum* 12.2 (1989): 199–211.

Sher, George. "Our Preferences, Ourselves." *Philosophy and Public Affairs* 12 (Winter 1983): 34–50.

Sherwin, Susan. "A Feminist Approach to Ethics." *The Dalhousie Review* 64.4 (Winter 1984–85).

———. "Feminist and Medical Ethics: Two Different Approaches to Contextual Ethics." *Hypatia* 4.2 (Summer 1989): 57–72.

Shogan, Debra. *Care and Moral Motivation.* Toronto: OISE Press, 1988.

———. "Categories of Feminist Ethics." *Canadian Journal of Feminist Ethics* 1 (1986): 4–13.

Sichel, Betty A. "Beyond Genderized Ethics." *Philosophy of Education: Proceedings* 43 (1987): 185–193.

———. "Ethics of Caring and Institutional Ethics Committees." *Hypatia* 4.2 (Summer 1989): 45–56.

———. "Women's Moral Development in Search of Philosophical Assumptions." *Journal of Moral Education* 14 (October 1985): 149–161.

Simons, Margaret A. "Motherhood, Feminism, and Identity." *Hypatia* 2 (1984): 349–359.

Simons, Margaret A., and Benjamin, Jessica. "Simone DeBeauvoir: An Interview." *Feminist Studies* 5 (Summer 1979): 330–345.

Singer, Linda. "Interpretation and Retrieval: Rereading Beauvoir." *Hypatia* 3 (1985): 231–238.

Smith, David H., ed. *Respect and Care in Medical Ethics.* Lanham, Md.: Lanham University Press of America, 1984.

Smith, Ruth L. "Feminism and the Moral Subject." In *Women's Consciousness, Women's Conscience*, ed. Barbara Hilkert Andolsen et al., pp. 235–250. Minneapolis: Winston Press, 1985.

Soble, Alan. *Pornography: Marxism, Feminism and the Future of Sexuality.* New Haven, Conn.: Yale University Press, 1986.

Socoski, Patrick. "Are Dick and Jane Different Moral Beings: An Inquiry Into Sex-Specific Morality and Some Educational Implications." *Philosophical Studies in Education: Annual Proceedings of the Ohio Valley Philosophy of Education Society* (1984): 69–74.

Spelman, Elizabeth. "On Treating Persons as Persons." *Ethics* 88 (1977): 150–161.

Starhawk. *Dreaming the Dark.* Boston, Mass.: Beacon Press, 1988.

Stockard, Jean; Van de Kragt, Alphos J. C.; and Dodge, Patricia. "Gender Roles and Behavior and Social Dilemmas: Are There Sex Differences in Cooperation and Its Justification?" *Social Psychology Quarterly* 51.2I (June 1988): 154–163.

Straumanis, Joan. "Duties to Oneself: An Ethical Basis for Self-Liberation?" *Journal of Social Philosophy* 15 (Summer 1984): 1–13.

Swanton, Christine, and Crosthwaite, Jan. "On the Nature of Sexual Harassment." *Australasian Journal of Philosophy* Supplement 64 (June 1986): 91–106.

Tapper, Marion E. "The Super Ego of Women." *Social Theory and Practice* 12 (Spring 1986): 61–74.

Tavris, Carol. *Anger: The Misunderstood Emotion.* New York: Simon and Schuster, 1982.

Tomm, Winnie. "Autonomy and Interrelatedness: Spinoza, Hume, and Vasubandhu." *Zygon: Journal of Religion and Science* 22 (December 1987): 459–478.

———. "Gender Factor or Metaphysics in a Discussion of Ethics." *Explorations: Journal for Adventurous Thought* 6 (Fall 1987): 5–24.

Tong, Rosemarie. "Feminism, Pornography and Censorship." *Social Theory and Practice* 8 (Spring 1982): 1–18.

———. *Women, Sex, and the Law.* Totowa, N.J.: Rowman and Allanheld, 1984.

Trebilcot, Joyce, ed. *Mothering: Essays in Feminist Theory.* Totowa, N.J.: Rowman and Allanheld, 1983.

Tronto, Jean C. "Beyond Gender Difference to a Theory of Care." *Signs* 12 (Summer 1987): 644–663.

———. "Political Science and Caring: Or, The Perils of Balkanized Social Science." *Women and Politics* 7 (Fall 1987): 85–98.

Valverde, Mariana. "Beyond Gender Dangers and Private Pleasures: Theory and Ethics in the Sex Debate." *Feminist Studies* 15.2 (Summer 1989): 237–254.

Vetterling-Braggin, Mary, ed. " 'Femininity,' Resistance, and Sabotage." In *Femininity, Masculinity, and Androgyny: A Modern Philosophical Discussion.* Totowa, N.J.: Littlefield, Adams, 1982.

Von Morstein, Petra. "Epistemology and Women in Philosophy: Feminism Is a Humanism." In *Gender Bias in Scholarship: The Pervasive Prejudice*, ed. Winnie Tomm and G. Hamilton, pp. 147–165. Waterloo, Ontario, Canada: Wilfrid Laurier University.

Warren, Mary Ann. "The Moral Significance of Birth." *Hypatia* 4.3 (Fall 1989): 46–65.

Warren, Virginia L. "Feminist Directions in Medical Ethics." *Hypatia* 4.2 (Summer 1989): 73–87.

Weil, Simone. "Reflections on the Right Use of School Studies with a View to the Love of God." In *Waiting for God*, trans. Emma Craufurd, pp. 113, 115. New York: G. P. Putnam's Sons, 1951.

Weinzweig, Marjorie. "Pregnancy Leave, Comparable Worth, and Concepts of Equality." *Hypatia* 2.1 (Winter 1987): 71–101.

Weldhen, Margaret. "Ethics, Identity and Culture: Some Implications of the Philosophy of Iris Murdoch." *Journal of Moral Education* 15 (May 1986): 119–126.

Whitbeck, Caroline. "A Different Reality: Feminist Ontology." In *Beyond Domination*, edited by Carol Gould, pp. 64–88. Totowa, NJ: Rowman and Allanheld, 1983.

———. "Fetal Imaging and Fetal Monitoring: Finding the Ethical Issues." *Women and Health* 13.1/2 (1987): 47–57.

———. "Love, Knowledge, and Transformation." *Hypatia* 2 (1984): 393–405.

Wider, Kathleen. "Women Philosophers in the Ancient Greek World: Donning the Mantle." *Hypatia* 1 (Spring 1986): 21–62.

Williams, Delores S. "Women's Oppression and Lifeline Politics in Black Women's Religious Narratives." *Journal of Feminist Studies* 1.2 (Fall 1985): 59–71.

Wilson, Leslie. "Is a 'Feminine' Ethic Enough?" *Atlantis* 13 (Spring 1988): 15–23.

Wolf, Susan. "Above and Below the Line of Duty." *Philosophical Topics* 14 (Fall 1986): 131–148.

Wolgast, Elizabeth. *The Grammar of Justice*. Ithaca, N.Y.: Cornell University Press, 1987.

Wood, J. T. "Different Voices in Relationship Crises: An Extension of Gilligan's Theory." *The American Behavioral Scientist* 29.3 (January/February 1986): 273–301.

Young, Iris. "Humanism, Gynocentrism, and Feminist Politics." *Hypatia* 3 (1985): 173–183.

———. "The Ideal of Community and the Politics of Difference." *Social Theory and Practice* 12 (Spring 1986): 12–13, 150, 151–52, 179, 204.

———. "Impartiality and the Civic Public." In *Feminism as Critique*, ed. S. Benhabib and D. Cornell, pp. 60–67. Cambridge: Polity Press, 1987.

Zimmerman, Michael E. "Feminism, Deep Ecology, and Environmental Ethics." *Environmental Ethics* 9.1 (Spring 1987): 21–44.

CONTRIBUTORS

ELIZABETH ANN BARTLETT is Associate Professor of Political Science at the University of Minnesota, Duluth, with an adjunct appointment in the Department of Women's Studies. She is the editor of Sarah Grimke's *Letters on the Equality of the Sexes and Other Essays*. She has published articles on feminist theory in *Women's Studies International Forum* and *The Journal of Ideology* and has written several papers on Albert Camus in comparison with other theorists including Hannah Arendt, Adrienne Rich, and Audre Lorde.

CHARLOTTE BUNCH, feminist author, organizer, teacher, and activist, has been a leading figure in the women's movement for over two decades. The first woman resident fellow at the Institute for Policy Studies in Washington, D.C., she was a founder of D.C. Women's Liberation and of *Quest: A Feminist Quarterly*, a journal of feminist theory which she edited during the 1970s. Her writings have appeared widely, and she has edited seven anthologies including *Class and Feminism*, *Learning Our Way: Essays in Feminist Education*, and *International Feminism: Networking against Female Sexual Slavery*. Her latest book is a collection of her essays from 1968 to 1986 titled *Passionate Politics: Feminist Theory in Action*. Recently she has been the Director of a new Center for Global Issues and Women's Leadership at Rutgers University.

CHESHIRE CALHOUN is Associate Professor of Philosophy at the College of Charleston, Charleston, S.C. She is coeditor with Robert C. Solomon of *What is an Emotion?* and has written on the emotions and feminist issues in moral theory.

LORRAINE CODE is Professor of Philosophy at York University in North York, Ontario. In addition to numerous articles in theory of knowledge and feminist theory, she is the author of *Epistemic Responsibility* and coeditor of *Changing Patterns: Women in Canada* and of *Feminist Perspectives: Philosophical Essays on Minds and Morals*. Her book on feminism and epistemology is forthcoming.

EVE BROWNING COLE is Assistant Professor of Philosophy, Humanities, and Classics at the University of Minnesota, Duluth. Her research interests include ancient Greek philosophy and culture, feminist philosophy, and ethics. She is the author of articles on ancient Greek life and thought, sexism in the history of philosophy, and ancient views on the intelligence and character of (nonhuman) animals. Her book *Philosophy and Feminist Criticism* is forthcoming.

SUSAN COULTRAP-McQUIN is Associate Professor of Women's Studies at the University of Minnesota, Duluth. She has recently published *Doing Literary Business: American Women Writers in the Nineteenth Century*, which examines the role of professional ethics in relationships between authors and publishers. Her research interests include 19th-century American women, publishing, feminist ethics, leadership, and professionalism.

ROBIN S. DILLON is Assistant Professor of Philosophy at Lehigh University, where she teaches ethical theory, engineering ethics, and feminist theory, and is a codirector of the Women's Studies Program. Her research interests include moral emotions, feminist ethics, and applied ethics. She is writing a book about the nature and moral importance of self-respect.

MAUREEN FORD is working on her doctoral studies in philosophy of education at the Ontario Institute for Studies in Education, in Toronto. She has published on gender and education in *Eidos* and coedited a special issue of *Resources for Feminist Research* titled "Women and Philosophy." She teaches science and history for the North York Board of Education, secondary-school level.

ELLEN L. FOX is a doctoral candidate in philosophy at the University of North Carolina, Chapel Hill. Her dissertation concerns moral issues in friendship, in particular the preservation of genuine connectedness, as opposed to individual autonomy, in relations between friends. Her research interests include ethics, social and political philosophy, and feminism. She is Assistant Professor of Philosophy at California State University, Chico.

MARILYN FRIEDMAN teaches philosophy at Washington University. She has published both feminist and "mainstream" articles in the areas of ethical theory, applied ethics, and social philosophy. Her book on feminism, personal relationships, and moral theory is forthcoming.

SARAH LUCIA HOAGLAND is Professor of Philosophy and Women's Studies at Northeastern Illinois University in Chicago. She is author of *Lesbian Ethics: Toward New Value*, which is excerpted in this anthology, and she coedited with Julia Penelope *For Lesbians Only: A Separatist Anthology*.

RITA MANNING is the token witch in the Philosophy Department at San Jose State University. She has published widely in philosophy, on subjects ranging from Aristotle's philosophy of mind to ethical theory. She is currently writing essays about our place in the natural world and a book on feminist ethics.

KATHLEEN MARTINDALE teaches in the English Department at York University, Ontario. She was the editor of *Feminist Ethics*, an interdisciplinary journal of ethics. She is the author of numerous articles on feminist ethics and literary theory, and is preparing a book on feminist critical theory, *Resisting Subjects*.

MARY C. RAUGUST started law school when her last child grew up and it seemed like it was time to find a new twist to work, after thirty years in medicine. When school is finished she will be a consultant in personal injury for individuals, litigators, and Native Americans affected by environmental pollution on their reservations. Working in the Kennedy Aging Project was another instance of the womanly tendency to break the departmental or disciplinary boundaries that men have set, to combine areas of knowledge and fields of interest, and to try to make work (almost) as whole as life is.

ROGER J. RIGTERINK is Associate Professor of Philosophy at the University of Wisconsin Center, Fond du Lac. He teaches both in a traditional college setting and at the Taycheedah Correctional Institute, a state-run women's prison. His publications have been in the areas of philosophy of mind, epistemology, and bioethics. In addition he has coauthored a paper on punishment with one of his students from the correctional institute.

DIANNE ROMAIN lives with her love, three cats, one gnawing rat, and countless spiders in a chilly but charming old farmhouse on a grassy hill in western Sonoma County. She teaches philosophy and liberal studies at Sonoma State University. She integrates her interests in feminism, creative and critical thinking with her concerns about nuclear buildup, U.S. foreign policy in Central America, and human treatment of nonhuman animals and the environment. Through art and play, teaching, writing, traveling, and giving public lectures, she explores how to lead a good life in a troubled world.

SARA RUDDICK is the author of *Maternal Thinking: Toward a Politics of Peace* and coeditor of *Working it Out* and *Between Women*. She teaches at Eugene Lang College of the New School for Social Research.

PATRICIA WARD SCALTSAS did her graduate studies at the University of Chicago and University College, London. She is part-time tutor in philosophy at the Open University and in the Extra-Mural and Philosophy Departments of Edinburgh University, Scotland. Her research interests include moral and political philosophy, feminist theory, and 18th- and 19th-century arguments for women's rights. She held a British Academy Research Grant for autumn term 1989 at the Institute for Research on Women, Rutgers University.

SUSAN SHERWIN is Associate Professor of Philosophy and Women's Studies at Dalhousie University. Her principal research and teaching interests are in the areas of feminism, ethics, and health-care ethics. Her recent publications include "Feminist and Medical Ethics: Two Different Approaches to Contextual Ethics," "Feminist Ethics and In Vitro Fertilization," and "Feminism, Ethics, and Caring." She is at work on a book on feminist ethics and health care, to be published in 1991.

DEBRA SHOGAN is Associate Professor in the Department of Leisure Studies at the University of Alberta. She is responsible for a senior seminar in feminist ethics in the University of Alberta's Women's Studies Program. Debra is the author of *Care and Moral Motivation*.

WINNIE TOMM coordinates the Women's Studies Program at the University of Alberta. Her published works include *The Effects of Feminist Approaches on Research Methodologies*, which she edited; *The Pervasive Prejudice: Gender Bias and University Research*, coedited with Gordon Hamilton; "Theories of Human Nature in Spinoza, Vasubandhu, and Feminism"; and numerous other works in ethics and the history of philosophy.

MARGARET URBAN WALKER is Associate Professor of Philosophy at Fordham University in New York City. Her teaching and research interests include moral philosophy, feminist theory, and Wittgenstein. She has published papers on moral agency, judgment, and responsibility, and is developing a relational ethics of responsibility for vulnerable, situated, and attached moral agents.

JULIE K. WARD teaches ancient Greek philosophy and feminist theory at Loyola University of Chicago. She has published papers in ancient philosophy and is working on a series of papers on autonomy and the body.

INDEX